Microsoft®
Word For Windows™

Version 2

D1363587

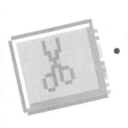

Step
by Step

Microsoft
P R E S S

PUBLISHED BY
Microsoft Press
A Division of Microsoft Corporation
One Microsoft Way, Redmond, Washington 98052-6399

Library of Congress Cataloging-in-Publication Data
Microsoft Word step by step : the Windows edition / Microsoft.
        p. cm.
    Includes index.
    ISBN 1-55615-467-4
    1. Microsoft Word for Windows (Computer program) 2. Word
processing--Computer programs. I. Microsoft Corporation.
Z52.5.M523M52 1991
652.5'536--dc20   91-35557
                                                   CIP

Printed and bound in the United States of America.

    4 5 6 7 8 9 MLML 7 6 5 4 3 2

Distributed to the book trade in Canada by Macmillan of Canada, a division of Canada Publishing Corporation.

Distributed to the book trade outside the United States and Canada by Penguin Books Ltd.

Penguin Books Ltd., Harmondsworth, Middlesex, England
Penguin Books Australia Ltd., Ringwood, Victoria, Australia
Penguin Books N.Z. Ltd., 182-190 Wairau Road, Auckland 10, New Zealand

British Cataloging-in-Publication Data available.

All names of companies, products, street addresses, and persons contained herein are part of a completely fictitious scenario or scenarios and are designed solely to document the use of a Microsoft product.

PostScript® is a registered trademark of Adobe Systems, Inc. Macintosh® is a registered trademark of Apple Computer, Inc. dBASE®, dBASE II®, dBASE III®, and dBASE IV® are registered trademarks, and dBASE III PLUS™ is a trademark of Ashton-Tate Corporation. HP® and LaserJet® are registered trademarks of Hewlett-Packard Company. DisplayWrite® and IBM® are registered trademarks of International Business Machines Corporation. Helvetica®, Times®, and Times Roman® are registered trademarks of Linotype AG and/or its subsidiaries. 1-2-3® and Lotus® are registered trademarks of Lotus Development Corporation. WordStar® is a registered trademark of MicroPro International. Microsoft®, the Microsoft logo, MS®, MS-DOS®, and Multiplan® are registered trademarks, and Toolbar™ and Windows™ are trademarks of Microsoft Corporation. WordPerfect® is a registered trademark of WordPerfect Corporation.

This book was produced using Microsoft Word.

Contents

About This Book   ix

Getting Ready   xiii

Part 1   Basic Skills

Lesson 1   **Creating a New Document**   3

The Document Window
Typing Text
Deleting, Replacing, and Moving Text
Making the Document Look Great
One Step Further
Saving a Document
Lesson Summary
Preview of the Next Lesson

Lesson 2   **Copying and Moving Text**   21

Opening a Document
Moving and Copying Text to a New Location
Scrolling Through a Document
Moving and Copying Text Using the Toolbar
    Moving Text a Long Distance
Checking the Spelling in a Document
One Step Further
Lesson Summary
Preview of the Next Lesson

Part 2   Everyday Tasks Made Easy

Lesson 3   **Using Indents, Margins, and Lists**   41

Setting Indents and Creating Lists
    Using the Toolbar to Set Indents
    Creating Bulleted and Numbered Lists
Setting Custom Indents

Setting Margins with the Ruler
One Step Further
Lesson Summary
Preview of the Next Lesson

Lesson 4   **Working with Commands and Dialog Boxes   58**

Using Commands in Word
Using Word Dialog Boxes
Using Keys to Choose Commands and Options
Locating Information in Help
    If You Are Familiar with WordPerfect Commands
One Step Further
Lesson Summary
Preview of the Next Lesson

Lesson 5   **Storing Formatting as Styles   77**

Storing Formatting as a Style
Applying Styles
Changing a Style
One Step Further
Lesson Summary
Preview of the Next Lesson

Lesson 6   **Proofing a Document   88**

Finding and Replacing Text
    Finding and Replacing Formatting
Using the Thesaurus
Checking Grammar and Spelling
    Adding Words to a Custom Dictionary
Creating an Envelope
One Step Further
Proofing Tips
Lesson Summary
Preview of the Next Lesson

Lesson 7   **Adding Page Numbers, Headers, and Footers   105**

Inserting Page Numbers
Printing Text and Page Numbers on Each Page
Changing Headers or Footers Within a Document
One Step Further

Lesson Summary
Preview of the Next Lesson

Lesson 8 **Working with Windows 118**

Windows Basics
Displaying More Than One Document at a Time
Copying Text from One Document to Another
Moving and Sizing Windows
One Step Further
Lesson Summary
Preview of the Next Lesson

Part 3 Arranging Text and Graphics

Lesson 9 **Creating Tables and Charts 139**

Creating a Table
Inserting and Deleting Rows and Columns
Polishing the Look of the Table
   Merging Cells
   Centering Text and Centering the Table
   Adding Borders and Shading
Creating Charts
One Step Further
Tips About Tables
Lesson Summary
Preview of the Next Lesson

Lesson 10 **Creating Columns 156**

Creating Columns
Varying the Number of Columns Within a Document
   Inserting Section Breaks
   Creating Columns in Each Section
Getting an Overview of the Layout
One Step Further
Lesson Summary
Preview of the Next Lesson

Lesson 11 **Adding Graphics and Emphasizing Text 174**

Inserting and Sizing Graphics

Framing a Graphic
Making Changes to Graphics
Working with WordArt
Framing and Sizing Text
One Step Further
Lesson Summary
Preview of the Next Lesson

Part 4 Managing and Printing Files

Lesson 12   **Finding and Printing Multiple Files   201**

Using the Find File Command
Searching for Files
Searching for Files by Using Summary Information
Working with Multiple Files
One Step Further
Lesson Summary
Preview of the Next Lesson

Lesson 13   **Creating Merged Documents   210**

Merging Documents: Basic Techniques
Working with Data Files
Working with Main Documents
    Inserting Field Names in the Main Document
Merging Documents
Attaching an Existing Data File
Tips for Merging Documents
One Step Further
Lesson Summary

Appendixes

Appendix A   **Installing Word   229**

Appendix B   **Installing and Selecting a Printer   232**

Appendix C   **Converting Documents To or From Other Formats 239**

Appendix D   **New Features in Word   243**

Appendix E   **Other Ways to Save Time in Word   245**

Glossary   247

Index   257

About This Book

Microsoft Word® for Windows™ is a full-featured word processor designed to help you work more efficiently—whether you spend several hours a day at the computer or use word-processing software only occasionally.

Microsoft Word Step by Step shows you how Word can make your everyday work easy. You can use *Step by Step* in a classroom setting, or use it as a tutorial to learn Word at your own pace and at your own convenience. Most lessons provide a sample document for you to practice on. The documents contain information about Word—ideas and suggestions for getting your work done more quickly. If you print the document at the end of each lesson, you can create a personal quick reference notebook about Microsoft Word.

Finding the Best Starting Point for You

This book is designed both for new users who are learning Microsoft Word for the first time, and for experienced users who want to learn about the new features in Word for Windows version 2.0. If you are familiar with other Microsoft Word products, such as Word for the Macintosh or Word 5.5 for the PC, you'll have a head start on the basics of Word for Windows version 2. Among the new features you'll want to learn about are the Toolbar™ buttons, which carry out the most common commands with a click of the mouse, and the "drag and drop" feature, which enables you to copy or move text by dragging selected text with the mouse and dropping it where you want.

The modular design of this book offers you considerable flexibility in customizing your learning. Lessons 1 through 4 teach very basic skills. To decide if you need to work through those lessons, scan the summary at the end of each. You can go through the other lessons in any order, skip lessons, and repeat lessons later to brush up on certain skills. You start most lessons by opening a practice file from the Practice Files disk. You then rename the practice file, so that the original file remains unchanged while you work on your own version.

The following table recommends starting points based on your word-processing experience.

If you are	Follow these steps
New to word processing	Read "If You are New to Word Processing," in "Getting Ready," later in this book.
	Next, work through lessons 1–4 in order. Work through the other lessons in any order.
New to the mouse	Read "If You are New to the Mouse," in "Getting Ready," later in this book.
	TIP: The sample documents that you can print at the end of each lesson often give special tips for keyboard users.
New to Word for Windows and unfamiliar with other Word products	Work through lessons 1–4 in order. Work through the other lessons in any order.
Familiar with Word for the Macintosh or Word 5.5 for the PC	Read the summaries at the end of lessons 1, 2, 3, and 4. You may not need to work through these lessons.
An experienced Word for Windows user	Read the summaries at the end of lessons 1 and 2. Note the Toolbar buttons.
	Next, read the summaries at the end of lessons 3 and 4. Note the Toolbar buttons.
	Work through the other lessons in any order. Finally, read Appendix D, "New Features in Word," for further information.

Using This Book as a Classroom Aid

If you're an instructor, you can use *Microsoft Word Step by Step* for teaching Word to novice users and for teaching the new features of Word for Windows version 2.0 to experienced users. You can choose from the lessons to customize courses for your students.

If you plan to teach the entire contents of this book, you should probably allow one and a half to two days of classroom time, to allow for discussion, questions, and any customized practice you may create.

Conventions Used in This Book

Keyboard Conventions

- Names of keys are in small capital letters; for example, TAB and SHIFT.

- A plus sign (+) between two key names means that you must press those keys at the same time. For example, "Press SHIFT+SPACEBAR" means that you hold down the SHIFT key while you press the SPACEBAR.

- A comma (,) between two key names means that you must press those keys sequentially. For example, "Press ALT, F, O" means that you first press and release the ALT key, then the F key, and then the O key.

Other Features of This Book

Print

- Many commands can be carried out by clicking a button at the top of the Word window. If a procedure instructs you to click a button, a picture of the button appears in the left margin, as it does here.

- Text in the left margin summarizes main points, gives tips, or provides additional useful information.

- You'll find optional "One Step Further" exercises at the end of most lessons. These exercises are less structured than the lessons themselves to help you practice what you learned in the lesson and to let you experiment a bit on your own.

TROUBLESHOOTING:
- **If you get unexpected results as you work** If what happens on the screen is not what you expected, look for a troubleshooting note below the step where the problem occurred. Troubleshooting notes are marked in the left margin, as shown here.

Cross-references to Microsoft Word Documentation

Microsoft Word Step by Step will help you learn about your Word documentation. At the end of each lesson, you'll find references to the documentation that comes with Word. If you work through a lesson that teaches skills you use frequently and want to know more about, check the chapter or online lesson mentioned at the end of the *Step by Step* lesson. You'll find cross-references to the following Word documentation.

Microsoft Word Getting Started Describes the features in Word, explains how to set up Word on your computer system, how to start and quit Word, and how to get the most out of the documentation provided with Word. It also includes special information for users upgrading from earlier versions of Microsoft Word for Windows.

Microsoft Word User's Guide   Contains background information, procedures, and examples for using the basic and advanced features in Word.

Microsoft Draw User's Guide   Shows how to create and modify line drawings and other graphics that you can add to Word documents.

Microsoft Graph User's Guide   Explains how to create and modify charts from tables of data. Using this feature, you can add column, bar, line, and pie charts to Word documents.

Online lessons   Introduce Word features and provide hands-on practice. Choose a basic or more advanced lesson, or use the index to get quick access to a topic.

Online Help   Provides information about Word features and gives instructions on performing specific tasks. Help also has documentation on WordBasic macros and fields and information for users switching from WordPerfect to Word. When the WordArt feature is running, WordArt Help displays complete documentation about creating special effects in your documents.

Templates   Word comes with a set of templates you can use to produce different kinds of documents, such as letters, memos, and business reports. The templates are located in the directory where you installed Word. For information on using templates, see Chapter 37, "Document Templates," in the *Microsoft Word User's Guide*.

Clip Art   Provides graphics that you can paste directly into Word or edit in Microsoft Draw. These graphics are located in the CLIPART subdirectory under the directory where you installed Word.

Getting Ready

This book shows you how to streamline your everyday work, using the features in Microsoft Word. Each lesson takes approximately 30 to 40 minutes, with optional practice available at the end of each lesson. There are several things you need to do before you begin the lessons. This portion of the book shows you how to install the practice files on your computer's hard disk and how to start Windows and start Word.

If you have not yet installed Windows or Word, you'll need to do that before you continue with the lessons. If you need instructions for installing Windows, see your Windows documentation. If you need instructions for installing Word for Windows version 2.0, see Appendix A, "Installing Word," or see your Word for Windows version 2.0 documentation.

Installing the Step by Step Practice Files

Inside this book you'll find a disk named "Microsoft Word for Windows Step by Step Practice Files." These files should be copied onto your hard drive into a directory named PRACTICE. A special program on the Practice Files disk will do this automatically for you.

To copy the practice files onto your hard drive

1   Insert the disk into drive A: of your computer.

2   At the system prompt (usually "C:\") type **a:lessons** Do not type a space between "a:" and "lessons."

3   Follow the instructions on the screen. You can press ESC at any time to exit the Step by Step setup program.

The Step by Step setup program displays a message asking where you want to install the practice files. Then the files are copied from the floppy disk into the directory that you specify and are stored in a subdirectory called PRACTICE. You'll need to remember the name of the drive and directory where the practice files are stored, so you can open a file for each lesson. It's best to place the PRACTICE subdirectory in the directory that contains the Word for Windows program. This is normally the WINWORD directory.

Later, as you work through the lessons, make sure to follow the instructions for renaming the practice files so that you can go through a lesson more than once if you choose to do so.

Starting Word

You can start Word from the system prompt, or you can start Word from within Windows.

To start Word from the system prompt

1 At the system prompt (usually C:\), change to the directory that contains Word for Windows by typing **cd** *directory name*

2 Type **win winword**

3 Press ENTER.

Proceed to the next section, "Working in Word."

To start Windows

The following section assumes you are new to Windows. If you already know how to use Windows, you can go directly to the next section, "Working in Word."

Follow these steps to start Windows from the system prompt (usually C:\). The appearance of your screen may be different from the illustrations that follow, depending on your particular setup.

1 At the system prompt, type **win**

2 Press ENTER.

While Windows is active, everything on your screen is displayed in a *window*. In later lessons you'll learn to make each window the size you want and move it anywhere you want on your screen. You can have many windows open at the same time.

To start Word from within Windows

You can start all of your applications, including Microsoft Word for Windows, from Program Manager. Program Manager displays icons that you can use to start applications. Double-clicking an icon often displays another window that contains a group of related icons.

The following procedure shows the sequence that you work through to start Word from within Windows. Depending on your particular setup, you may not need to go through the entire sequence as described here. If you do not see the icon shown in step 1, look for the icon shown in step 2. If you do not see it, look for the icon shown in step 3.

1 Double-click the icon shown below to display the Program Manager window.

Program Manager

2 Double-click the Word for Windows 2.0 icon, shown at the far right in the following illustration. The icons on your screen may be arranged differently.

3 To start Word, double-click the Microsoft Word icon.

Working in Word

When you start Microsoft Word for Windows, a new document called *Document1* appears in a *document window*. The document window is Word's equivalent of a sheet of paper in a typewriter: It is where you type your text. The buttons and ruler you see at the top the window are the easy way to work on your documents. By using the mouse to click a button, select an option from a list, or adjust margins and indents on the ruler, you can change the way your document looks, check the spelling of the document, or perform any number of other common word-processing tasks.

The Word window

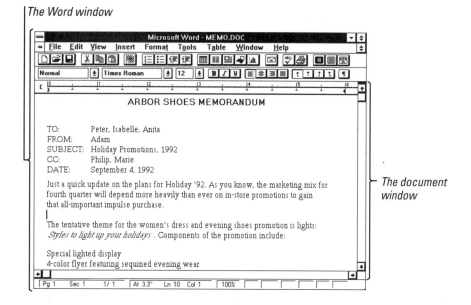

The document window

The rows of buttons and the ruler at the top of the Word window are really three separate items. You can display or hide them independently of each other should you need more viewing room on your screen. They are designed to speed your everyday work. It's usually most convenient to display all three.

Click Toolbar buttons to carry out commands such as opening, saving, and printing.

Use the ribbon to format documents, for example, to add bold, italic, or underlining.

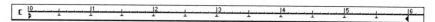

Use the ruler to set tabs or adjust margins and indents.

If You Are New to Using the Mouse

The Toolbar, ribbon, and ruler were designed for working with the mouse. By moving the mouse pointer over a button or to a location on the ruler and then pressing a button on the mouse itself, you can create great-looking documents quickly and easily.

The mouse controls a pointer on the screen. You move the pointer by sliding the mouse over a flat surface in the direction you want the pointer to move. You usually don't press the mouse button while you're moving the mouse. If you run out of room to move the mouse, lift it and then put it down. The pointer doesn't move while the mouse is not touching the flat surface.

Moving the mouse pointer across the screen does not affect the document; the pointer simply indicates a location on the screen. When you press the the mouse button, something happens at the location of the pointer. Throughout these lessons, you will be pressing the left mouse button.

When the mouse pointer passes over different parts of the Word window, it changes shape, indicating what it will do at that point. You'll work with the following mouse shapes during the *Step by Step* lessons.

Pointer shape	Significance
I I	The pointer is in the text area. This is sometimes called the "I-beam" pointer. In italic text, this pointer slants to make positioning and selecting easier. You use this pointer to indicate where you want to begin typing.
▶	The pointer is in the menus, inactive windows, scroll bars, ribbon, ruler, or Toolbar. You can choose a menu and command, click a button, or drag a tab stop marker.

Pointer shape	Significance
	The pointer is in the selection bar or the style name bar along the window's left edge. You can select a line, paragraph, or the entire document. This pointer also appears in table selection bars.
	The pointer appears after you press the Help key (SHIFT+F1). You can point to a command name or a region on the screen and click to view a Help topic about the item you clicked.
	The pointer is in a window border. You can change the size of a window vertically. A similar two-headed arrow indicates you can size a graphic or frame.
	You can change the size of a window horizontally. A similar two-headed arrow indicates you can size a graphic or frame.
	You can change the size of a window diagonally. A similar two-headed arrow indicates you can size a graphic or frame.
	This pointer appears when positioned over a frame, indicating you can drag the frame to a new position.
	The pointer is over a column in a table. Click to select the column.
	A small, dotted box and dotted insertion point appear when you select text or a graphic and press a mouse button to drag the selection itself to a new location, where you "drop," or insert, it.

Experiment

Take a moment to test drive the mouse. Do not press the mouse button, but simply slide the mouse so that the pointer moves around the Word screen.

1   Slide the mouse until the pointer is over the buttons at the top of the screen. Note the left-pointing arrow.

2   Slide the mouse around the large open area in the center of the screen, called the "document window." This is the area in which you type text. Note that the pointer looks like an I-beam.

3   Slide the mouse so the pointer is on the left edge of the document window. Note the right-pointing arrow. In Lesson 1, you'll learn a shortcut that uses this right-pointing arrow.

Using the mouse pointer

Moving the mouse and pressing the mouse button are the only skills you need to master the basic skills of *pointing, clicking, double-clicking,* and *dragging.* There are four basic mouse actions that you will use throughout these lessons.

Pointing Moving the mouse to place the pointer on an item is called pointing.

Clicking Pointing to an item on your screen and then quickly pressing and releasing the mouse button is called clicking. You select items on the screen and move around in a document by clicking.

Double-clicking Pointing to an item and quickly pressing and releasing the mouse button twice. This a convenient shortcut for many of the tasks you'll do in Word.

Dragging Holding down the mouse button as you move the pointer is called dragging. You can use this technique to select text in documents.

Adjusting the speed of the mouse

If you are new to using the mouse, you may want to slow the mouse down a bit until you get accustomed to moving it around the screen and clicking. The speed of the mouse is controlled by the Windows program. The settings stay in effect until you or another Windows user changes them. For assistance in changing the speed at which the mouse pointer moves and the speed at which it registers the press of the mouse button, see your Windows documentation.

If You Are New to Word Processing

Each time you start Word, you will either create a new document—a letter, memo, report—or work on a document that you or someone else has already created. There are several basic stages to creating a document. Steps 2a, 2b, and 2c are usually done a little at a time, alternating with one another.

Step 1 Typing

Typing text in Word is very similar to typing on a typewriter. There are, however, some important differences that can save you time. For example, when you type enough words to reach the end of a line, Word automatically moves to the next line. This is called *wordwrap*. With wordwrap, you do not have to watch for the end of the line. You will not need to press ENTER unless you want to start a new paragraph or create a blank line in the document. If a complete word will not fit when you reach the end of a line, Word automatically moves the last whole word you typed to the next line.

If you often type columns of numbers, you will find Word much easier to use than a typewriter. You do not need to set up tabs to create the columns. Word has a table feature that displays a grid of columns and rows on the screen. You type your information into the boxes that you see on the screen to organize it automatically in columns and rows. The grid does not print; it simply helps you organize information.

Step 2a Editing

Great writers often say their secret to success lies in rewriting their text, changing their mind, trying out a different word—in other words, *editing* the text. This is where a word processor is a great asset. If you change your mind after you write something, you can replace what you've written, add text, or delete the text you do not want.

Whichever the case, Word adjusts the spacing of the text—making more room for text that you add and closing up empty spaces left when you remove text. Your reader will never know a change was made. That's the beauty of word processing.

Step 2b Formatting

Formatting is the term used for controlling the appearance of the document. Formatting in Word includes several features available on many typewriters, such as applying bold, italic, or underlining, and centering text. It also includes other changes that Word makes easy, such as changing the number of columns in the document.

Step 2c Adding special touches

Word makes it easy to dress up a document. For example, you can add pictures and charts, create special effects with text, or type text once and have Word automatically insert the text in the top or bottom margin of every page in your document.

Step 3 Checking the spelling and grammar

Word can quickly compare each word in your document to a standard dictionary and highlight words that are not found. Word can also highlight possible grammatical errors. Word makes suggestions for correcting both types of errors, which you can accept or ignore. You can also make your own changes.

Step 4 Storing the document for safekeeping

The thoughts we hold in our memory are more likely to be lost than the thoughts we write down and file in an orderly way. This is also true of computers. When you create a new document, the information you type exists only in your computer's memory until you save it on the hard disk that is built into your computer or on a floppy disk that can be inserted and removed from your computer. Information held in memory can be lost if the power to your computer goes off. Saving a document stores it away on disk.

Step 5 Printing

You'll have many opportunities to print documents during these lessons. If you can't print documents, or if your document prints on a different printer than you expected, read through Appendix B, "Installing and Selecting a Printer," at the end of this book.

Step 6 Removing the document from the screen

When you are through working on the document, you save it on a disk and if you are ready, print it. Then you can *close* the document; that is, you remove the document from the screen of the computer. You'll no longer see it on the screen; it remains stored on the hard disk until you open it again.

Step 7 Displaying the document on the screen again

Perhaps you need to do more work to a document, or perhaps it was so good the first time that you want to use some of the text in another document. (Sharing text between documents is another way word processors can save you time.) To display a document on the screen, you *open* it. This puts a copy of the document on the screen. The real document remains safe on your hard disk.

After you make changes to the copy of the safely stored document, you have a choice. You can either replace the original with your new version—this is called *overwriting*—or you can save your version with a different name. If you save your version with a different name, you will have two versions of the document—the original and the revised document with the new name.

This completes the cycle. Every time you begin work in Word, you will either create a new document, as in step 1, or you will open an existing document, as in step 7, and then move on to step 2.

If a Lesson Directed You to "Getting Ready"

If your screen did not look like the illustration at the start of a lesson, or if you could not find the PRACTICE subdirectory, the lesson directed you to this troubleshooting section. You do not need to work through this section unless a lesson directed you to do so.

Displaying the list of practice files

You begin most of the lessons by opening one of the sample documents that came on the Step by Step Practice Files disk. The practice files should be stored on your hard drive, in a subdirectory called PRACTICE.

1 On the Toolbar, click the Open button.

Clicking the Open button displays the Open dialog box, where you select the name of the document to open. You must also tell Word where the document is stored, that is, on which drive and in which directory.

2 If the box labeled "Drive" does not display the drive where the practice files are stored, click the arrow next to the box and then click the name of the correct drive.

Most users would have the PRACTICE subdirectory stored on drive C.

3 In the box under "Directories," find the name of the directory where the PRACTICE subdirectory is stored. You may have to click the up or down arrow next to the box to see all the directories in the list. When you find the name of the directory, double-click it to open the directory and display the PRACTICE subdirectory.

The WINWORD directory is a likely location for the PRACTICE subdirectory.

4 Double-click the PRACTICE subdirectory to open it.

When you open the PRACTICE subdirectory, the names of the Step by Step practice files (the sample documents) are listed in the box under File Name. Click the up or down arrow next to the box to see all the names.

You are ready to open a file to work on. Return to the lesson to get the name of the file and continue from there. To open the file, click the file name, and then click the OK button.

If the directory that contains the PRACTICE
subdirectory is not open, double-click it.

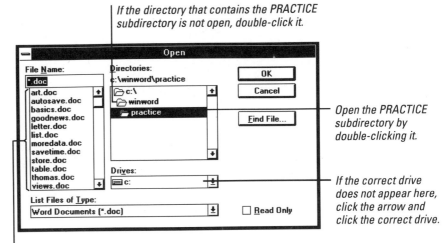

Open the PRACTICE
subdirectory by
double-clicking it.

If the correct drive
does not appear here,
click the arrow and
click the correct drive.

Click the name of the document you want to open.

Changing your screen display to match the illustrations

Word makes it easy for users to set up the Word screen to suit their working style. If
you share your computer with others, previous users may have changed the screen
setup. You can easily change it back, so the screen matches the illustrations in the
lessons. Use the following methods for controlling the screen display.

If buttons or the ruler are missing at the top of the screen

If buttons or the ruler are missing at the top of the screen, previous users may have
hidden them to make more room for text. You can easily display the buttons and ruler
as indicated below.

If you do not see the Toolbar, click the View menu, then click the word Toolbar.

If you do not see the ribbon, click the View menu, then click the word Ribbon.

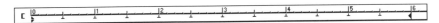

If you do not see the ruler, click the View menu, then click the word Ruler.

If the vertical scroll bar is not displayed

If you do not see the vertical scroll bar, a previous user may have hidden the scroll bar to make more room for text. You can easily display it again.

1   Click the Tools menu, then click the word Options.

2   Under Category, click the View icon.

3   Click the Vertical Scroll Bar check box so that an "X" appears, indicating it is selected.

If the Vertical Scroll Bar option was already checked, complete step 4 and then see the following procedure, "If Word does not fill the screen."

4   Click the OK button.

If Word does not fill the screen

A previous user may have made the Word window smaller to allow quick access to another application. You can enlarge the Word window by doing the following.

▶   Click the Maximize button to the far right of the Microsoft Word title.

The Maximize button

If the right edge of the Word window is hidden so that you cannot see the Maximize button, point to "Microsoft Word" in the title bar at the top of the screen and then hold down the left mouse button. Continue holding down the mouse button and drag the title bar to the left until you see the Maximize button.

If the document does not fill space that Word allows

The last time Word was used, the user may have displayed the document in a smaller size, to get an overview of a document. To see your document at the normal size, click the Zoom 100 Percent button on the Toolbar.

Zoom 100 Percent

Click here.

If the text seems unusually large or small

The last person to use Word may have "zoomed" in or out to get a different perspective on the document. To see your document at a normal size, click the Zoom 100 Percent button on the Toolbar.

Zoom 100 Percent

If you see the "top edge" of the page on the screen

The last person to use Word may have worked in page layout view, which displays one page of text on the screen. To return to normal view for the lesson, click the Zoom 100 Percent button on the Toolbar.

If you see words in brackets

If you see {TIME...} or {SYMBOL..} or {DATE...} in the document, you are looking at the codes that instruct Word to insert a certain type of information. You can hide the codes and view the information that Word inserts in place of them without changing the document in any way. To hide the codes, click the View menu, then click the term Field Codes.

If you see "¶" throughout the document

Show/Hide ¶

You are viewing the paragraph marks that indicate the end of paragraphs. You may also be viewing other nonprinting symbols that mark spaces or locations where the TAB key was pressed. The symbols do not affect the way the document prints. Many users work with the symbols on all the time. If you prefer to hide the symbols, you can do so without affecting the document in any way. To hide the symbols, click the Show/Hide ¶ button on the ribbon, as shown below.

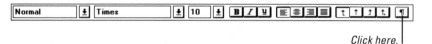

Click here.

1 Basic Skills

Lesson 1   Creating a New Document

Lesson 2   Copying and Moving Text

Creating a New Document

With the options available in Word for Windows, it's easy to create documents and make them look the way you want. In this lesson, you will type a short document and then experiment with the many formatting and editing options available with a simple click of the mouse button. When you're comfortable using the options, you will apply formatting to your name and address, creating and saving a personalized letterhead that you can use each time you start a letter. At the end of the lesson, your document will look similar to the following illustration.

Pat Tanner
555 Plaza Ave.
Middletown, CO 54230

This lesson explains how to do the following:

- Type text in a new document window
- Select text to edit or format
- Use the buttons in the Word window to perform common word-processing tasks
- Delete, replace, and move text
- Change the appearance of text and its position on the page
- Name and save your document for future use
- End your Word session

Estimated lesson time: 40 minutes

The Document Window

If you haven't started Word yet, work through "Getting Ready," earlier in this book. Then return to this lesson.

When you start Word, you see the basic Word window, with a new, empty document automatically opened for you. The document window is Word's equivalent of a sheet of paper in a typewriter: It is where you type your text. The new document is preset to use standard 8.5-by-11-inch paper, with 1.25-inch left and right margins, and 1-inch top and bottom margins.

Across the top of the Word window are the tools and features you'll use to do most of your word-processing tasks. The new Toolbar makes everyday tasks easy. Just click on the Toolbar for one-step access to common tasks such as saving and printing documents or creating tables. The ribbon and ruler, located below the Toolbar, make it easy to format text or adjust margins and indents.

Above the Toolbar is the menu bar, which gives you access to all the commands in Word. You'll learn more about menus and commands in later lessons; the first lessons concentrate on the buttons you see at the top of the Word window.

Buttons on the Toolbar make common tasks quick and easy.

Menus on the menu bar display groups of command names.

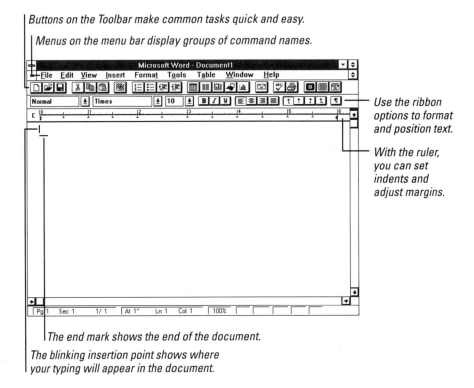

Use the ribbon options to format and position text.

With the ruler, you can set indents and adjust margins.

The end mark shows the end of the document.

The blinking insertion point shows where your typing will appear in the document.

Typing Text

If you are new to word processing, see "Getting Ready," earlier in this book.

You can begin typing in the empty document window, just as you would on a clean sheet of paper. The blinking insertion point, which is already positioned for you at the top of the window, shows where the text you type will appear. As you type, the insertion point moves to the right, leaving behind a stream of text.

Type your name and address

Follow the instructions below to begin this document as you would begin a typical letter. If you make a mistake as you type, press the BACKSPACE key to delete the mistake, and then type the correct text.

1   Type your name and press ENTER.

2   Type your street address and press ENTER.

3   Type your city, state, and ZIP code and press ENTER.

4   Press ENTER to create a blank line.

5   Type the letter salutation, using the name of someone you know. Then press ENTER.

In this book and in the Microsoft Word User's Guide, *text that you are to type appears in bold.*

For example, type **Dear Maria,** and then press ENTER.

6   Press ENTER to create a blank line.

Your screen should look similar to the following illustration.

Type a paragraph of text

Although you can press ENTER at the end of a short line of text as you have been doing, you do not need to press ENTER when you type longer paragraphs. As your typing reaches the right margin, Word automatically moves to the next line as you type. This is known as *wordwrap*. Press ENTER only to begin a new paragraph or to create a blank line.

▶ Type the paragraph below without pressing ENTER. If you make a mistake as you type, press the BACKSPACE key to delete the mistake, and then type the correct text or ignore the mistake and correct it later.

Word is a great place to work. Working in Word is easier than typing on a typewriter. Nothing is on paper until you print your document. You can correct mistakes, and delete, add, or move text as you go. You don't have to press the Enter key at the end of every line because Word wraps the text between the margins.

Display paragraph marks and special symbols

When you typed the inside address for the letter, Word inserted a paragraph mark (¶) each time you pressed ENTER. You can see paragraph marks on the screen if they are not already displayed.

Show/Hide ¶

▶ Click the Show/Hide ¶ button at the right end of the ribbon, as shown below.

To do this, point to the button shown below and quickly press and release the left button on the mouse. You'll use the left mouse button throughout these lessons.

If you're new to using the mouse, see "Getting Ready," earlier in this book.

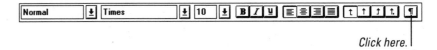

Click here.

In Word, a paragraph can be any amount of text, from a word or two, as in your name, to several lines. Even a blank line is a paragraph in Word; it's called an *empty paragraph*. Word also displays small dots that represent the spaces between words, created when you press the SPACEBAR. Paragraph marks and dots are nonprinting symbols. They will not appear in printed documents.

Your document should look similar to the following illustration. Your text may appear different than the illustration, depending on the printer that is currently selected.

Blank line, or "empty paragraph"

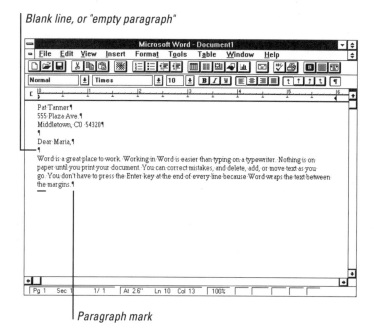

Paragraph mark

You can work with the paragraph marks and space marks displayed or hidden, simply by clicking the Show/Hide ¶ button. Many people find it easier to work with the marks displayed, so they can see, for example, how many empty paragraphs fall between lines of text. Some users work with paragraph marks displayed all the time. As you continue through this lesson, try working with the paragraph marks displayed. Hide them whenever you want to see how your text will look when printed.

Insert text into the practice paragraph

You can easily insert new text anywhere in a document. For example, the next procedure changes "easier" to "much easier" in the practice paragraph.

1   Position the I-beam pointer just before the word "easier" as shown in the following illustration and then click. This inserts the blinking insertion point where you want to begin typing. If you are working with paragraph and space marks displayed, click immediately to the right of the space mark.

Click here.

Pat Tanner
555 Plaza Ave.
Middletown, CO 54320

Dear Maria,

Word is a great place to work. Working in Word is easier than typing on a typewriter. Nothing is on paper until you print your document. You can correct mistakes, and delete, add, or move text as you go. You don't have to press the Enter key at the end of every line because Word wraps the text between the margins.

2   Type **much** and then press SPACEBAR to insert a space between "much" and "easier."

Word makes room in the document for the new word.

Deleting, Replacing, and Moving Text

You can delete, replace, or rearrange text before printing the document. To indicate which text you want to change, you must first *select* it. Once you've selected text, you can click a button to do something to the text. This is called "select then do." It's an important concept in Word.

Selected text is highlighted, that is, shown in white letters against a dark background or in dark letters against a colored background. How selected text looks depends on your Windows settings.

Select and delete a word

You can always press BACKSPACE to delete characters if you make a mistake as you type. After you've typed a paragraph or a document, it's easier to use the following procedure to delete, or "cut," text, whether it's one word or a number of paragraphs.

1   In the second line of the practice paragraph, position the I-beam pointer over the word "and." Then double-click—two quick clicks.

Dear Maria,

Word is a great place to work. Working in Word is much easier than typing on a typewriter. Nothing is on paper until you print your document. You can correct mistakes, and delete, add, or move text as you go. You don't have to press the Enter key at the end of every line because Word wraps the text between the margins.

The word is highlighted to show that it is *selected*. When you double-click a word, Word also selects the space that follows. This keeps the spacing correct after you delete a word.

Cut

2 On the Toolbar, click the Cut button as shown below. This removes the word from the text.

| Click here to cut the selected text.

The text in the document moves over to fill the space.

Change your mind

A handy feature in Word is the Undo button, which reverses, or "erases," your last action. (For this reason, the symbol on the button looks like a pencil eraser.) For example, clicking the Undo button will put back into your document the word that you just cut. Whenever something happens that is confusing or is not what you intended, click the Undo button as the *next* action.

▶ On the Toolbar, click the Undo button to undo your last action.

Undo

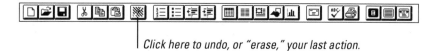

| Click here to undo, or "erase," your last action.

If this did not put the word back in the paragraph, you may have pressed another key before you clicked the Undo button. Undo reverses only the last action that you took.

Select text and replace it

Double-clicking a word selects it, as you have seen. You can select any amount of text by dragging across it with the mouse. Once you've selected text, the next text you type—regardless of its length—replaces the selection. Typing new text does not, however, replace unselected text. New text is simply inserted where the insertion point is. Use the following procedure to select a phrase in your practice paragraph and replace it with new text.

1 In the practice paragraph, drag to select the phrase "at the end of every line," as shown in the following illustrations.

Dear Maria,

Word is a great place to work. Working in Word is much easier than typing on a typewriter. Nothing is on paper until you print your document. You can correct mistakes, and delete, add, or move text as you go. You don't have to press the Enter key at the end of every line because Word wraps the text between the margins.

Point here, hold down the left mouse button ...

Dear Maria,

Word is a great place to work. Working in Word is much easier than typing on a typewriter. Nothing is on paper until you print your document. You can correct mistakes, and delete, add, or move text as you go. You don't have to press the Enter key at the end of every line because Word wraps the text between the margins.

... and drag to here. Release the mouse button.

TROUBLESHOOTING: **If you didn't select the amount of text that you wanted**   Click outside the selection and then try again. As you drag, keep the mouse pointer in the line of the text that you want to select.

2   Type the following words: **to end a line and start a new one**

Remember, you can click the Undo button right away if you want the original words back in the paragraph. You can even "undo" an undo.

TROUBLESHOOTING: **If your typing erased part of the word "because"**   If Word typed over the text outside the selection, Word is in overtype mode, a setting some users prefer. For these lessons, press the INS key on the numeric keypad to turn off overtype mode.

3   Check the spacing before and after the new text you typed. To add a space, position the insertion point and press the SPACEBAR.

Tip   You can drag to select any amount of text, as you have seen in this lesson. Some users find it easier to click where they want the selection to begin, then, while holding down the SHIFT key, click where they want the selection to end. Word selects everything between the first place you clicked and the second place you clicked. You can also adjust any selection by holding down the SHIFT key and clicking where you want the selection to end.

Select text and move it

The new "drag and drop" feature in Word makes it easy to move text to a new location, simply by dragging it where you want it. The following procedure shows how to move the second sentence to the end of the paragraph by selecting the sentence and dragging it.

1   Select the sentence "Working in Word is much easier than typing on a typewriter." Make sure you select the period and the space that follows the sentence.

2   Position the mouse pointer over the selection until the pointer turns into a left-pointing arrow.

The arrow indicates that your next click will do more than reposition the insertion point.

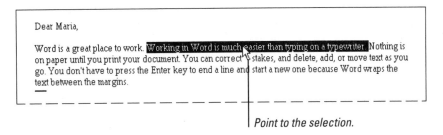

Point to the selection.

3   Hold down the left mouse button. A small, dotted box and a dotted insertion point appear. Drag until the dotted insertion point is at the end of the paragraph, as shown below. Then release the mouse button.

Drag the dotted insertion point to here.

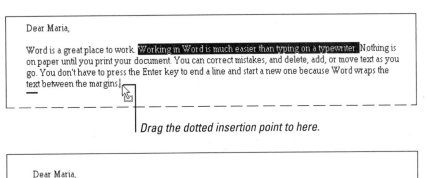

The selection is inserted in the new location
when you release the mouse button.

4   Click anywhere outside the selected text to remove the highlighting. Then click in front of the sentence you just moved and press the SPACEBAR to insert a space.

Making the Document Look Great

When you change the look of text—by centering it or making it bold or italic, for example—you are *formatting* it. The concept of "select then do" is important in formatting. You first select the text you want to format and then you apply the formatting. You can apply more than one format to selected text.

Bold, italic, and underlining are formats you can apply or remove quickly by clicking buttons on the ribbon. Just as the Show/Hide ¶ button displays or hides paragraph marks, these buttons apply formatting or remove it. For example, you can select text and then click the Bold button to apply bold formatting. Later, you can select the text again and click the Bold button to remove the formatting.

Sometimes it's difficult to see the result of your formatting while the text is selected. You can click outside the selected text to remove the highlighting and look at the formatting. You must select the text again if you want to apply more formatting to it.

The next procedures encourage you to experiment with formatting your name and address. You can create results similar to the following:

Pat Tanner
555 Plaza Ave.
Middletown, CO 55555

<u>**Marina Rocco**</u>
Via Verdi
I - 20100 Milano

Julien Beaumarchais
56, avenue Paul Doumer
F - 75016 Paris

Experiment with selecting entire lines of text

You need to select your name and address for the next portion of the lesson. Although you can always drag to select text, there's a faster way to select entire lines of text.

At the left of every paragraph, there's an invisible selection bar. By clicking in the selection bar, you can select an entire line. You can also drag the mouse pointer down the selection bar to select several lines at once.

1 Position the mouse pointer to the left of your name. When the mouse pointer changes to an arrow pointing toward your name, the mouse pointer is in the selection bar. Click to select the line that you are pointing to.

```
Pat Tanner
555 Plaza Ave.
Middletown, CO  54320

Dear Maria,
```

Click to select the line.

2 Continue experimenting by pointing to the left of other lines of text and clicking to select them one at a time.

3 Try using the selection bar to select several lines of text. Point to the left of your name, hold down the mouse button, and drag down the selection bar to select your name and address. Release the mouse button when all the lines are selected.

Drag down the selection bar to select several lines.

Change the look and position of the address

1 Make sure your name and address are selected.

2 Experiment by clicking the following buttons on the ribbon.

The Bold, Italic, and Underline buttons each apply formatting the first time you click them and remove the formatting when you click them again.

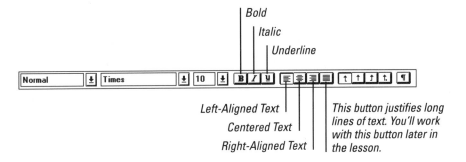

Note The button next to the Right-Aligned Text button *justifies* text; that is, it adds space between words in a paragraph to make the lines even on both the left and right margins. The lines in the address are too short to see that happen: Word aligns the text on the left but does not add the space required to extend the text to the right margin. Later in this lesson you can select your practice paragraph and experiment with the Justified Text button.

Change the look and size of the letters in your name

Select your name and take a moment to look at the buttons that you've been clicking. They reflect the formatting that you've applied to text that is currently selected. For example, if you formatted your name bold, the Bold button appears pressed down.

Word also shows the *font* and *point size* that the text will print in. The font is the design of the text characters (letters and numbers); the point size is their size. You can change the font and point size for selected text by displaying a list and choosing from it.

1   Select your name if it is not already selected.

2   To display the list of fonts, click the down arrow next to the Font box.

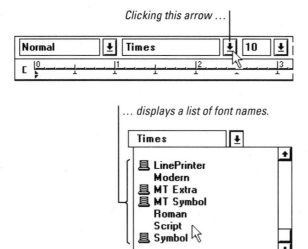

The names in your list may be different from those in this illustration. Font names that have a printer symbol next to them can be printed by your printer.

3   Click one of the font names in the list.

TROUBLESHOOTING: **If you see symbols or lines instead of your name**   Some fonts are for specific uses and convert your text to symbols or lines. To see your name again, select another font.

4   If you'd like to continue experimenting with fonts, repeat steps 2 and 3 to select other fonts.

5   To display a list of point sizes for the font you've selected, click the down arrow next to the Points box.

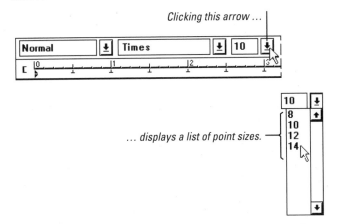

Clicking this arrow ...

... displays a list of point sizes.

6   Click one of the point sizes.

Experiment with fonts and point sizes until you are comfortable selecting them. Later in the lesson you'll have time to make the text look just the way you want.

Note   A point is a measurement used in the publishing industry. There are 72 points in an inch, 36 points in half an inch, and 18 points in a quarter of an inch.

Add a new paragraph

Word "stores" formatting information in the paragraph mark at the end of each paragraph. When the insertion point is at the end of a paragraph that has formatting applied to it, pressing ENTER copies the paragraph mark to the next line and carries the formatting into the new paragraph.

1   Click to position the insertion point at the end of your address, as shown in the following illustration.

2   Press ENTER.

3   Type your phone number.

Note that the phone number has the same formatting as the paragraph above it.

Tip   If you do not want a new paragraph to have the formatting of the one preceding it, press CTRL+Q before you begin typing the new paragraph. This removes, or *clears*, the formatting.

Format your personal letterhead

▶ Experiment with fonts and point sizes and apply formatting to your name, address, and phone number until they look the way you want for your personal letterhead.

Note   Your printer may not be able to print both underlining and bold, or other combinations of formatting, if they are applied to the same word. Check your printer documentation for any limitations.

One Step Further

You have learned three ways to select text. You can double-click to select a word, you can drag to select any amount of text, or you can use the selection bar to select one or more lines of text. If you'd like to practice these and other basic skills in your practice paragraph, try the following:

▶ Practice selecting one word at a time by double-clicking a word. If Word does not select the word, try again, changing the speed at which you click.

▶ Practice selecting several words or a few sentences by dragging across the text. Keep making selections of various lengths until you feel comfortable with dragging. To select text that spans two or more lines, you can point where you want the selection to start and hold down the mouse button. Drag straight down to the last line you want in the selection, and then drag to the left or right to select the text you want in the last line. Release the mouse button.

▶ Select the words "on a typewriter." Then use the Cut button to remove the text.

▶ Apply bold, italic, or underlining, or change the font or point size of one character of text, the entire sample paragraph, or anywhere in between. Vary the size of your selections and experiment with different formats.

▶ Select the practice paragraph and experiment with the Left-Aligned Text, Centered Text, Right-Aligned Text, and Justified Text buttons. The Justified Text button adds space between words until the text is even on both margins.

▶ Experiment with the Undo button by selecting text, applying formatting, and then clicking the Undo button. Word reverses the last action you took, so you need to click the button immediately to undo an action.

▶ Select a word, phrase, or sentence and drag it to a different place in the paragraph. If you don't like the changes, click the Undo button.

▶ Correct any typing errors. If you need to delete characters, click just after the characters you want to delete and press the BACKSPACE key. If you need to insert characters, click where you need to insert the characters and then type. If you want to replace characters, you can select the letters you want to replace and then type as you did earlier in this lesson.

Saving a Document

The work you've done is currently stored in the computer's memory. To save the work for future use, you must give the document a name and store it on a disk.

You can delete the practice paragraph now and save only your name, address, and if you want, phone number, to use later as your personal letterhead. You'll be able to use the letterhead over and over, each time you begin a letter. Before you save the document, make sure the letterhead looks the way you want.

Delete the practice paragraph

1 Use the selection bar to the left of the practice paragraph to select all the lines in the practice paragraph.

2 On the Toolbar, click the Cut button to delete the paragraph from the document.

Cut

Save the document

Use the following procedure to save the document in the same directory with the Step by Step practice files. During the procedure, Word displays a *dialog box*. You use dialog boxes to give Word more information about what you want to do.

1 On the Toolbar, click the Save button. The Save button has a symbol that looks like a disk; when you click Save, you save a document to a disk.

Save

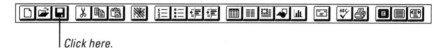

│ *Click here.*

2 Word displays a dialog box. The insertion point is automatically positioned in the box under the label File Name, so you can type a name for the document. Type your initials, with no periods or spaces, followed by the word **letter**

For example, if your initials were J.P., you would type the following without any spaces: **jpletter**

In later lessons, we'll write this instruction as "Type *your initials***letter**"

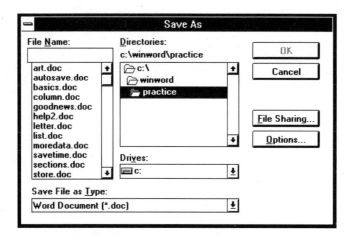

Document names can be no more than eight letters long. They cannot have spaces in them.

3 In the box under Drives, check to make sure that drive C: is selected, if that is where you stored your Step by Step practice files. If you need assistance, see "Getting Ready," earlier in this manual.

4 In the list under Directories, check to make sure that the Practice directory is selected. If it is not, select it by double-clicking it.

5 To close the dialog box and have Word save the document the way you've specified, click the OK button, or press ENTER.

Word displays the summary information dialog box. Although the information is optional, you will find it very useful later when you want to locate documents. You'll learn about the categories in this dialog box in a later lesson.

6 Type in each box as shown in the following illustration. Press TAB to move from box to box. Do not press ENTER until you've finished typing, because ENTER chooses the OK button and closes the dialog box.

7 When you've finished filling in the information, close the dialog box by clicking the OK button.

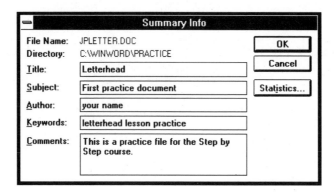

When you click the OK button in the Summary Info dialog box, Word saves the new document, along with the summary information, on disk.

It is best to name and save a document soon after you start working on it. After that, you should continue to save the document as you work. The Save button on the Toolbar makes this quick and easy to do. It's a good idea to save a document every 15 minutes or so as you work. This ensures that your work will not be lost if the power to your computer is interrupted. After you've named a document and saved it for the first time, Word no longer displays the dialog box when you click the Save button. Word simply saves the current version of the document in place of the old version.

Quit Word

To end your Word work session, you'll use a Word command. Word commands are organized into groups, called menus, which are listed on the menu bar at the top of the Word window. Choosing a command instructs Word to perform a given action. You choose commands by opening the appropriate menu and then clicking the command you want.

1 On the menu bar at the top of the screen, click the word "File."

Word opens the File menu.

Click the File menu.

2 To end your Word session, choose the Exit command by clicking it.

In future lessons and in the Word documentation, the procedure for quitting Word will be shortened to read "From the File menu, choose Exit." This is the standard phrasing for choosing commands. It means that you open the menu by clicking its name on the menu bar and then choose a command by clicking it.

Lesson Summary

To	Do this
Create a new paragraph or blank line	Press ENTER.
Insert text into existing text	Position the insertion point where you want the new text and then type.
Display or hide paragraph marks	Click the Show/Hide ¶ button on the ribbon.

To	Do this
Select a word	Double-click the word you want to select.
Select any amount of text	Drag over the text you want to select, or click where you want the selection to begin, hold down SHIFT, and then click where you want the selection to end.
Select entire lines	Point to the left of the line in the selection bar and then click. To select more than one line, select a line and then drag down the selection bar.
Delete text	Select the text and then click the Cut button on the Toolbar.
Replace text	Select the text and then type new text.
Move text	Select the text and then drag the selection to a new location.
Apply bold, italic, or underlining, or align text	Select the text and then click buttons on the ribbon.
Change a font or point size	Select the text, click the down arrow next to the Font or Points box, and then click a font or point size.
Reverse an action	Click the Undo button immediately after an action.
Save a new document	Click the Save button and then type a name that has a maximum of eight letters.
End a Word session	Choose Exit from the File menu.

For more information on	See the *Microsoft Word User's Guide*
Creating and formatting a simple document	"Your First Word Document"
The Word window	Chapter 1, "The Word Workplace"
Opening and saving documents	Chapter 2, "Opening, Saving, and Deleting Documents"
Typing and editing text	Chapter 3, "Typing and Revising a Document"

Preview of the Next Lesson

In the next lesson, you'll open an existing document and learn how to take advantage of work that's already done by copying useful text and changing it slightly. You'll also learn how to move text using the buttons on the Toolbar. At the end of the lesson, you'll use the Word spelling checker. Finally, you'll print a document for use in your quick reference notebook.

Copying and Moving Text

By copying and moving text, you can easily take advantage of work you've already done. For example, you can copy text, edit it, and use it again in a different location. You can also rearrange text by moving a word, sentence, or paragraph from one location to another.

During this lesson, you'll copy and move text a short distance using the mouse, and move text longer distances within a document using buttons on the Toolbar. You'll also check the spelling in the document using the Word spelling checker. The printed document, which contains tips and shortcuts for selecting text using the mouse or keyboard, will be the first page in your quick reference notebook about Word.

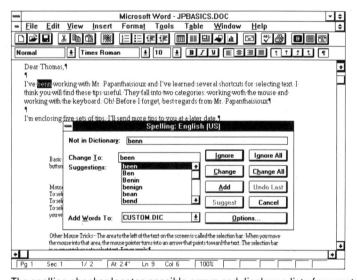

The spelling checker locates possible errors and displays a list of suggested alternatives.

This lesson explains how to do the following:

- Open an existing document
- Move text to a new location in a document
- Copy text to a new location in a document
- Scroll through a document
- Check and correct spelling

Estimated lesson time: 30 minutes

Start Word

For instructions about starting Word, see "Getting Ready," earlier in this book.

If you haven't already started Word, do the following.

1   At the C:\ prompt, type **win** and press ENTER.

2   Double-click the Program Manager.

3   Double-click the Word group icon if the group is not open.

4   Double-click the Microsoft Word icon.

Opening a Document

As you learned in Lesson 1, a new, empty document window is displayed when you start Word. You can also open an existing document—one that you or a co-worker has already created—and work on it in the same way you work on a new document. To open an existing document, you need to tell Word the name of the document and where it's located. You do this by using a button on the Toolbar.

Open a document

Open

1   To display a list of existing documents, click the Open button on the Toolbar.

   | *Click here.*

Word displays a dialog box, where you can select the name of the document you want. The dialog box you see may look different from the following, depending on where the Step by Step files are stored.

If the directory that contains the PRACTICE subdirectory is not open, double-click it.

Open the PRACTICE subdirectory by double-clicking it.

If the correct drive does not appear here, click the arrow and click the correct drive.

| *Click the name of the document you want to open.*

2 In the box labeled "Drives," make sure the drive where the Step by Step practice files are stored is displayed. Click the down arrow next to the box to see and select other drives.

3 In the box labeled "Directories," make sure the directory where the practice files are stored is open. If it is not, double-click it.

4 In the box labeled "Directories," double-click PRACTICE. This is the subdirectory where the Step by Step practice files are stored.

If you do not see PRACTICE in the list of directories, see "Getting Ready," earlier in this book, for assistance.

5 In the list under the label File Name, click BASICS.DOC.

6 Click the OK button.

Word closes the dialog box and displays the document BASICS.DOC. If you are a person who spots spelling errors at a glance, you'll see several in this document. Ignore them for now. At the end of this lesson, you'll use the Word spelling checker to correct them.

If you share your computer with others who use Word for Windows, the screen display may have been changed since your last lesson. The display is easily customized. For the illustrations in this lesson, the ruler was hidden to show you a few more lines of text. You do not need to hide the ruler as you work. If your screen does not look similar to the following illustration—with the exception of the ruler—see "Getting Ready," earlier in this book.

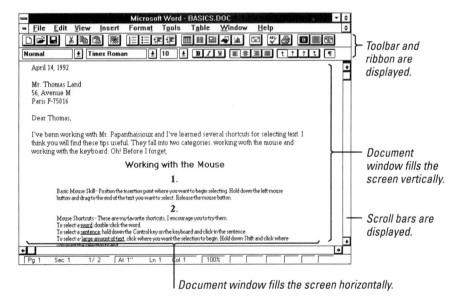

Toolbar and ribbon are displayed.

Document window fills the screen vertically.

Scroll bars are displayed.

Document window fills the screen horizontally.

Save the document with a new name

In this lesson and the ones that follow, you will begin by giving the practice document a new name. When you rename a document, it's like making a copy of it to work on: Any changes you make do not affect the original. This way, if you want to go through a lesson again, the original practice document will still be intact.

To choose a command, click the menu name at the top of the window, and then click the name of the command.

1 From the File menu, choose Save As (ALT, F, A).

Word displays a dialog box where you can type a new name for the document. For more information about using this dialog box, see Lesson 1.

2 Under File Name, type *your initials***basics**

Remember, this means that you type your initials with no space between them, followed by the word "basics." For example, if your initials were J.P., you would type **jpbasics**

Italic indicates text that you supply; bold indicates text you should type exactly as it appears.

3 Click the OK button.

4 When Word displays the summary information dialog box, select the name in the author box and type your own name if it does not already appear there.

For more information about the Summary Info dialog box, see Lesson 1.

5 Click the OK button.

Display paragraph marks

Show/Hide ¶

It's useful to display paragraph marks as you copy and move text. Word stores formatting instructions in the paragraph marks. If you include the paragraph mark in your selection, the text keeps paragraph formatting, such as centering, as you move or copy it. Displaying the paragraph marks also lets you see at a glance how many blank lines, or "empty paragraphs," you have between paragraphs of text and how many spaces you have between words.

▶ If paragraph marks are not displayed on your screen, click the Show/Hide ¶ button on the ribbon.

Moving and Copying Text to a New Location

Using the "drag and drop" feature in Word, you can quickly move or copy text short distances within a document. As you learned in Lesson 1, you simply select the text you want to move, then use the mouse to drag it to a new location on the screen. Using a similar procedure, you can make a copy of selected text and then insert the copy in a new location.

Drag a word to a new location

The address in the sample document is incorrect. "Paris" should be at the end of the line instead of at the beginning. Use the following procedure to move the word, using the "drag and drop" skill you learned in Lesson 1.

1   In the inside address, select the word "Paris" by double-clicking it.

2   Point to the middle of the selected word and, holding down the mouse button, drag the dotted insertion point to the end of the line of text. Release the mouse button to move the selection.

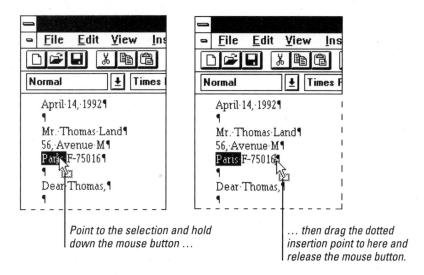

Point to the selection and hold down the mouse button ...

... then drag the dotted insertion point to here and release the mouse button.

3   After you move text, it's a good idea to check the spacing. In this case, you need to add a space before "Paris." Position the insertion point before "Paris" and press the SPACEBAR.

Copy text using the mouse

Copying text with the mouse is similar to moving text with the mouse. You can use the following procedure to quickly copy "Mr. Papanthaisioux" and insert it at another location in the letter.

1   Position the insertion point at the end of the first paragraph in the body of the letter.

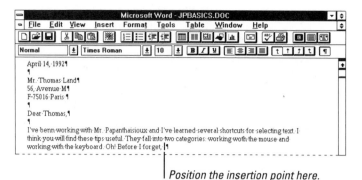

Position the insertion point here.

2   Type **best regards from** and press the SPACEBAR.

3   Drag to select "Mr. Papanthaisioux" in the first sentence of the letter.

4   Hold down the CTRL key on the keyboard, and point to the selected text and hold down the mouse button. Drag the dotted insertion point to the end of the paragraph. Release the key and the mouse button.

A copy of the selected text is inserted; the original remains where it was, unchanged.

5   Check the spacing. If you need to add a space before "Mr. Papanthaisioux," position the insertion point and press the SPACEBAR. Then add a period at the end of the sentence.

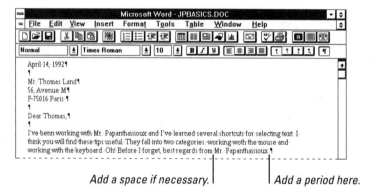

Add a space if necessary. | | *Add a period here.*

Scrolling Through a Document

The sample document you're working on contains more text than you can see on the screen at one time. To see the rest of the text, you need to *scroll* through the document. Scrolling means moving text across the screen to bring the text that's currently above or below the window into view. You use the *scroll arrows* and *scroll box* located on the *vertical scroll bar* to move the document text through the window.

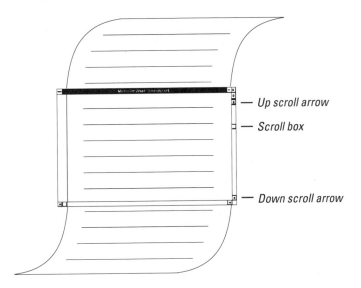

— Up scroll arrow

— Scroll box

— Down scroll arrow

You can use any of three methods for scrolling, depending on how quickly you want to move through the document. You can scroll line by line, window by window, or you can jump immediately to the beginning, middle, or end of the document.

Scroll line by line

Each time you click a scroll arrow, Word changes the screen to show you one more line.

1 Click the down scroll arrow once to see the line of text that is currently below the window display. Click the down scroll arrow a few more times.

2 Click the up scroll arrow a few times to see the text that is currently above the window display.

3 Try scrolling very quickly line by line—text will "roll" by. Point to the down scroll arrow and hold down the mouse button. To stop scrolling, release the mouse button.

Word scrolls past the end of the text and displays the blank space just beyond the end of the text. The next procedure shows you a fast way to get back to the top of the screen.

Tip When you scroll to the end of the document, you may notice a dotted line that extends across the page. This indicates a page break. Word automatically adjusts the page break as you add or delete text.

Jump to a different part of the document

The following procedure shows you a quick way to jump to the beginning, middle, or end of a document, or anywhere in between.

1 Point to the scroll box and drag it to the top of the scroll bar. (You cannot drag it off the scroll bar.)

Word displays the beginning of the document.

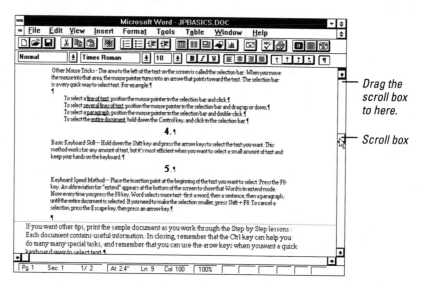

Drag the scroll box to here.

Scroll box

2 To see the end of the document, drag the scroll box to the bottom of the scroll bar.

This method offers an advantage, in addition to speed, over scrolling line by line: It always stops at the last line of text or slightly below the last line. You cannot scroll well beyond the text.

Tip You can drag the scroll box to any location on the scroll bar. For example, if you wanted to work on text that was in the middle of the document, you could drag the scroll box halfway down the scroll bar.

Scroll window by window

Sometimes you need to move faster than line by line, but you don't need to scroll very far—the text you need to see is in the window area above or below the text currently displayed. The following procedure shows you the best shortcut for this situation.

1 To see the window of text above what you are currently viewing, click in the scroll bar above the scroll box.

2 To see the window of text below what you are currently viewing, click below the scroll box.

Practice for a moment

You've learned three ways to scroll. If you frequently create documents that are longer than one-half page, scrolling will be a basic skill for you.

1 Click the up or down scroll arrow to scroll line by line.

2 Practice dragging the scroll box to various positions on the scroll bar—first to the top, then to the middle, then to the bottom.

3 Click in the scroll bar above or below the scroll box to move one window at a time toward the beginning or end of the document. Make sure you click in the scroll bar.

4 When you've finished practicing, scroll to the beginning of the document.

TROUBLESHOOTING: **If a line appears across the window** If a horizontal, double line appears, dividing the document window in half, it means you double-clicked the *split box,* which divides the screen display for special purposes. When the document window is not divided, the split box is located at the top of the scroll bar. To remove the horizontal line, point to the solid black bar in the middle of the scroll bar (the split box), between the two scroll arrows. When the mouse pointer changes to a double-headed arrow, double-click.

Moving and Copying Text Using the Toolbar

You've learned a quick way to move and copy text using the mouse, but in both cases, you could see the final destination for the text on the screen. If you need to move or copy text to a location you cannot see in the document, you can use buttons on the Toolbar to store the text until you display the new location.

The following illustration shows how you can use the Copy and Paste buttons on the Toolbar to insert text in a new location. When you copy text, Word stores the copy on the *Clipboard* —a temporary storage area. The text remains on the Clipboard until you cut or copy other text.

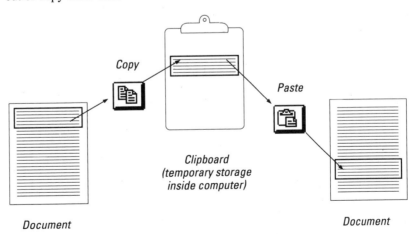

Copy

Paste

Clipboard
(temporary storage
inside computer)

Document

Document

Copy and edit a heading

Remember, the area to the left of the text is called the "selection bar."

In this procedure, you'll make a copy of the heading "Working with the Mouse," scroll to see the location where the heading is needed, insert the text, and change the last word so you have a new heading, "Working with the Keyboard."

1 Select "Working with the Mouse" by pointing to the left of it and clicking.

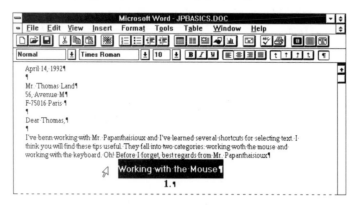

Copy

2 On the Toolbar, click the Copy button

Click here.

You see no change in the document, but Word has made a copy of the selected text and placed it on the Clipboard.

3 Click the down scroll arrow repeatedly to scroll line by line. Stop when the bold "**4**" is in the middle of the screen.

4 Position the insertion point in front of the bold "**4**."

You will have Word insert text here. When the new text is inserted, the text that follows the insertion point will move down to make room.

TROUBLESHOOTING:

If you accidentally select the entire line   When you try to position the insertion point at the beginning of a line, it is easy to accidentally select the whole line. This happens when the pointer is in the selection bar, at the left of the line. To remedy this, click well outside the selection to remove the highlighting and then try again. Always make sure the I-beam pointer, not the arrow pointer, is displayed before you click to position the insertion point.

Paste

5   On the Toolbar, click the Paste button. The Paste button looks like the Clipboard that is currently storing a copy of the text.

| *Click here.*

Word inserts a copy of the heading. The copy is centered because the paragraph mark, which stores paragraph formatting, was included in the selection.

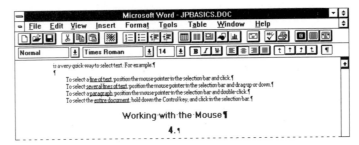

Edit the new heading

▶   Double-click "Mouse" in the new heading, and type **Keyboard** to complete the new heading, as shown in the following illustration.

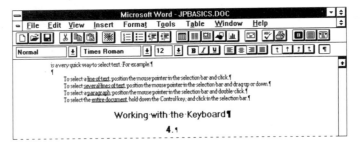

Moving Text a Long Distance

Moving text a long distance is similar to copying text a long distance, as you just did. The Toolbar provides buttons to make this easy. The difference is that instead of storing a copy of the text on the Clipboard, you remove the text from the document and store it on the Clipboard. Then you scroll to where you want to insert the text and paste it back into the document.

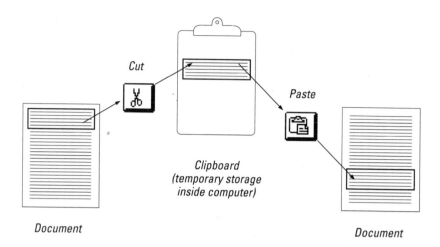

Clipboard
(temporary storage
inside computer)

Document   Document

Move text from the end of the document to the beginning

Use the following procedure to move the last sentence in the document to the beginning of the document.

1   Click the down scroll arrow until you can see "Sincerely."

2   Select the line that begins "I'm enclosing five sets of tips ..."

3   On the Toolbar, click the Cut button.

Cut

Word removes the text from the document and stores it on the Clipboard.

4   Drag the scroll box to the top of the scroll bar to move quickly to the top of the document.

5   Position the insertion point in front of the bold heading "Working with the Mouse."

Word will move this heading down, to make room for the text you insert.

Paste

6   On the Toolbar, click the Paste button to insert the text from the Clipboard.

7   Position the insertion point at the beginning of the line you just moved and then press ENTER to create a blank line.

Your document should look similar to the following illustration.

```
┌─────────────────────────────────────────────────────────────┐
│ ▄                 Microsoft Word - JPBASICS.DOC         ▼ │ ▲│
│ ▄ File  Edit  View  Insert  Format  Tools  Table  Window  Help │ ▼│
│ ─────────────────────────────────────────────────────────── │
│ [□][☞][▤] [✄][▣][▣] [▨] [☰][☷][≣][≣] [▦][▤][▨][≈][▦] [▱] [✓][▤] [▣][▤][▣] │
│ [Normal    ][±] [Times Roman  ][±] [10][±] [B][I][U] [≣][≣][≣][≣] [↑][↑][↑][↑] [¶] │
│ ┌───────────────────────────────────────────────────────┐ ▲│
│ │ April·14,·1992¶                                         │ │
│ │ ¶                                                       │ │
│ │ Mr.·Thomas·Land¶                                        │ │
│ │ 56,·Avenue·M¶                                           │ │
│ │ F-75016·Paris·¶                                         │ │
│ │ ¶                                                       │ │
│ │ Dear·Thomas,¶                                           │ │
│ │ ¶                                                       │ │
│ │ I've·benn·working·with·Mr.·Papanthaisioux·and·I've·learned·several·shortcuts·for·selecting·text.·I· │ │
│ │ think·you·will·find·these·tips·useful.·They·fall·into·two·categories:·working·woth·the·mouse·and· │ │
│ │ working·with·the·keyboard.·Oh!·Before·I·forget,·best·regards·from·Mr.·Papanthaisioux¶ │ │
│ │ ¶                                                       │ │
│ │ I'm·enclosing·five·sets·of·tips.·I'll·send·more·tips·to·you·at·a·later·date.¶ │ │
│ │              Working·with·the·Mouse¶                    │ ▼│
└─────────────────────────────────────────────────────────────┘
```

Save the document

Save

▶ On the Toolbar, click the Save button.

Word saves the current version in place of the previous version. You will not see any change to the document or the screen display.

Checking the Spelling in a Document

Before you print the document, you'll want to check for typos and spelling errors. With the Word spelling checker, you can do a quick and thorough job of *proofing* the document.

When you check the spelling in a document, Word compares each word in the document to a standard dictionary. The spelling checker may find words such as your name, your company name, or a technical term that are spelled correctly but that are not in the standard dictionary. You can ignore these words as you check the spelling. In Lesson 6, you'll learn how to add such words to a custom dictionary.

Word not only displays the misspelled word in the dialog box but also highlights the word in the document. You can read the sentence that contains the word to help determine the correct spelling. If a word is spelled incorrectly, you have two choices for correcting it: You can type it correctly if you are sure of the spelling, or you can select the correct spelling from a list of suggestions.

Word begins checking the spelling at the insertion point and checks downward from there.

Check the spelling

1   Scroll to the beginning of the document and position the insertion point in front of the first line (the date).

Spelling

2   On the Toolbar, click the Spelling button.

Click here.

Word displays the Spelling dialog box when it finds a word that is not in its dictionary.

Word highlights the mispelled word in the text ...

... and displays the word in the dialog box.

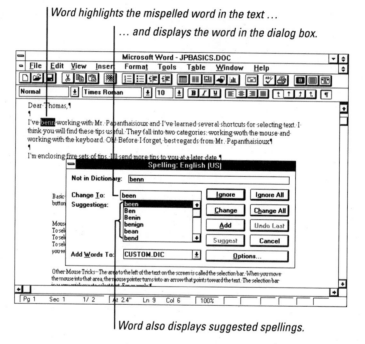

Word also displays suggested spellings.

3   If you read the sentence that contains the selected misspelling, you'll see that "benn" should be "been." Word already suggests that spelling in the Change To box. Click the Change button.

Word corrects the spelling in the document and selects the next misspelled word.

4   "Papanthaisioux" is a proper name that is spelled correctly. To have Word ignore this instance of the name and all future instances in this document, click the Ignore All button.

5 Continue checking and correcting the spelling in the document.

For this word	Do this
woth	Click "with" in the list of suggested spellings, then click the Change button.
Ctrl	"Ctrl" is a technical term—an abbreviation for the Control key. It is spelled correctly but is not in the Word standard dictionary. Click the Ignore All button.
many	Note that the label for the first box in the dialog box has changed to "Repeated Word." If you check the sentence that contains the selection, you'll see that there are two "many's" in a row. Click the Delete button.
arow	The spelling you want is the first suggestion Word makes. Click the Change button.
youneed	This is a typo that you'll have to correct yourself, using the following steps: • Click "youneed" in the dialog box. Word copies the word to the Change To box, where you can select and edit text just as you do in the document. • Press the left arrow key to position the insertion point between "you" and "need" in the Change To box. • Press the SPACEBAR to insert a space. • Click the Change button.

6 Click the OK button when the spelling check is complete.

Tip You can create custom dictionaries for words that are unique to your business so that Word recognizes technical terms and proper names that you frequently use. There will be more information about the spell checker in Lesson 6, "Proofing a Document."

Save the document

Save

▶ On the Toolbar, click the Save button.

Word saves the current version of this document in place of the previous version. You won't see a change in the screen display.

Print the document

If you are the only person who uses this computer and you have not printed a document using a Windows application, you may not have installed or selected a printer. If this is the case, take a moment and work through Appendix B,"Installing and Selecting a Printer." For complete instructions about installing and setting up a printer, see your Windows documentation. If you share this computer with others, it's likely that the printer is installed and ready to use.

Print

1 Make sure the printer is on.

2 On the Toolbar, click the Print button.

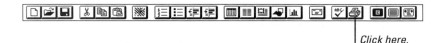

| Click here.

Word displays a message telling you that the document is being printed.

Tip Clicking the Print button on the Toolbar always prints the entire document. Occasionally, you may want to print just a page or two from a long document, instead of printing all the pages. This is easy to do. For information about printing, see Chapter 4, "Printing a Document," in the *Microsoft Word User's Guide*.

One Step Further

▶ Try combining the skills you learned in Lesson 1 with the scrolling skills you learned in this lesson. Scroll to display the text under each bold number. The text under each number is currently 8 points in size. Select all the text under a number and change the point size to 10.

To do this quickly, change the point size for all the text under one number, and then select all the text under another number and press F4. This is the Repeat key. Word repeats the last action you took—in this case, changing the point size. (For convenience, scrolling and selecting do not count as "actions.") After you've changed the point size for all text under the numbers, click the Print button on the Toolbar if you'd like to print the document with the changes.

If you want to continue to the next lesson

1 From the File menu, choose Close.

Remember, click the File menu, then click the Close command.

2 If a message is displayed asking if you want to save changes to the document, choose the No button. You do not need to save the changes you made to the document after you printed it.

Choosing this command closes the active document; it does not exit the Word program. If no other documents are open, the menu bar changes to display two menus: File and Help.

If you want to quit Word for now

1   From the File menu, choose Exit.

2   If a message is displayed asking if you want to save changes to the document, choose the No button. You do not need to save the changes you made to the document after you printed it.

Lesson Summary

In this lesson you used the following Toolbar buttons:

To	Do this
Open an existing document	On the Toolbar, click the Open button, and then select the document name from the list displayed under File Name in the dialog box. If you don't see the document name, check to make sure the correct drive and directory are selected.
Move text a short distance	Select the text. Position the mouse pointer over the selection, drag the dotted insertion point to a new location, and release the mouse button.
Copy text a short distance	Select the text, hold down the CTRL key, and drag the dotted insertion point to a new location.
Move text to a location not currently visible	Select the text, click the Cut button on the Toolbar, scroll to the new location, and then click the Paste button to insert the selection.
Copy text to a location not currently visible	Select the text, click the Copy button on the Toolbar, click to position the insertion point, and then click the Paste button.
Scroll through a document	Click the scroll arrows on the scroll bar, drag the scroll box, or click above or below the scroll box.
Check and correct the spelling in a document	On the Toolbar, click the Spelling button and then change or ignore words as Word selects them.

For more information on	See the *Microsoft Word User's Guide*
Moving and copying text	Chapter 3, "Typing and Revising a Document"
Scrolling through a document	"Your First Word Document"
Opening and saving documents	Chapter 2, "Opening, Saving, and Deleting Documents"
Checking the spelling of a document	Chapter 14, "Proofing a Document"

For an online lesson about	Do this
Moving text and checking spelling	Click the Help menu. Click Getting Started. Click Basic Skills. Click Basic Editing. Click Moving Text or Checking Spelling. Follow the instructions on the screen. To exit a lesson at any time, click the Control button, then click Exit.

Preview of the Next Lesson

In the next lesson, you'll learn to add bullets or numbers to lists. You'll also learn how to indent paragraphs and how to set page margins. At the end of the lesson, you'll have another document for your quick reference notebook.

Part

2 Everyday Tasks Made Easy

Lesson 3 *Using Indents, Margins, and Lists*

Lesson 4 *Working with Commands and Dialog Boxes*

Lesson 5 *Storing Formatting as Styles*

Lesson 6 *Proofing a Document*

Lesson 7 *Adding Page Numbers, Headers, and Footers*

Lesson 8 *Working with Windows*

Using Indents, Margins, and Lists

By default, the left and right margins in a Word document are set to 1.25 inches. Word automatically aligns text with the left margin. If you prefer different settings, you can use the mouse to indent text and adjust the margins. You can also use the mouse to indent lists and add bullets or numbers to them. In this lesson, you'll quickly indent two lists and then add numbers to one list and bullets to the other. You'll set paragraphs off from the rest of the text by giving them custom indents. Finally, you'll change the margins and print another document for your quick reference notebook.

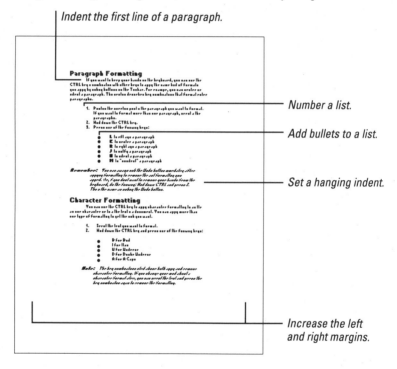

Indent the first line of a paragraph.

Number a list.

Add bullets to a list.

Set a hanging indent.

Increase the left and right margins.

This lesson explains how to do the following:

- Set left, right, and first-line indents
- Create bulleted or numbered lists
- Change the size of the margins
- View an entire page on the screen

Estimated lesson time: 30 minutes

Setting Indents and Creating Lists

You can quickly indent the left edge of one or more paragraphs simply by clicking a button on the Toolbar. You can also use Toolbar buttons to add bullets or numbers to lists automatically.

Open a sample document

If you haven't already started Word, do so now. For instructions about starting Word, see "Getting Ready," earlier in this book.

Open

1 On the Toolbar, click the Open button.

2 Under Directories, make sure the PRACTICE directory is open. If it is not, select the drive where the Step by Step practice files are stored and open the appropriate directories.

For information about opening a sample document, see Lesson 2.

3 In the list of file names, click LIST.DOC.

If you do not see LIST.DOC in the list of file names, check to be sure the correct drive and directory are selected. If you need help, see "Getting Ready."

4 Click the OK button.

If you share your computer with others who use Word for Windows, they may have changed the screen display since your last lesson. If your screen does not look similar to the following illustration, see "Getting Ready."

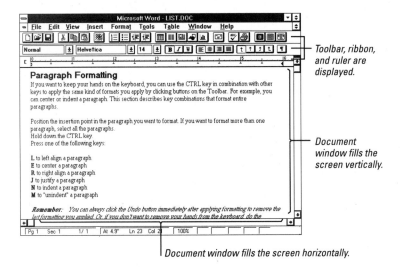

Toolbar, ribbon, and ruler are displayed.

Document window fills the screen vertically.

Document window fills the screen horizontally.

Save the document with a new name

Give the document a new name so the changes you make in this lesson will not overwrite the original document.

1 From the File menu, choose Save As.

2 Under File Name, type *your initials*list

For example, type **jplist**

3 Choose the OK button.

4 When Word displays the summary information dialog box, select the name in the author box and type your own name if it does not already appear there.

5 Choose the OK button.

Using the Toolbar to Set Indents

With buttons on the Toolbar, you can quickly indent one or more paragraphs. Each time you click the Indent button, Word indents the selected paragraph a half inch. Word has preset, or "default," tab stops every half inch, so you are actually indenting to the next tab stop. The Toolbar also has an Unindent button if you decide that you've indented a paragraph too far.

Indents affect entire paragraphs. If you want to indent one paragraph, simply position the insertion point in the paragraph before you set the indent. If you want to indent several paragraphs, select them before you set the indent.

Experiment with the Indent and Unindent buttons

1 Click anywhere in the paragraph below the heading "Paragraph Formatting."

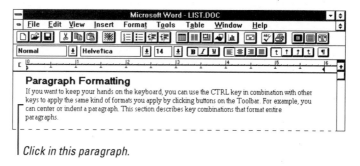

Click in this paragraph.

Indent

2 On the Toolbar, click the Indent button.

Click here.

3 Try clicking the Indent button again a time or two.

Each time you click the button, Word indents the paragraph 0.5 inch and wraps the text in the paragraph to fit.

Unindent

4 Try moving the paragraph back to the left by clicking the Unindent button on the Toolbar. Click the Unindent button until the paragraph reaches the left margin—it will not move beyond the margin.

| *Click here.*

Indent several paragraphs

1 Select the next three paragraphs of the sample document, as shown in the following illustration.

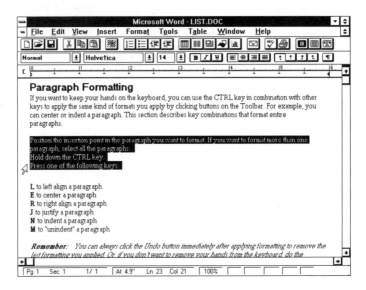

2 On the Toolbar, click the Indent button to indent the selected paragraphs 0.5 inch.

3 Select the next group of paragraphs, beginning with "L to left align ..." as shown in the following illustration.

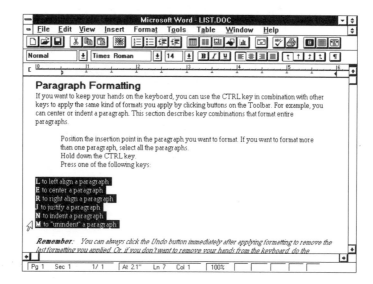

4 On the Toolbar, click the Indent button twice to indent the selected items 1 inch.

Creating Bulleted and Numbered Lists

Bulleted and numbered lists are common elements in many documents. Bullets clearly separate listed items from one another, emphasizing each point; numbers show sequence. Using buttons on the Toolbar, you can quickly turn a series of paragraphs into a bulleted or numbered list.

Create a bulleted list

1 Make sure the list that begins "L to left align ..." is still selected.

2 On the Toolbar, click the Bulleted List button.

Bulleted List

Click here.

Word inserts a bullet in front of each selected paragraph and adjusts the indents to separate the text from the bullets.

Position the insertion point in the paragraph you want to format. If you want to format more than one paragraph, select all the paragraphs.
Hold down the CTRL key.
Press one of the following keys:

- **L** to left align a paragraph
- **E** to center a paragraph
- **R** to right align a paragraph
- **J** to justify a paragraph
- **N** to indent a paragraph
- **M** to "unindent" a paragraph

If you see codes instead of bullets   If you do not see bullets, but see "{symbol...}" instead, you are viewing the codes that produce the bullets. To see the bullets, click View on the menu bar, and then click the Field Codes command.

Show/Hide ¶

If you're working with paragraph marks displayed   The arrow that you see between the bullet and the text is a tab character. Word automatically inserts tab characters to align the text. To see the text as it will print, hide the paragraph marks and tab characters by clicking the Show/Hide ¶ button on the ribbon.

Create a numbered list

1   Select the paragraphs directly above the bulleted list, as shown in the following illustration.

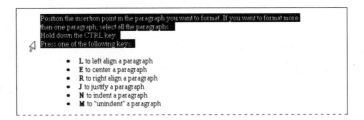

Numbered List

2   On the Toolbar, click the Numbered List button.

Click here.

Word numbers the list and adjusts the indents to separate the text from the numbers. Notice that when the paragraph is longer than one line, as it is in step 1, Word indents the second line of text to align with the one above.

Tip   Although the Toolbar buttons are the quickest way to create a numbered or bulleted list, many more options are available through the Bullets And Numbering command on the Tools menu. For example, if you want a different type of bullet, or if you want paragraphs numbered with letters instead of numerals, you can select from a large collection of symbols and then use the command to apply the bullet or numbering system that you want. You can also use the command to remove bullets from a selected list. You'll have a chance to experiment with these options in Lesson 4. For more information about this feature, see Chapter 28, "Adding Bullets and Numbers," in the *Microsoft Word User's Guide*.

Setting Custom Indents

Clicking the Toolbar buttons is the fastest way to adjust a left indent in half-inch increments. Sometimes, though, you may want to indent the right edge of a paragraph or indent only the first line. Or you may want to indent a paragraph to the 0.75-inch mark instead of 0.5. You can use the ruler at the top of your screen to set custom indents such as these. The ruler is preset to show inches. Each inch is divided into eighths.

The triangular markers on the ruler control the indents of the paragraph that you've selected. If you have not made a selection, the markers control the indents for the paragraph that contains the insertion point.

The left side of the ruler has two triangles. The top one controls the first line of the paragraph; the bottom one controls the entire left edge of the paragraph. The triangle on the right side of the ruler controls the right edge of the paragraph.

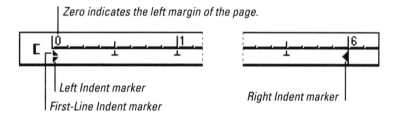

Zero indicates the left margin of the page.

Left Indent marker

First-Line Indent marker

Right Indent marker

TROUBLESHOOTING: **If the zero does not appear on the ruler**   The ruler can show either indents or margins. If zero is not visible on the ruler, it means that the ruler has been set to display margins instead of indents. If this is the case, click the double triangles to the left of the ruler to display indent markers and to have zero indicate the left margin.

Set a custom left indent

In the following procedure, you'll drag the bottom triangle on the ruler, called the *Left Indent marker,* to adjust the entire left edge of the paragraph, including the first line.

Clicking the scroll arrow scrolls the document line by line.

1   Click the down scroll arrow until the paragraph that begins "Remember: ..." is near the ruler, as shown in the following illustration.

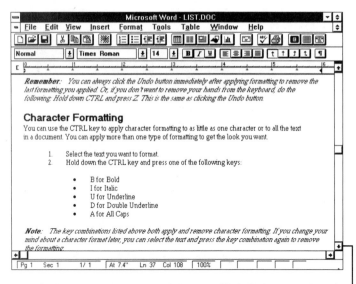

Click here until the paragraph formatted in italic is next to the ruler.

2   Click in the paragraph that begins with the word "Remember."

Note that when the I-beam pointer or insertion point is in italic text, it slants to the right, making it easier to select text.

3   Point to the Left Indent marker—the bottom triangle on the left side of the ruler. Drag the marker just past the 0.5-inch mark on the ruler and then release the mouse button. The top triangle will move with the bottom triangle.

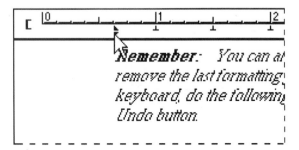

When you release the mouse button, the text moves to align with the Left Indent marker.

TROUBLESHOOTING: **If only the top triangle moves**   Both the bottom and top markers should move when you drag the bottom one. If only the top marker moves, it means the mouse pointer dragged the top triangle instead of the bottom. On the Toolbar, click the Undo button. Then, point to the bottom triangle and try again.

Set a right indent

▶ With the insertion point still in the italic paragraph, drag the marker at the right end of the ruler, called the *Right Indent marker*, to the 5.5-inch mark.

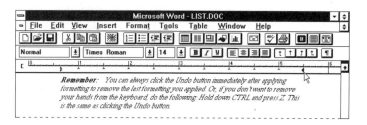

Set a hanging indent

The top triangle on the left is called the *First-Line Indent marker*. This marker controls only the first line of a paragraph.

▶ With the insertion point still positioned in the italic paragraph, drag the First-Line Indent marker to zero.

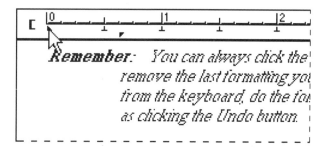

The first line extends to the left of the paragraph, with the rest of the paragraph "hanging" below it. This creates what is called a *hanging indent*.

TROUBLESHOOTING: **If both triangles moved** Only the top, or First-Line Indent, marker should move. If both markers move, it means the mouse pointer dragged the bottom triangle instead of the top. On the Toolbar, click the Undo button. Then, point to the top triangle and try again.

Indent the first line

1 Click in the paragraph under the heading "Character Formatting."

2 Drag the First-Line Indent marker (the top triangle) to the 0.5-inch mark.

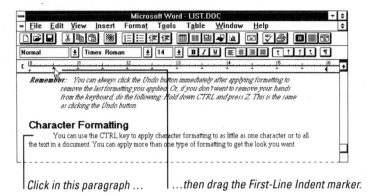

Click in this paragraph ...   *...then drag the First-Line Indent marker.*

Indent another paragraph

Working with the ruler is a useful skill. Take a minute to practice.

1 Scroll down to display all of the paragraph that begins with the word "Note," and then click in that paragraph.

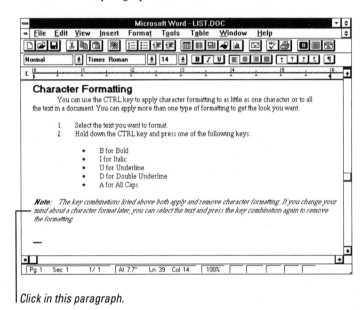

Click in this paragraph.

2 Drag the Left Indent marker (the bottom triangle) just past the 0.5-inch mark.

3 Drag the Right Indent marker to the 5.5-inch mark.

4 Drag the First-Line Indent marker (top triangle) to zero.

The paragraph should look similar to the following illustration.

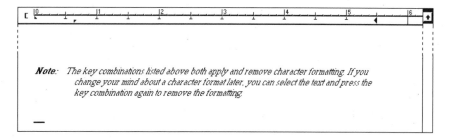

Further customize the left indent

Usually, dragging the Left Indent marker (the bottom triangle) moves the entire left side of the paragraph, including the first line. Sometimes, though, you may want to move the bottom triangle by itself. Here's a chance to try it.

1 Make sure the insertion point is still in the paragraph that begins "Note."

2 Drag the Left Indent marker to 1 inch.

The First-Line Indent marker also moves.

3 Hold down SHIFT and drag the Left Indent marker to 0.75, or 3/4, inch. Then release the mouse button and the SHIFT key.

The first line does not move. The paragraph should look similar to the following.

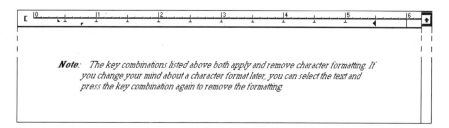

Tip If you know the exact measurements that you need for indents and you prefer to type the measurements instead of dragging markers on the ruler, you can use the Paragraph command on the Format menu. You'll learn more about this command in the next lesson.

Setting Margins with the Ruler

You've seen how you can use the ruler to set indents. The ruler can also display margin markers, which you can drag to change the page margins. You can display the entire page on the screen and see the effect that changing the margins has on the layout of the page.

Display the margin boundaries on the ruler

Indents are measured from the left margin. When you display indents on the ruler, zero indicates the left margin. On the other hand, margins are measured from the left edge of the page, so when you display margins on the ruler, zero indicates the left edge of the page.

▶ Click the symbol at the left end of the ruler to display the margin markers.

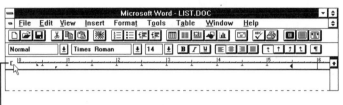

Click here to display the margin markers.

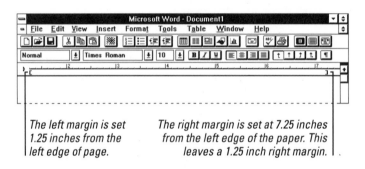

The left margin is set 1.25 inches from the left edge of page.　　*The right margin is set at 7.25 inches from the left edge of the paper. This leaves a 1.25 inch right margin.*

The ruler changes to display brackets, which mark the margins. The left edge of the text aligns under the 1.25-inch mark. Zero on the ruler now marks the edge of the page. This will be easier to see after the next procedure.

View the whole page

Word provides several ways of viewing a document, so you can concentrate on different aspects of your work. When you are setting margins with the ruler, you'll find it helpful to see the entire page at once. You can do that with the click of a button.

Changing your view of the document does not affect the document itself in any way. It only affects the way the document is displayed on the screen.

▶ On the Toolbar, click the Zoom Whole Page button.

Zoom Whole Page

Click here.

Word displays the entire page on the screen. The ruler adjusts to match the size of the display.

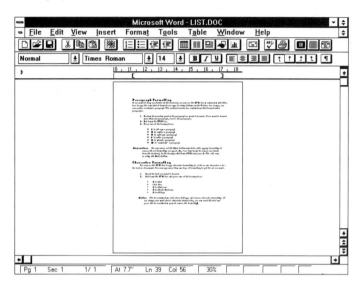

Adjust the margins

1   To adjust the left margin, drag the left bracket to number 2 on the scale. This creates a 2-inch left margin.

Drag the left margin marker to 2.0 inches.

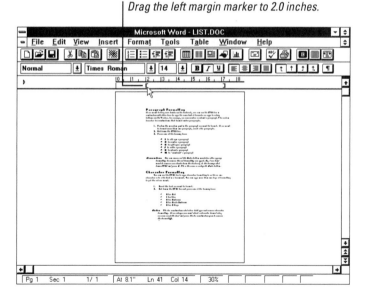

2 Drag the right margin marker to 6.5. The paper is 8.5 inches wide, so this creates a 2-inch right margin.

Drag the right margin marker to 6.5 inches.

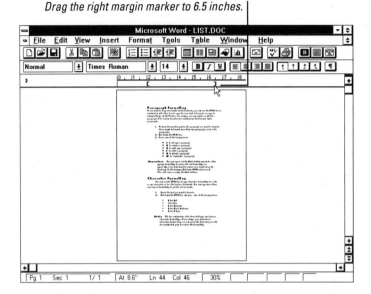

Switch back to normal view

▶ On the Toolbar, click the Zoom 100 Percent button to enlarge the display to its normal size.

Zoom 100 Percent

Click here.

Change the ruler display to show indents again

▶ To see the triangular indent markers on the ruler again, click the triangular symbol at the left end of the ruler.

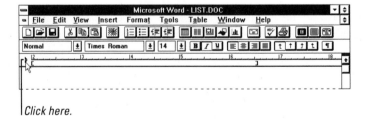

Click here.

The ruler adjusts to show the three indent markers. Zero once again marks the left margin and a vertical line on the ruler marks the right margin.

Tip   If you know the exact measurements that you want for the margins, you can choose the Page Setup command on the Format menu and type them in. You can also use the Page Setup command to set top and bottom margins. If you want different parts of your document to have different margins, you can divide the document into sections and set different margins for each. For more information about setting margins, see Chapter 9, "Margins, Paper Size, and Page Orientation," in the *Microsoft Word User's Guide*.

Save the changes

Save

▶   On the Toolbar, click the Save button. Word saves this version of the document in place of the previous version.

Remember that you will not see a change in the document or screen display as Word saves the document.

Print the document

The sample document you've been working on explains how you can format text as bold, italic, underlined, or centered without taking your hands off the keyboard. It also tells how to choose the Undo command without taking your hands off the keyboard. You can print this document and add it to your quick reference notebook.

Print

1   Make sure the printer is on.

2   On the Toolbar, click the Print button.

One Step Further

▶   Click at the end of the document and type a list of your own. It could be as simple as the days of the week or the names of the people in your family. Press ENTER after each item in the list, so each item is in its own paragraph. Then use buttons on the Toolbar to do any of the following:

- Use the Bulleted List button to add bullets to your list.

- Select the list and use the Numbered List button to change the bullets to numbers. Word will display a message asking if you want to replace the bullets with numbers. Click the Yes button.

- Select and cut one or more items from your numbered list. Then use the Numbered List button to renumber the list. Add one or more items and then renumber the list again.

▶   Scroll to the top of the document. (Dragging the scroll box is the fastest method.) Click in the paragraph under "Paragraph Formatting," and indent the first line to 0.5 inch.

If you want to continue to the next lesson

1   From the File menu, choose Close.

2   If Word displays a message asking if you want to save changes, click the No button. You do not need to save the changes made while experimenting.

Choosing this command closes the active document; it does not exit the Word program.

If you want to quit Word for now

1   From the File menu, choose Exit.

2   If Word displays a message asking if you want to save changes, click the No button.

This command closes the document and quits Word.

Lesson Summary

In this lesson you used the following Toolbar buttons:

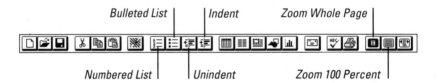

To	Do this
Set indents	Click the Indent or Unindent button.
Set custom indents	Drag the triangular indent markers on the ruler to set the first-line, left, and right indents.
Create bulleted lists	Click the Bulleted List button.
Create numbered lists	Click the Numbered List button.
Set margins	Click the symbol at the left end of the ruler to display the margin markers. Then drag the markers.
View an entire page	Click the Zoom Whole Page button.
Return to normal view	Click the Zoom 100 Percent button.

For more information on	See the *Microsoft Word User's Guide*
Setting indents	Chapter 7, "Paragraph Formatting"
Creating bulleted or numbered lists	Chapter 28, "Adding Numbers and Bullets"
Setting margins	Chapter 9, "Margins, Paper Size, and Page Orientation"

Preview of the Next Lesson

In the next lesson, you'll work with Word menus, commands, and dialog boxes. These give you complete access to the many features in Word. You'll also experiment with the online Help system that is built into Word, which is designed to get you help quickly as you work.

Working with Commands and Dialog Boxes

In earlier lessons you used the Toolbar, ribbon, and ruler to format text. These features provide quick access to the most commonly used kinds of formatting. Many more options are available through Word commands.

Word commands are grouped together in *menus*. To choose a command, you display a menu and then choose a command name from the list. Many commands provide further choices. For example, if you choose the Page Numbers command on the Insert menu, you have the choice of printing page numbers at the top or bottom of the page. You select options such as these in dialog boxes. A *dialog box* is a means of "conversing" with Word; you select or type options that tell Word how to carry out a command.

In this lesson, you'll learn about menus, commands, and dialog boxes by using the Character and Paragraph commands on the Format menu. You'll also use Word online Help, which provides both background information and step-by-step instructions.

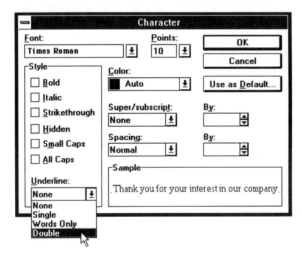

Dialog boxes display the options for a command.

This lesson explains how to do the following:

- Work with Word commands and dialog box options
- Use Word online Help

Estimated lesson time: 35 minutes

Open a sample document

For help on opening a sample document, see Lesson 2.

As you have seen in previous lessons, when you click the Open button on the Toolbar, Word displays a dialog box. Many dialog boxes display lists of items. The Open dialog box, for example, displays an alphabetical list of file names. You scroll through the list of names by clicking the up and down scroll arrows next to the list, just as you scroll through a document.

Open

1 On the Toolbar, click the Open button.

2 Under Directories, make sure the PRACTICE directory is open. If it is not, select the drive where the Step by Step practice files are stored and open the appropriate directories.

3 In the list box labeled "File Name," click the down scroll arrow as shown below until you see WORDHELP.DOC.

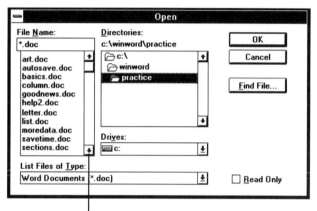

Click here until you see WORDHELP.DOC.

If you do not see WORDHELP.DOC in the list of files, check to be sure the correct drive and directory are selected. If you need assistance, see "Getting Ready," earlier in this book.

4 Click WORDHELP.DOC.

5 Click the OK button.

If you share your computer with other Word users, they may have changed the screen display. To begin this lesson, the Toolbar, ribbon, and ruler should be displayed at the top of the screen. The ruler should display approximately 6 inches, or the equivalent. Word and the sample document should completely fill the screen. If you need assistance in changing the screen display, see "Getting Ready," earlier in this manual.

Save the document with a new name

Give the document a new name so the changes you make in this lesson will not overwrite the original document.

1   From the File menu, choose Save As (ALT, F, A).

2   Under File Name, type *your initials***help**

For example, type **jphelp**

3   Choose the OK button.

4   When Word displays the summary information dialog box, select the name in the author box and type your own name if it does not already appear there.

5   Choose the OK button.

Using Commands in Word

A *command* is an instruction to Word to perform an action such as copying text, making text bold, or printing a document. The buttons on the Toolbar, which you have used in earlier lessons, provide quick and easy access to the most frequently used commands in Word. All of the commands in Word, including those on the Toolbar, are available through the menus on the menu bar.

Take a quick guided tour of the menus

If you're the type of learner who likes overviews, this section is for you. You can take a minute to browse the menus and get oriented. You'll display each group of commands, but you will not actually choose any. If you prefer to jump in feet first, skip this procedure and begin with "Get information about a command."

To browse the menus, click the menu names as instructed in the following steps. If you accidentally click a command on the menu, you can press the ESC key or click the Undo button on the Toolbar.

Menu names

1   Click the File menu to see the commands.

These commands affect the entire document. You cannot undo these commands. Note the bottom of the menu. The names of the last files you worked on appear on this menu. Clicking the name of a file opens it. It's a quick way to start work on a file you recently used.

Some command names are followed by an *ellipsis*—three dots. The ellipsis indicates that more information is needed to carry out the command. When you choose a command that has an ellipsis, Word displays a dialog box—a special window containing the options for that command. A command without an ellipsis after its name is carried out immediately.

The key combinations to the right of some command names are the keyboard shortcuts for choosing those commands. The key combinations appear on the menu as a reminder.

2   Click in the document text to close the menu and then click the Edit menu.

You use these commands to change the text in your document in some way. Many of the commands on this menu are unavailable now and appear dimmed because you do not have any text selected. The Cut, Copy, and Paste commands perform the same function as the buttons on the Toolbar.

3   Click in the document text to close the menu and then click the View menu.

These commands affect the way a document is displayed in the window as well as the way the Word window is set up. The Toolbar, Ribbon, and Ruler commands display or hide that feature, giving you a bit more room on the screen. A check mark shows that a command is currently "on," or active.

4   Click in the document text and then click the Insert menu.

This menu lists items that can be inserted in a document.

5   Click in the document text and then click the Format menu.

These commands affect the finished look of the document. For example, the Border command places boxes or lines around a paragraph, picture, or table.

6   Click in the document text and then click the Tools menu.

If Word has a miscellaneous category, this is it. The commands are a collection of special tools. The Spelling command is the same as the button you used on the Toolbar in Lesson 2.

7   Click in the document text and then click the Table menu.

Most of the commands on this menu are unavailable now and appear dimmed because you are not currently working in a table. Tables make it easy to create side-by-side paragraphs of text or perfectly aligned columns of numbers. In many ways, tables replace tabs as a way to create and align columns and rows of text. The commands you need to create and work with tables are located here. You'll work with tables in a later lesson.

8   Click in the document text and then click the Window menu.

You can have more than one document open at a time, each in its own window. You can see several documents at once in small windows, or one document at a time in a large window. You use this menu to control the display of the windows. You'll use these commands in a later lesson.

9   Click in the document text and then click the Help menu.

Word has online Help built into it. You can get specific information about whatever you're doing at the moment. The commands on this menu give you lists of steps, background information, or short lessons with hands-on practice. Using

Help is a great habit to develop. You get quick answers without ever turning away from the screen. You'll work with Help in this lesson and in the lessons to come.

10 Click in the document text to close the menu.

Get information about a command

Word's online Help system contains a description of every command. You can read about a command before you actually use it. Use the following procedure to learn about the Zoom command.

1 Hold down the SHIFT key while you press the F1 key once.

In the *Microsoft Word User's Guide,* this is written as "Press SHIFT+F1."

This key combination adds a question mark to the mouse pointer, indicating that you will choose a command for information only.

TROUBLESHOOTING: **If Word displays a window of text instead of a question mark**   Pressing only the F1 key or holding it down too long while pressing SHIFT displays the Help window. To hide the Help window, click in the document text. Then try step 1 again.

2 Click the View menu.

3 Click Zoom.

Word displays a Help window that describes the Zoom command and shortcuts or options related to that command. The Help window has its own scroll bars, separate from the document window scroll bars; you can scroll through the Help window in the same way you scroll through a document window.

You'll learn more about the Help window later in this lesson. For now, click the down scroll arrow in the Help window to read more about the Zoom command.

4 When you finish reading about the Zoom command, click in the document text. If the Help window fills the screen, hold down the ALT key and press F4. Either method hides the Help window.

Using Word Dialog Boxes

For many commands, Word displays a dialog box, where you select options that specify how the command should be carried out. Dialog boxes vary according to what kind of information is needed. Most of them, however, have certain features in common, such as check boxes, lists, and command buttons.

When Word displays a dialog box, you select or type the options you want Word to use. Then you choose the command button—usually the OK button—that tells Word to carry out the command using the options you specified. Or, if you change your mind while the dialog box is displayed, you can choose the Cancel button, and Word will not carry out the command. When you choose the Cancel button, no change is made to the document.

For most commands, you must identify the text you want the command to act on before you choose the command. This is the "select then do" concept you learned in Lesson 1.

Choose a command

The ribbon provides buttons and boxes for the most frequently used character formats—such as bold, italic, and underlining, which you can apply to as little as one character of text. There are many other character formats available through the Character command. In this procedure you'll apply formatting using that command.

1   Select the bold heading "For information about dialog boxes."

Remember, you can drag to select the text in a paragraph, but it's faster to use the selection bar.

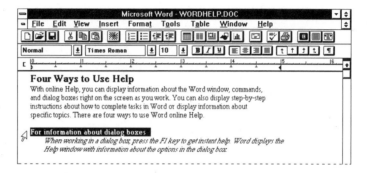

2   From the Format menu, choose Character.

Remember that this means to click the Format menu at the top of the screen and then click the Character command.

Word displays the Character dialog box, which contains all the options available in Word for formatting characters. Some of these options, such as font, point size, bold, and italic, also appear on the ribbon; you used them in earlier lessons.

A sample of your selection appears in the lower-right corner of the dialog box. As you select options, Word formats the sample to show you the effect before you apply the formatting to the document.

The settings in the dialog box identify which formats are currently applied to the selected text.

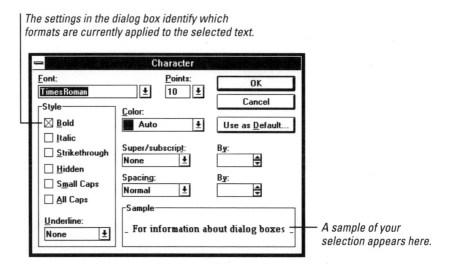

A sample of your selection appears here.

Select options using check boxes

Dialog boxes often include check boxes such as those grouped together under the label "Style." The settings reflect the current formatting of the selected text. For example, an "X" appears in the Bold check box, indicating that the selection is currently formatted bold. To specify options you want Word to use, you can select or clear one or more check boxes.

1   Click the Bold check box to remove, or *clear,* the formatting. Note the change in the sample.

2   Experiment with the check boxes. Start with Italic and work with each of the check boxes. Click each one once to select the formatting and then click the box again to clear the formatting. Try selecting different combinations of check boxes. Watch the sample change to show the formatting.

Note that selecting the Hidden option places a dotted line under the sample text; this indicates the characters can be hidden. You use the hidden text format for text you don't want to appear on the screen, that you don't want to appear in the printed document, or both. For example, you could format notes to yourself or a co-worker as hidden text.

3   When you finish experimenting, select the Bold check box and make sure the other check boxes are clear. Only the Bold check box should have an "X" in it.

Select options from a list

When several alternatives are available for one option, they are frequently stored on a drop-down list. You display the list by clicking the down-pointing arrow.

1   Click the down arrow next to the Underline box.

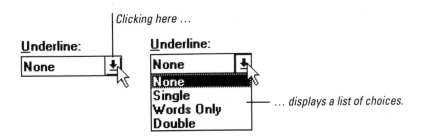

Clicking here ...

... displays a list of choices.

2 Experiment by clicking one of the choices in the list and then viewing the effect on the sample. Then, click the down arrow again and click a different kind of underline.

3 When you finish experimenting, click the down arrow and click the option for a double underline.

Type an option in a text box

Note the difference between the Underline box and the Points box. The down arrow does not touch the Points box, indicating that you can either type in the box or select from a list of options. If you move the mouse pointer over the Points box, you'll see that the pointer changes to the I-beam you've used when typing text in the document.

You'll recall from Lesson 1 that the size of characters is measured in points. For example, the text you are reading right now is a 10-point font. The heading "Type an option in a text box" is a 12-point font.

1 Next to the Points box, click the down arrow to display the list of point sizes.

2 Suppose that you want 16 points, and it does not appear in the list. First, select the measurement that is currently in the Points box by dragging across it. Then type **16**. Make sure you type the number "1" on the keyboard, not the lowercase letter "L."

3 To see the effect on the sample, you must move to another option within the dialog box. For example, click in the Font box. You'll see an increase in the size of the letters in the sample, depending on the capabilities of the currently selected printer.

4 If you change your mind after seeing the sample, it's easy to change the point size. Select the measurement in the Points box again.

5 Type **11**

Make sure you type the number "1", not the lowercase letter "L."

6 Click in the Font box to see the effect.

Get Help about dialog box options

F1 is the Help key.

When you are working in a dialog box, you can read about the options by pressing the F1 key.

1 With the Character dialog box still open, press the F1 key.

Word displays a Help window that describes the command and the dialog box options. The Help window may look slightly different from the following illustration, but the procedures described in this lesson are basically the same.

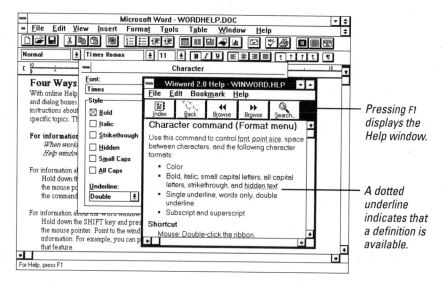

Pressing F1 displays the Help window.

A dotted underline indicates that a definition is available.

2 In the Help window, point to the phrase "point size." When the mouse pointer changes to resemble a hand, hold down the mouse button to display and read a definition of the term.

3 Click the down arrow on the Help window scroll bar to read more about the dialog box options.

TROUBLESHOOTING: **If the Help window disappears** If you accidentally click outside the Help window instead of clicking the down scroll arrow, Help is hidden behind the Word window. If this occurs, press F1 to display Help again.

4 To hide the Help window, click in the document window, not in the dialog box. If the Help window completely fills the screen, you can hold down the ALT key and press F4 to close the Help window.

If you accidentally click the dialog box, click the Help window again and then click the document window.

Tip In a later lesson you'll learn to size and move the Help window so you can read about the available options as you work in the dialog box.

Complete the command

Clicking the OK button in a dialog box carries out the command using the options you've selected. On the other hand, clicking the Cancel button returns you to your document without carrying out the command—none of the changes you indicated in the dialog box will occur.

▶ To complete the command after selecting dialog box options, click the OK button.

In the *Microsoft Word User's Guide,* this is phrased "Choose the OK button." You *choose* a command or button either by clicking it or by pressing keys on the keyboard.

If you choose the OK button and then change your mind, there's always the Undo button on the Toolbar.

You may wonder about the Use As Default button. It stores the settings in the dialog box as your default, or preset, settings. These settings will be used for future documents; that is, whenever you open a new document and begin typing, your text will automatically have the formatting options that were chosen when you clicked the Use As Default button.

TROUBLESHOOTING: **If you accidentally chose the Use As Default button**   Click the No button when Word displays a confirmation message.

Tip   Pressing ENTER is the same as clicking whichever button in a dialog box has a bold outline—usually the OK button. Pressing ESC is the same as clicking the Cancel button.

Choose another command

Another command you may use frequently is the Paragraph command. Options you set with the command affect entire paragraphs. You worked with indents, a paragraph format, in Lesson 3. That option and more are available through the Paragraph command.

For example, in Lesson 3 you learned two ways to set indents. You clicked the Indent button on the Toolbar to indent paragraphs to the default tab stop, which is 0.5 inch. You also set custom indents by dragging the triangular markers on the ruler.

If you know the exact measurement you want for indents, the Paragraph dialog box offers a third alternative. You can type or select exact measurements and preview the effect on a sample paragraph displayed in the dialog box. In this procedure, you'll set the left and right indents to 0.6 inch.

1   Select the italic paragraph under the heading "For information about dialog boxes," as shown in the following illustration.

To quickly select an entire paragraph, you can move the mouse pointer into the selection bar, point to any line of the paragraph, and double-click.

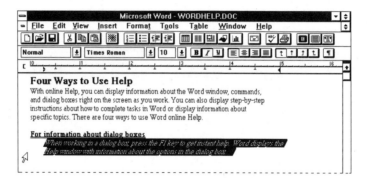

2 From the Format menu, choose Paragraph.

Word displays the Paragraph dialog box. In the lower-right corner is a sample, which gives you a preview of the options as you set them. This dialog box shows you the current formatting of the selected text. For example, the paragraph currently has a 0.25-inch left indent.

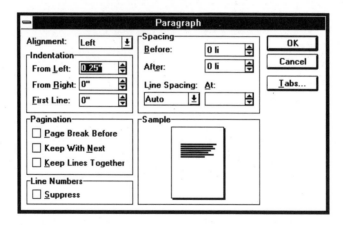

3 The options for indentation are grouped together. Click the up arrow next to the box that is labeled "From Left" until 0.6" is displayed in the text box.

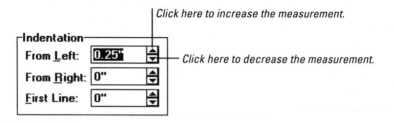

Click here to increase the measurement.

Click here to decrease the measurement.

The number in the From Left box increases each time you click the up arrow, indicating how far the selected text will be indented from the left margin. Note that the sample has changed to reflect the setting.

4 Click the up arrow next to the From Right box until 0.6" is displayed in the text box.

Tip By default, indents are set in inches. If you prefer a different unit of measurement, you can drag to select the text in the box and then type a measurement. For example, you can type **1.5 cm** for 1.5 centimeters. Word converts the measurement to inches when you choose the OK button.

Add spacing before the paragraph

Instead of pressing ENTER to add blank lines before and after a heading or text paragraph, you can make the spacing part of the paragraph's formatting. Later, if you need to move the paragraph to another location in the document, the correct spacing travels with it. This method also gives you more flexibility. You can increase spacing by a fraction of a line, for example, by 1.5 or 1.75 lines.

▶ Under Spacing, click the up arrow in the Before box until "1 li" is displayed. This will add one line of space before the paragraph.

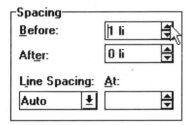

Remember to check the sample in the lower-right corner of the dialog box to see the results.

Tip Word is preset to measure the space before or after a paragraph in lines. If you prefer a different measurement, you can drag to select the text in the box and then type the measurement that you want; for example, you can type **9 pt** for 9 points.

Change the line spacing within a paragraph

Word is preset to create single-spaced lines. When the Auto setting is used, Word automatically enlarges the line spacing if necessary to accommodate a large font size or a graphic. If you prefer a different line spacing, you can change the setting.

1 Click the down arrow under Line Spacing. This displays the spacing options.

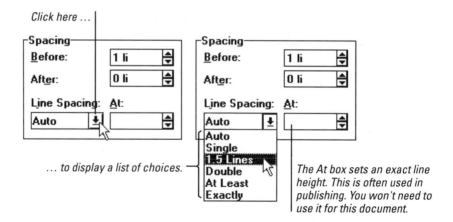

Click here ...

... *to display a list of choices.*

The At box sets an exact line height. This is often used in publishing. You won't need to use it for this document.

2   Select the 1.5 Lines option by clicking it.

3   To apply the formatting and close the dialog box, choose the OK button.

4   To get a better look at the formatting, click outside the selection to remove the highlighting.

Tip   If you want to change the line spacing for an entire document, use the Select All command on the Edit menu to select the entire document and then choose the Paragraph command and set the spacing.

Save

Save the document

▶   On the Toolbar, click the Save button.

Word saves the current version of the document in place of the previous version.

Using Keys to Choose Commands and Options

This book teaches the mouse method for working with Word. Sometimes you may prefer to choose commands and dialog box options using the keyboard. This is easy to do. Work through the following procedure to learn the keyboard method for working in Word.

Choose commands and options using keys

1   Take a moment to look at the menu bar and note the underlined letters in menu names, such as Table and Format.

2   Click the Format menu to see that underlined letters also appear in command names, such as Character.

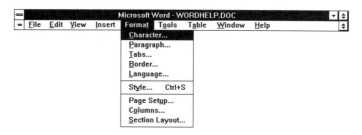

3 Click the Character command to see underlined letters in the names of the dialog
box options, such as Font, Points, and Small Caps.

Holding down the ALT key and pressing an underlined letter chooses that menu,
command, or option.

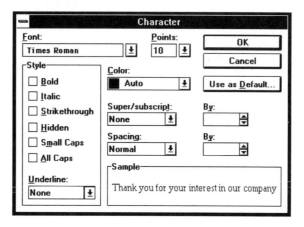

4 To use the keyboard to select options from a drop-down list, press ALT plus the
underlined letter of the option to display the list. For example, to select from the
Points list, press ALT+P. Then press the DOWN ARROW on the keyboard to select the
item you want.

5 To close the list, either press ALT plus another underlined letter to move to another
location in the dialog box, or press ENTER to complete the command.
−or−
To close the dialog box without completing the command, press ESC.

Note The *Microsoft Word User's Guide* lists the keystrokes for menus and commands at the end of every command. For example, to choose the Open command on
the File menu, you hold down the ALT key while pressing the F key and then the O key.
An instruction such as this is written "From the File menu, choose Open (ALT, F, O)."
These lessons will use this convention from now on, so the commands you see in this
book will match those in the documentation. You can use the mouse or the keyboard
to choose the commands, whichever you prefer.

Locating Information in Help

You can quickly search the online Help topics for the information that you need. Once you display a topic, you can click phrases that have solid underlines to jump to related topics. You can click a button to retrace your path through Help, backtracking through the topics.

Search for a topic in Help

You've learned three ways to set indents—with a command, with the ruler, and with the Toolbar. Later, as you are working, you may want a quick reminder about how to set indents. You can search Help for information.

1 Press the F1 key.

Pressing F1 displays the Help window. You could click any of the underlined topics and browse for information, but it's often faster to have Word search for what you need.

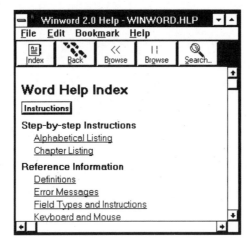

2 Click the Search button.

You'll begin your search at the top of this dialog box and work your way toward the bottom of the dialog box. The dialog box on your screen may look slightly different from the illustrations.

3 Type **indent** but do not press ENTER.

As you type, Word searches for categories of information associated with the word "indent," and displays those categories in the middle box.

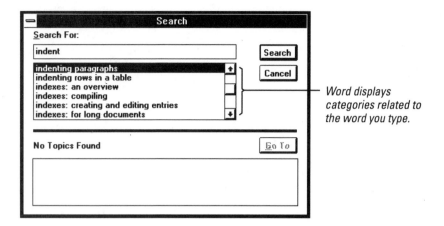

Word displays
categories related to
the word you type.

4 In the middle box, click the category "indenting paragraphs" if it's not already
selected.

5 Click the Search button to show the topics.

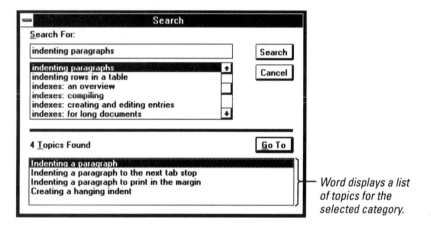

Word displays a list
of topics for the
selected category.

6 In the bottom box, click "Indenting a paragraph" and then click the Go To button.

Word displays information about indenting a paragraph.

7 Use the down scroll arrow in the Help window to view information about indenting
paragraphs.

Jump to a related topic

If you do not see what you need in a Help topic, you can click any underlined phrase
in the topic to jump to related information.

1 Click the down scroll arrow to scroll through the Help window text until you see
the underlined phrase "Indenting a paragraph to the next tab stop."

2 To jump to this related topic, point to the phrase. When the mouse pointer changes to resemble a hand, click the underlined phrase.

Word displays information about the topic. Take a moment to scroll through the topic, reading any definitions.

Return to the previous topic

You can backtrack through the Help topics that you've displayed.

1 Click the Back button in the Help window.

Word displays the previous topic.

2 When you finish reading the topic, click in the document to hide the Help window.

If You Are Familiar with WordPerfect Commands

If you are accustomed to working in WordPerfect, the Word online Help system can ease the transition to Word commands. In the Help system, you can choose a WordPerfect command name to read about the Word procedure, or you can watch as Word demonstrates the appropriate procedure.

Find the Word equivalent of a WordPerfect command

1 Select the paragraph that follows "Four Ways to Use Help."

2 From the Help menu, choose WordPerfect Help (ALT, H, W).

3 In the Command Key box, click "Indent->." You may need to scroll the list to see this command.

Help displays information about the command you select.

4 For a demonstration of the command, click the Demo option on the right side of the box, then click the OK button.

Tip The dialog box that Word displays when you choose WordPerfect Help from the Help menu includes a button labeled Automatic Keys. You can click this button to learn the Word commands you need for your daily work. When you choose this button, the Help system demonstrates Word commands automatically as you need them, when you press WordPerfect key combinations. When you no longer need the automatic demonstrations, choose the WordPerfect Help command from the Help menu and click the Disable Automatic button. The lessons in this book are designed to work with Automatic Help disabled.

One Step Further

▶ If you'd like to experiment with other character formatting options, select the document title "Four Ways to Use Help." Then, from the Format menu, choose Character. Experiment with the Spacing option to get special effects in the title of the document. When you select the Expanded or Condensed options, Word automatically expands or condenses the space between the characters by a certain amount. You can "fine-tune" the spacing by adjusting the measurement in the "By" box. This box shows the measurement in points.

▶ Experiment with the Color option in the Character dialog box. (From the Format menu, choose Character to display the box.) You can see the effect of different options on the sample. When you finish experimenting, leave the color set to Auto. The Color options are listed alphabetically. You may need to scroll up in the list to select Auto.

▶ Find out more about using color in Word by pressing F1 and searching for information about "color." Click in the document when you are ready to hide the Help window.

▶ In Lesson 3, you added bullets and numbers to lists by clicking buttons on the Toolbar. The Bullets And Numbering command on the Tools menu offers you a wide variety of additional options and formats. To experiment with this command, scroll to the end of the sample document and select all of the tips. From the Tools menu, choose Bullets And Numbering. At the top of the dialog box, click either the Bullets or the Numbered List option button and experiment with the various formatting options until you get the look you like.

▶ Most commands are designed to do one very specific action. However, some commands act like a toggle switch. Choosing the command once turns the command on; choosing the command again turns it off. A check mark next to the command name indicates that the command is "on." To experiment with a command that toggles on and off, click the View menu and note that there's a check mark by the Ruler command (as well as by other commands), indicating the ruler is currently on, or displayed. Click the Ruler command and note that the ruler no longer appears at the top of the screen. To display the ruler again, from the View menu, choose Ruler.

If you want to continue to the next lesson

You'll work with this document in the next lesson, too. You do not need to close it now.

If you want to quit Word for now

1   From the File menu, choose Exit (ALT, F, X).

2   If Word displays a message asking if you want to save changes, choose the No button. You do not need to save any of the changes you made while experimenting.

Lesson Summary

To	Do this
Choose commands	Click the menu name and then click the command name.
Select options in a dialog box	First, select options by clicking them or typing in text boxes. Then choose the OK button to complete the command.
Get Help about a command	Press SHIFT+F1 and then click the command name.
Get Help about a dialog box	While the dialog box is open, press F1.
Search Help for information	Press F1 and then click the Search button. In the Search dialog box, select the topic you want information about.

For more information on	See the *Microsoft Word User's Guide*
Choosing commands and working in dialog boxes	Chapter 1, "The Word Workplace"
Character formatting	Chapter 6, "Character Formatting"
Paragraph formatting	Chapter 7, "Paragraph Formatting"
Using online Help	Chapter 5, "Using Help and Online Lessons"

For an online lesson about	Do this
Choosing commands and working in dialog boxes	Click the Help menu. Click Getting Started. Click The Word Screen. Click Commands and Dialog Boxes.
	Follow the instructions on the screen.
	To exit a lesson at any time, click the Controls button and then click Exit.

Preview of the Next Lesson

In the next lesson, you'll continue your work on this sample document. You'll learn how to take advantage of the formatting you've already done by storing the formatting for later use. You'll learn how to apply combinations of formatting quickly and consistently throughout a document. At the end of the lesson, you'll have another document to add to your quick reference notebook.

Storing Formatting as Styles

In the last lesson you formatted two paragraphs—a heading and a text paragraph. Now you'll learn a quick way to make other paragraphs look just like the formatted ones. Although you could select another paragraph and change it to match a formatted paragraph—applying italic, setting left and right indents, and setting 1.5 line spacing, for example—it's much faster to take advantage of the work you've already done.

By selecting a formatted paragraph and giving that particular combination of formats a name, you can store all the formatting that you applied to that paragraph. This is called creating a *style*. You can apply the identical formatting to other paragraphs by "labeling" other paragraphs with the style name. The illustrations below show the effect of applying two styles.

Store this formatting as a style ...　　　　*... and apply the style to other paragraphs.*

This lesson explains how to do the following:

- Store a combination of formats as a style
- Apply a style to one or more paragraphs
- Change the definition of a style

Estimated lesson time: 30 minutes

If WORDHELP.DOC is not open

For this lesson, you will continue to work on your version of WORDHELP.DOC, the document you formatted in Lesson 4. If the document is not open, or if you did not work through Lesson 4, do the following.

Open

1 On the Toolbar, click the Open button.

2 Under Directories, make sure the PRACTICE directory is open. If it is not, select the drive where the Step by Step practice files are stored and open the appropriate directories.

3 Under File Name, click the name of the document you worked on in Lesson 4 (*your initials*HELP.DOC). If you did not work through Lesson 4, click HELP2.DOC.

4 Click the OK button.

If you share your computer with other Word users, they may have changed the screen display. Before you begin this lesson, make sure the Toolbar, ribbon, ruler, and scroll bars are displayed. The ruler should display approximately 6 inches, or the equivalent. The Word window and the sample document should completely fill the screen. If you need assistance in changing the screen display, see "Getting Ready," earlier in this book.

If you are using HELP2.DOC

Save the document with a new name so the changes you make in this lesson will not overwrite the original document.

1 From the File menu, choose Save As (ALT, F, A).

2 Under File Name, type *your initials***help2**

For example, type **jphelp2**

3 Choose the OK button.

4 When Word displays the summary information dialog box, select the name in the author box and type your own name if it does not already appear there.

5 Choose the OK button.

Display paragraph marks

Show/Hide ¶

Styles are stored in paragraph marks at the end of paragraphs. When you work with styles, it is a good idea to display paragraph marks. Displaying the marks makes it easier to select paragraphs accurately and helps ensure that you don't accidentally delete a paragraph mark and with it, the paragraph's formatting.

▶ On the ribbon, click the Show/Hide ¶ button if paragraph marks are not currently displayed.

Storing Formatting as a Style

The following procedure shows you how to name and store a combination of formats so that you can apply those formats with a click of the mouse. By storing combinations of formats as styles, you save time and you get identical formatting throughout your document.

Store the formatting of the heading as a style

Use the following procedures to define two new styles: one for the headings and one for the text paragraphs. When you name a style, think of a name that helps you recall what the style is for. Style names can be up to 24 characters in length. They can include numbers, letters, and spaces.

1   Scroll to the top of the document and select the heading "For information about dialog boxes," which is formatted with a double underline.

2   In the style box on the ribbon, drag to select the current style name "Normal," so you can replace it with a new style name.

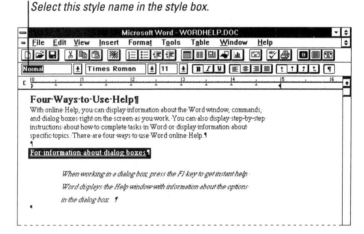

Select this style name in the style box.

3   Name the style by typing **bold underline** in the box. The text you type replaces the selected text.

4   Press ENTER. You will not see a change in the document, but Word has stored the formatting of the paragraph as the "bold underline" style.

Store the formatting of the text paragraph as a style

*You can select an
entire paragraph by
double-clicking in the
selection bar.*

1   Select the italic text paragraph, which is formatted with 1.5 line spacing.

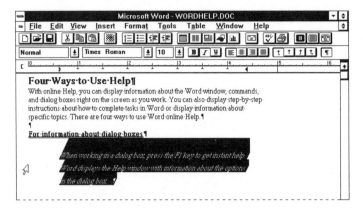

2   In the style box, drag to select the current style name for this paragraph, "Normal,"
so you can replace it with a new style name.

3   Type **indent/1.5** to remind you that the style indents the paragraph and changes the
line spacing to 1.5 lines.

Type the style name here.

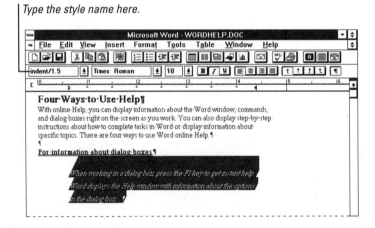

4   Press ENTER to store the formatting.

Applying Styles

Once you've created a style, you can apply it to any number of paragraphs in the document. Applying a style to a paragraph gives it the same formatting as the paragraph
you used as the model for that style. Styles affect entire paragraphs; you can't apply a
style to part of a paragraph.

Apply the heading style

In the following procedure, you'll apply the bold underline style to the next heading in the document.

1 To see more of the headings, scroll down until the formatted heading, "For information about dialog boxes," is at the top of the screen.

2 Select the next heading, "For information about Word commands," which appears after the italic paragraph.

3 To display the list of styles, click the down arrow next to the style box.

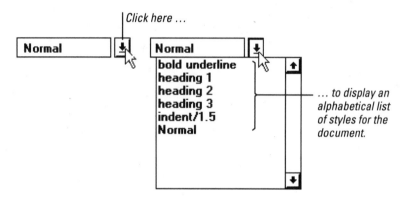

Click here ...

... to display an alphabetical list of styles for the document.

This displays the styles you've created along with some of the standard styles that Word provides: for example, the Heading 1, Heading 2, and Heading 3 styles. You will see what these styles look like in the One Step Further section at the end of this lesson.

4 Click the "bold underline" style name.

Word applies the formats stored with that name—bold, double-underlining, 11-point font size—to the selected text. Click outside the selection for a better look at the formatting.

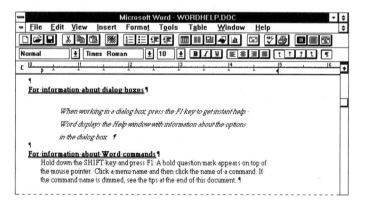

Apply another style

Apply the "indent/1.5" style to the next text paragraph in the document.

1 Select the paragraph that follows "For information about Word commands."

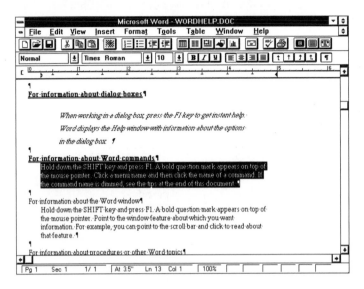

2 Click the down arrow next to the style box and then click the "indent/1.5" style.

Word applies all the formats stored with the style name—italic, left and right indents, 1.5 line spacing, and space before the paragraph. Click outside the selection for a better look at the formatting.

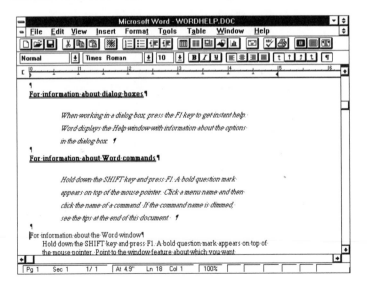

Apply the styles to the rest of the document

1 Click the down scroll arrow on the vertical scroll bar until you see the last two headings and the paragraph that follows each of them.

2 Apply the "bold underline" style to each heading and the "indent/1.5" style to the text paragraphs below each heading.

3 Click outside the selection for a better look at the formatting.

View the document

▶ Use the up scroll arrow to scroll line by line to the top of the document, noting the formatting as you go.

Changing a Style

Suppose after viewing the document, you decide that the text paragraphs would look better with justified lines, no right indent, and no italic. Instead of reformatting every text paragraph separately, all you need to do is change the style. Redefining the style changes the formatting of every paragraph that you applied the style to.

Reformat a styled paragraph

In the next procedure, you'll make quick adjustments to the options you set in the dialog boxes. When an option such as indents or italic appears in two places—a dialog box and the ribbon, ruler, or Toolbar—you can select or adjust the option in either place. The effect on the text is the same.

1 Select the first text paragraph that has the "indent/1.5" style.

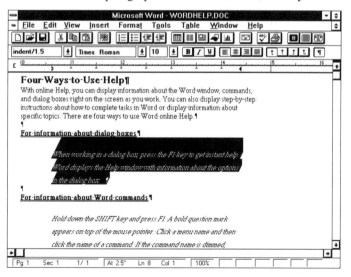

Justified Text

Italic

2 On the ribbon, click the Justified Text button.

Word justifies the text, adding space between words as necessary to make the lines extend to the right indent.

3 On the ribbon, click the Italic button.

Word removes the italic formatting from the paragraph.

4 Drag the Right Indent marker to 5 inches on the ruler, as shown in the following illustration.

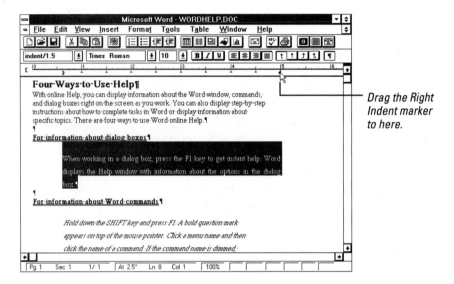

Drag the Right Indent marker to here.

Redefine the style

1 With the formatted paragraph still selected, drag to select the name "indent/1.5" in the style box.

2 Press ENTER.

3 When Word displays a message asking if you want to redefine the style, click the Yes button.

Every paragraph with the "indent/1.5" style changes to reflect the new formatting.

4 Click the down scroll arrow to scroll through the document line by line, viewing the results.

Search for a topic in Help

As you are working on a document, you may want more information about styles. You can get quick information through Help. Take a moment now to look at the information available about applying styles.

1 Press the F1 key to display the Help window.

2 Choose the Search button.

3 Type **style** but do not press ENTER.

Word displays all categories related to styles.

4 Select "styles: applying," and then choose the Search button to show topics.

Word displays a list of available topics. The dialog box on your screen may look slightly different from the one in the following illustration.

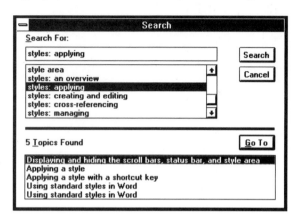

5 Select "Applying a style," and then choose the Go To button.

Word displays the topic, which includes several methods for applying styles. Remember that solid underlines indicate related topics. If you jump to a related topic, you can always click the Back button to return to a previous topic.

6 When you are ready to return to the document, click in the document window, or if the Help window fills the screen, hold down ALT and press F4.

Save the document

Save

▶ On the Toolbar, click the Save button.

Word saves the current version of the document in place of the previous version. You won't see a change in the screen display as Word saves the document.

Print the document

Print

The sample document describes the Help system and suggests ways to use it.

1 Make sure the printer is on.

2 On the Toolbar, click the Print button.

Word prints one copy of the document.

One Step Further

▶ Every paragraph in every document has a style, whether you apply one or not. Word uses the "Normal" style until you apply another style. Normal style is left-justified, no indents, single spacing. You can clear the formatting from a paragraph by applying Normal style to it. Select one of the paragraphs that has the "indent/1.5" style. Apply the Normal style by selecting it from the list of styles. You can click the Undo button after you have seen the effect.

▶ Experiment by creating another style. Select the text paragraph at the top of the document that begins "With online Help, you can ..." Format the paragraph using any of the formats on the Toolbar or ribbon, or using the Character and Paragraph commands on the Format menu. (Note that Word does not include bullets or numbers in a style.) Use the style box to name your style. Select any other paragraph and apply the style. You can click the Undo button after you've seen the results.

▶ Word provides other standard styles in addition to Normal. For example, the Heading 1, Heading 2, and Heading 3 standard styles are displayed when you open the style list on the ribbon. In addition to applying formatting, they are useful for automatically outlining a document. To see what these styles look like, try applying each in turn to the document title "Four Ways to Use Help."

If you want to continue to the next lesson

1 From the File menu, choose Close (ALT, F, C).

2 If Word displays a message asking if you want to save changes, click the No button. You do not need to save the changes made while experimenting.

Choosing this command closes the active document; it does not exit the Word program.

If you want to quit Word for now

1 From the File menu, choose Exit (ALT, F, X).

2 If Word displays a message asking if you want to save changes, click the No button. You do not need to save any of the changes you made while experimenting.

This closes the document and quits Word.

Lesson Summary

To	Do this
Create a style	Select the formatted paragraph and then type the style name in the style box on the ribbon.
Apply a style	Select the paragraphs you want to format and then select the style name in the style box on the ribbon and press ENTER.
Redefine a style	Format one of the styled paragraphs the way you want it to look, select the style name, and then press ENTER. Choose the Yes button to redefine the style.

For more information on	See the *Microsoft Word User's Guide*
Defining, naming, applying, and changing styles	Chapter 8, "Formatting with Styles"

For an online lesson about	Do this
Creating or modifying styles	Click Help. Click Learning Word. Click Formatting. Click Creating Styles or click Modifying Styles.
	Follow the instructions on the screen.
	To exit the lesson at any time, click the Controls button, and then click Exit.

Preview of the Next Lesson

In the next lesson, you'll learn how to add finishing touches to a letter. Using the Grammar command, you'll check the letter for any errors. Then you'll use a quick method to address and print an envelope. At the end of the lesson, you'll print another document for your quick reference notebook.

Proofing a Document

After you've written and formatted a document, you'll probably want to add a few finishing touches. For example, you'll probably want to *proof,* or check, the document one last time, to make sure there are no errors and that everything is in order. Also, if you've written a letter, you'll need to address an envelope. Word makes these final steps quick and easy.

You've already seen how simple it is to check for spelling errors using the Spelling button on the Toolbar. With the Word grammar checker, you can quickly find and correct both spelling errors and common grammatical or stylistic errors. The Word thesaurus helps you add interest and precision to your writing by suggesting synonyms or antonyms for selected words. With the Word search and replace features, you can quickly find text or formatting that you want to change. And Word makes addressing and printing an envelope almost as simple as clicking a button. In this lesson, you'll use these features to add finishing touches to a sample letter.

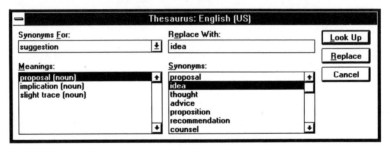

The Thesaurus dialog box lists alternatives for the selected word.

This lesson explains how to do the following:

- Find and replace text and formatting
- Find synonyms and related words using the Word thesaurus
- Check grammar and spelling using the grammar checker
- Address and print an envelope

Estimated lesson time: 35 minutes

Open

Open a sample document

1 On the Toolbar, click the Open button.

2 Under Directories, make sure the PRACTICE directory is open. If it is not, select the drive where the Step by Step practice files are stored and open the appropriate directories.

3 Double-click LETTER.DOC.

If you share your computer with other Word users, they may have changed the screen display. Before you begin this lesson, make sure the Toolbar, ribbon, and scroll bars are displayed. The Word window and the sample document should completely fill the screen. You can work with the ruler displayed or hidden; you will not need it for this lesson. For assistance in changing the screen display, see "Getting Ready," earlier in this book.

If you have a sharp eye for spelling and grammar errors, you'll notice several in this document. Don't correct them yet; you'll find and correct them later using the Word grammar feature.

Save the document with a new name

Give the document a new name so the changes you make in this lesson will not overwrite the original document.

1 From the File menu, choose Save As (ALT, F, A).

2 Under File Name, type *your initials***letter**

For example, type **jpletter**

3 Choose the OK button.

4 When Word displays the summary information dialog box, select the name in the author box and type your own name if it does not already appear there.

5 Choose the OK button.

Finding and Replacing Text

When you need to review or change text in a document, use the Find and Replace commands on the Edit menu. With these commands, you can quickly find—and, if necessary, replace—all occurrences of a certain word or phrase. For example, you may want to find every instance of a client's name in a report and add the name of the client's partner. Or you may need to change a code number or the name of a product.

Prepare to replace text

The letter on your screen was written by a person named Jane Box. For the purposes of this lesson, you need to replace Jane's name with your own. The following procedure shows you how to quickly find Jane's name and replace it.

1 From the Edit menu, choose Replace (ALT, E, E).

2 In the Find What box, type **Jane Box**

If you share you computer with others who have used the Find command or the Replace command in the current work session, the text they last searched for may appear in the Find What box. You can select the text and type over it.

3 If the Clear button is available—that is, if it does not appear dimmed—choose it so Word does not search for any formatting.

If the Clear button appears dimmed, the previous search did not involve formatting. You can proceed to the next step.

4 Click in the Replace With box and type your first and last name just as you would at the end of a letter.

If text is already in the Replace With box, select the text and type over it.

5 If the Clear button is available, choose it so Word does not format the replacement text.

6 If the Match Whole Word Only option is not selected, select it now.

This instructs Word to find only separate words, not characters embedded in other words. For example, Word will find "Jane Box," but would skip "Jane Boxer."

7 Select the Match Case option.

This instructs Word to match the capitalization pattern in the Find What box. With this option selected, for example, Word will find "Box," but skip any instances of "box."

Now that you have told Word what text to find and how to change it, use the next procedure to actually find and replace the specified text.

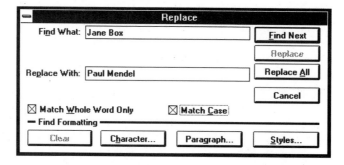

Find and replace the text

1 To begin the search, choose the Find Next button.

Word searches for and highlights "Jane Box."

2 Choose the Replace button.

Word replaces "Jane Box" with your name and returns to the beginning of the document.

Find and replace the company name

For the purposes of this lesson, you'll also want your real company or school name in place of "Arbor Shoes," a fictitious company.

1 In the Find What box, select the text if it is not currently selected and type **Arbor Shoes**

2 Select the text in the Replace With box and type your company or school name.

3 To begin the search, choose the Find Next button.

Word searches for and highlights "Arbor Shoes."

4 Choose the Replace button.

Word replaces "Arbor Shoes" with the name of your company or school, and returns to the beginning of the document.

5 To close the dialog box, choose the Cancel button.

Finding and Replacing Formatting

You can locate text that has a specific format, such as bold or underlining, and change the formatting as well as the text. You can also search for and change only the formatting, without changing the text. For example, if you formatted the titles of publications as bold and wanted to make them italic instead, you could find any bold text and change the bold to italic.

Specify which formatting to find and replace

Throughout the sample document, book titles and special terms appear in bold. Take a minute and scroll through the document to view the formatting. Then return to the beginning and use the following procedure to change the bold words to italic.

1 From the Edit menu, choose Replace (ALT, E, E).

2 Delete the text in the Find What box by selecting it (if it is not currently selected) and pressing the BACKSPACE key.

3 Choose the Character button at the bottom of the dialog box.

4 Choose the Bold option under Style.

An "X" appears next to Bold, indicating that the option has been selected.

5 Choose the OK button.

6 Select your company or school name in the Replace With box and delete it by pressing the BACKSPACE key.

7 Choose the Character button again and then select the Italic option.

8 Choose the OK button to return to the Replace dialog box.

Now that you've specified what formatting Word should find and replace, you are ready to start the search.

Word indicates it will search for bold formatting...

... and replace it with italic.

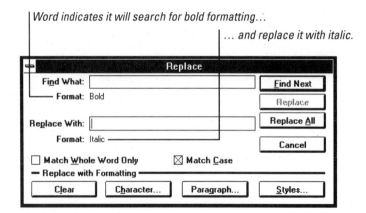

Find and replace formatting

1 In the Replace dialog box, choose the Replace All button.

You will not see the changes in the document until you complete the next step.

2 Choose the Close button to return to the document and see the changes.

Scroll through the document and note that the text that was bold is now italic.

Using the Thesaurus

Using the Word thesaurus helps you add precision and variety to your writing. Like a printed thesaurus, the Word thesaurus provides synonyms (words with a similar meaning) and sometimes antonyms (words with an opposite meaning) for a particular word. It also provides lists of related words and different forms of the selected word. For example, the word "work" can be used as a noun or as a verb; the thesaurus lists synonyms for both forms. When you select a word and then choose the Thesaurus command, Word displays the Thesaurus dialog box, where you can quickly search through a wide range of synonyms and related words until you find exactly the word you want.

Important   The Setup program you use to install Word on your computer gives you the option to install or not install the Word proofing commands, which include the Thesaurus, the Grammar checker, and the Spelling checker. If you chose to install these commands, they appear on the Tools menu; otherwise, they do not. You can run the Word Setup program again and specify that you want to install the proofing commands only. For more information on the Setup program, see *Microsoft Word Getting Started.*

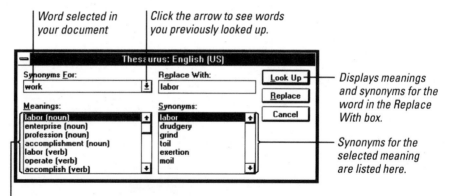

Word selected in your document

Click the arrow to see words you previously looked up.

Displays meanings and synonyms for the word in the Replace With box.

Synonyms for the selected meaning are listed here.

Different meanings for the word are listed here.

Look up a word in the thesaurus

Suppose you want to find an alternative to the word "excellent" and insert it in the document. The following procedure shows you how. First you will use the Find command to find the word "excellent"; then you'll use the Thesaurus command to select a synonym.

1   From the Edit menu, choose Find (ALT, E, F).

2   Type **excellent**

3   Choose the Clear button so Word does not search for any formatting.

4   Choose the Find Next button.

Word finds and highlights the word "excellent."

5   Choose the Cancel button to close the Find dialog box.

6   From the Tools menu, choose Thesaurus (ALT, O, T).

Word displays the Thesaurus dialog box.

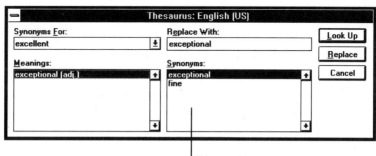

Words with similar meanings

7 In the Replace With box, Word suggests "exceptional." Assume that "exceptional" is the term that you want to use. Choose the Replace button.

Word replaces "excellent" with "exceptional" and closes the Thesaurus dialog box.

Replace another word

The following procedure shows how you can find an alternative to the word "suggestions."

1 In the sentence that follows "exceptional," select the word "suggestions," as shown in the following illustration.

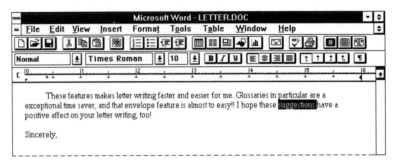

2 From the Tools menu, choose Thesaurus (ALT, O, T).

Note that Word does not display alternatives for "suggestions." Instead, it displays the singular form of the word, "suggestion." This indicates that you can look up alternatives for the singular form.

3 Choose the Look Up button to see alternatives for the singular form of this word.

Word lists the synonyms. "Idea" would be a good alternative, but you'll need to add an "s" to the end of it.

4 Select "idea" to have Word copy it to the Replace With box.

5 In the Replace With box, click at the end of "idea" and type **s**

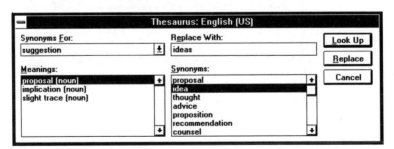

6 Choose the Replace button.

Word replaces "suggestions" with "ideas."

Checking Grammar and Spelling

The Grammar command identifies sentences in your document that have possible grammatical errors or a nonstandard writing style. For many types of errors, the Grammar command suggests ways to correct the sentence. You can choose the correction you want to make and have Word change the sentence in your document. You can also make changes directly in your document and then continue checking.

While checking your document for grammatical errors, Word also checks spelling. If a questionable word is found, the Spelling dialog box is displayed over the Grammar dialog box so you can correct the misspelling. Word then continues the grammar check.

The grammar checker provides a quick and convenient way to find many common grammatical errors. However, remember that no grammar checker is a replacement for a careful reading of the document.

Check the grammar and spelling

Word normally checks all of your document, beginning at the insertion point. Although you can position the insertion point anywhere in the document, in this lesson you'll position it at the top.

Dragging the scroll box is a fast way to scroll.

1   Scroll to the top of the document.

2   Position the insertion point at the beginning of the line that shows the date.

3   From the Tools menu, choose Grammar (ALT, O, G).

   This starts both the grammar checker and the spelling checker.

4   The spelling checker finds the street name "Doumer," which is correctly spelled. Choose the Ignore button.

   The Grammar dialog box displays a sentence that appears to have an error. When possible, Word suggests ways to change the sentence and sometimes provides a brief explanation of the error. In this case, the suggestion to use "is" instead of "are" is the correction you want.

Sentence that contains the possible error

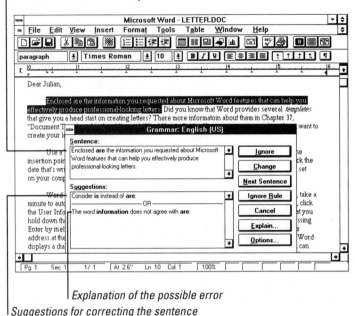

Explanation of the possible error
Suggestions for correcting the sentence

5   Choose the Change button.

Word replaces "are" with "is" and continues checking the document.

The next error Word finds is a spelling error: "informatoin." Word displays the error and the suggested correction in the Spelling dialog box.

6   Choose the Change button.

Word changes "informatoin" to "information" and continues checking the document.

The next error Word finds is a grammatical error. The sentence that Word highlights has no verb and so is not a complete sentence. Word explains the error, but you need to make the correction yourself.

7   Click in the document to make it active. Then point to the space after the word "There" and click again to position the insertion point as shown in the following illustration.

This step removes the highlighting from the sentence and positions the insertion point, ready for typing.

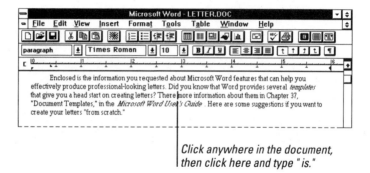

*Click anywhere in the document,
then click here and type "is."*

8   Type **is** and a space.

9   Choose the Start button in the Grammar dialog box to continue the check.

10 For each error that Word finds, do the following:

When Word suggests	Do this
Using "make" instead of "makes"	Choose the Change button.
Using "an" instead of "a"	Choose the Change button.
Using "too" instead of "to"	Choose the Change button.
Checking the appropriateness of the two punctuation marks	Delete the second exclamation point by doing the following: Click in the document. Click again, this time to the right of the extra exclamation point. Press BACKSPACE. Choose the Start button in the Grammar dialog box to continue
Using "effect" instead of "affect"	See the following procedure.

Get an explanation for a grammar rule

Word provides explanations for the suggestions that it makes. The following procedure shows how to read about a grammar rule before you make a change in your document.

1   With "Consider effect instead of affect" still displayed in the Grammar dialog box, choose the Explain button.

Word displays a window with an explanation of the grammar rule.

Double-click here to close the Grammar Explanation window.

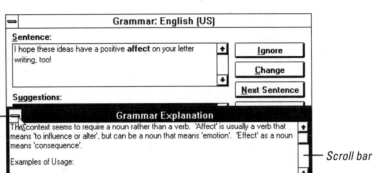

2 Scroll down to see more of the explanation.

3 When you finish reading about the grammar rule, double-click the horizontal bar in the upper-left corner of the window.

4 Choose the Change button.

If your name or company name is not in the Word dictionary, Word selects it and displays the Spelling dialog box. The next section of this lesson shows how to add your name or your company name to a custom dictionary.

Adding Words to a Custom Dictionary

You often use words in your documents that are not likely to be in the Word dictionary—for example, specialized terms, product codes, acronyms and abbreviations, and proper names such as your name and names of business associates. If you don't want Word to question such words during spell checks, you can add them to a custom dictionary. You can use one or more custom dictionaries in addition to the standard main dictionary when you check your documents. Word can then check that the words entered in a custom dictionary are also correctly spelled.

To have Word consult a custom dictionary when checking spelling, make sure that the dictionary is open before you choose the Spelling or Grammar command. Word can check spelling more quickly if you close any custom dictionaries that are not needed to check a particular document.

Add names to a custom dictionary

The following procedure shows how you can add your name to a custom dictionary. If your name is composed of words found in the dictionary, such as Rob Stone, you may not need to add it to the custom dictionary.

1 If the spelling checker selects your first name or last name, choose the Add button.

2 If the spelling checker selects your company name, choose the Add button.

The next time you check a document that contains your name or your company name, Word will recognize the correct spelling.

3 If Word displays a message asking if you want to continue checking from the beginning of the document, choose the No button.

Word displays the readability statistics for the document, as described in the next procedure.

View the readability statistics for this document

In the Readability Statistics dialog box, Word displays information about the text that it checked. The readability statistics help you evaluate how easily your writing can be understood by the average adult reader. Most readability indexes assign a reading grade level. A Flesch Grade Level of 7, for example, indicates writing that can be understood by an average English-speaking reader who has completed seven years of education in the United States.

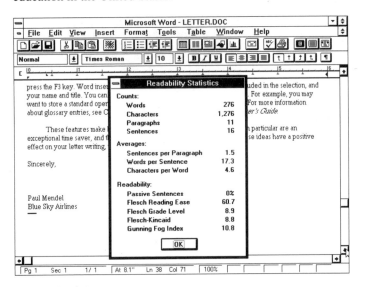

▶ Choose the OK button to return to your document.

TROUBLESHOOTING: **If you do not see the readability statistics** If the Readability Statistics dialog box did not appear, it means the option has been cleared. To display the statistics the next time you run the grammar checker, choose Options from the Tools menu. Scroll the list under Category to display the Grammar symbol and then click the Grammar symbol. Select the check box next to Show Readability Statistics After Proofing.

Creating an Envelope

If your printer can print on envelopes, you can automate the process of addressing them. You can store your return address so that Word prints it automatically on envelopes. You have a choice of printing an envelope at the time you address it, or storing the text for the envelope for printing when you print the letter. Even if your printer cannot print envelopes, you can work through the following procedure.

Create an envelope

Envelope

1 On the Toolbar, click the Envelope button.

Click here.

2 Position the insertion point in the Return Address box and type your name, if you want it to appear in the return address, and your address.

3 If you want to print on a different size envelope than that shown in the dialog box, click the arrow next to the Envelope Size box and then click the size you want.

4 Choose the Add To Document button.

5 If the return address you typed is different from the one that Word is currently storing, Word displays a message asking if you want to store the address for use later. Choose the Yes button if you want to use this return address in the future.

Word creates a new section at the top of the letter and inserts the inside address from the letter and your return address from the User Info dialog box. The text is positioned correctly for printing on the size of envelope you selected.

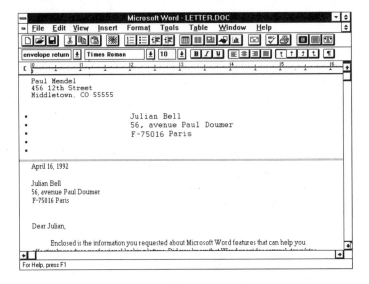

Save

Save the document

▶ On the Toolbar, click the Save button. Word saves this version of the document in place of the previous version.

Remember that you will not see a change in the document or screen display as Word saves the document.

If your printer can print envelopes

The sample document on your screen describes Word features that make letter writing faster and easier. If your printer can print envelopes, use the following procedure to print the document.

Print

▶ On the Toolbar, click the Print button.

The printer will wait for you to insert an envelope. If you do not insert one, the print job will be canceled.

If your printer cannot print envelopes

You can print the letter by itself using the following procedure.

1   From the File menu, choose Print (ALT, F, P).

2   In the From box, type **1** and in the To box, type **1**

The envelope is page 0; the letter is one page long and begins on page 1.

3   Choose the OK button to print the letter.

One Step Further

▶ You can find many alternatives to words and phrases by using the Thesaurus dialog box. Practice working with it by selecting any word in the sample document and then choosing Thesaurus from the Tools menu. Or you can type a word or phrase at the end of the document, select it, and then choose the command. Explore the numerous alternatives available by double-clicking words in the Synonyms or Related Words box. If you want another look at synonyms you've already seen, click the down arrow next to the Synonyms For box. Word displays all the words you've already looked up. Select the one you want to look at again. You can also look up entirely new words by typing a word in the Replace With box and clicking the Look Up button. For more information on using the Word thesaurus, see Chapter 14, "Proofing a Document," in the *Microsoft Word User's Guide.*

▶ Take a moment to browse the Help system for information about the Grammar checker. To do this, press F1, click the Search button, and type **grammar**. Select the category and topic that interests you. If Word does not locate topics, make sure you typed "grammar" correctly.

Proofing Tips

- If you're using the Replace command to make major changes to your document, it's a good idea to save your document before you start replacing. That way, if you don't like the results, you can close the document without saving the changes.

- Each time the grammar checker finds a sentence with a possible error, you can click the Ignore button or the Next Sentence button if you don't want to change anything. If you click Ignore, Word ignores the "error" it flagged and continues checking the sentence. If you click Next Sentence, Word skips to the next sentence. You can also specify which grammatical and stylistic rules Word applies when checking your documents. For more information about how to use and customize the grammar checker, see Chapter 14, "Proofing a Document," in the *Microsoft Word User's Guide*.

- You can use the proofing commands with more than one language in a single document. You can check the spelling, for example, of a document containing text in several different languages; Word can automatically check words using the appropriate dictionary for each language. For more information, see "Proofing Text in Different Languages," in Chapter 14, "Proofing a Document," in the *Microsoft Word User's Guide*.

If you want to continue to the next lesson

1   From the File menu, choose Close (ALT, F, C).

2   If Word displays a message asking if you want to save changes, click the No button. You do not need to save the changes made while experimenting.

Choosing this command closes the active document; it does not exit the Word program.

Save

If you want to quit Word for now

1   From the File menu, choose Exit (ALT, F, X).

2   If Word displays a message asking if you want to save changes, click the No button. You do not need to save any of the changes you made while experimenting.

Lesson Summary

To	Do this
Find and replace text	From the Edit menu, choose Replace. In the Replace dialog box, type the text you want Word to find. Clear or select any formatting. Type the replacement text Word should use and clear or select any formatting. Use the Find Next button to replace each occurrence.
Find and replace formatting	From the Edit menu, choose Replace. Use the buttons and options available in the Replace dialog box to specify the kind of formatting Word should find and what to replace it with. Then click the Find Next button to find and replace each occurrence of formatting.
Find a word or phrase	From the Edit menu, choose Find. Type the text you want Word to find and clear or select any formatting. Choose the Find Next button to find each occurrence.
Use the Word thesaurus	Select a word or phrase in the document and then choose Thesaurus from the Tools menu to see synonyms, related words, and, sometimes, antonyms.
Check grammar and spelling	From the Tools menu, choose Grammar. As Word flags possible grammar or spelling errors, make the suggested changes or ignore them.
Add words to the custom dictionary	During a spelling or grammar check, choose the Add button in the Spelling dialog box each time Word flags a correctly spelled word you want to add to a custom dictionary.
Address and print an envelope	After typing the letter, click the Envelope button on the Toolbar. Then choose the Add To Document button. Print the document right then by clicking the Print button. Or print the envelope when you print the letter.

For more information on	See the *Microsoft Word User's Guide*
Finding or replacing text and formatting	Chapter 12, "Finding and Replacing Text or Formatting"
Checking spelling and grammar, or using the thesaurus	Chapter 14, "Proofing a Document"
Creating envelopes	Chapter 4, "Printing a Document"

For an online lesson about	Do this
Checking spelling and grammar, or using the thesaurus	Click the Help menu. Click Learning Word. Click Proofing. Click a lesson title. Follow the instructions on the screen. To exit a lesson at any time, click the Controls button, and then click Exit.

Preview of the Next Lesson

In the next lesson you'll learn to automatically number pages. You'll also learn to add text, such as a company name or a chapter name, along with a page number in the top or bottom margin of every page in the document. You'll work with two sample documents in the next lesson. Both describe ways Word can help you save time.

Adding Page Numbers, Headers, and Footers

With Word, you can quickly and easily number the pages in your documents. All you do is choose a command and specify where on the page you want the number to print. Word inserts the page numbers and, if you add or delete text in the body of the document, automatically adjusts the page numbers for you.

You may want more information than just the page number to appear at the top or bottom of every page. For example, you may want the document title, or the author and date, or a graphic such as a company logo. Information such as this is called a *header* if it prints at the top of every page and a *footer* if it prints at the bottom. Word makes it easy to add headers and footers to your documents. You can even create different headers and footers for different parts of a document.

This lesson is in three parts. First you'll learn to insert page numbers automatically. Then you'll learn to print text as well as a page number on every page of a document. Finally, you'll change the text that appears in different sections of the document, producing footers like the ones in the following illustration.

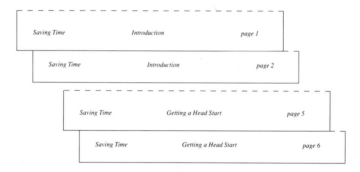

This lesson explains how to do the following:

- Insert page numbers in a document
- Create a header or footer that prints on every page
- Create different headers or footers for different sections of a document

Estimated lesson time: 30 minutes

Open a sample document

The following procedure provides a shortcut for opening documents.

Open

1 On the Toolbar, click the Open button.

2 Under Directories, make sure the PRACTICE directory is open. If it is not, select the drive where the Step by Step practice files are stored and open the appropriate directories.

3 Double-click STORE.DOC.

If you share your computer with other Word users, they may have changed the screen display. Before you begin this lesson, make sure the Toolbar, ribbon, ruler, and scroll bars are displayed. The ruler should display approximately 6 inches, or the equivalent. The Word window and the sample document should completely fill the screen. If you need assistance in changing the screen display, see "Getting Ready," earlier in this book.

Save the document with a new name

Give the document a new name so the changes you make in this lesson will not overwrite the original document.

1 From the File menu, choose Save As (ALT, F, A).

2 Under File Name, type *your initials***store**

For example, type **jpstore**

3 Choose the OK button.

4 When Word displays the summary information dialog box, select the name in the author box and type your own name if it does not already appear there.

5 Choose the OK button.

Inserting Page Numbers

The Page Numbers command is the quickest way to number the pages in your document. This command does not place a number on the first page. Instead the numbering begins with "2" on the second page. This is useful for letters, reports, and many other types of documents that normally do not number the first page.

You will not see the page numbers when you first insert them. They appear when you print the document or when you switch to another view.

Number all pages except the first

You can insert page numbers at the top or bottom of pages. You can align page numbers with the left or the right page margin, or center them between the margins. In the following procedure, you'll add page numbers to the upper-right corner of the page.

1 From the Insert menu, choose Page Numbers (ALT, I, U).

2 Under Position, select Top Of Page (Header).

3 Under Alignment, select Right.

4 Choose the OK button.

To see the page numbers, use the following procedure.

View the page numbers

Word provides several *views*—ways of looking at your document. You've been working in *normal view*, which is often the fastest view for typing and editing. *Page layout view* shows the document as it will print, with most of the elements, such as page numbers, in their exact positions on the page.

You'll notice several differences between normal view and page layout view. For example, in page layout view you can see the "edges" of each page. Also, the vertical scroll bar displays two more buttons at the bottom. You use these buttons, called the *Page Forward* and *Page Back* buttons, to quickly display the next or previous page.

1 From the View menu, choose Page Layout (ALT, V, P).

2 Click the Page Forward button to see pages 2 and 3.

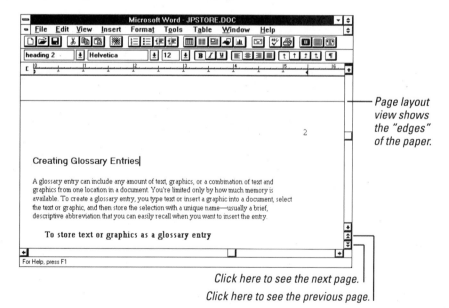

Page layout view shows the "edges" of the paper.

Click here to see the next page.

Click here to see the previous page.

TROUBLESHOOTING:

If you see the {Page} code instead of numbers If you see {Page} instead of numbers, Word is currently set to display field codes. To view the page numbers, from the View menu, choose Field Codes.

3   When you are through viewing the document, return to normal view by clicking the Zoom 100 Percent button on the Toolbar.

Zoom 100 Percent

Click here.

Save the document

Save

▶   On the Toolbar, click the Save button. Word saves this version of the document in place of the previous version.

Remember that you will not see a change in the document or screen display as Word saves the document.

Print the document

You can print the sample document now to see the page numbers. The document describes how to store frequently used text and graphics so that you never have to retype or create them again. You can easily insert them as often as you need in any document you create. Use the following procedure to print this information and add it to your quick reference notebook.

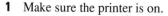

Print

1   Make sure the printer is on.

2   On the Toolbar, click the Print button.

Close the document

You'll work with a different document for the rest of this lesson.

▶   From the File menu, choose Close (ALT, F, C).

Printing Text and Page Numbers on Each Page

You've learned all you need to know to insert page numbers in a document. This portion of the lesson shows you how to print text such as the document name or chapter title on every page, in addition to the page number. To do this, you use the Header/Footer command. The Header/Footer command displays a separate *pane* of the document window, where you type the header or footer text.

A header or footer pane provides a clean space in which to type, along with symbols you can click to insert the page number, date, and time. If you make a mistake as you type, you can edit the text in a header or footer pane as you usually do. When you close the pane, Word inserts your typing in the top margin of each page if you created a header, or in the bottom margin of each page if you created a footer.

The following procedures show you how to create a footer that looks like the following illustration.

Open another sample document

1 On the Toolbar, click the Open button.

2 Under File Name, double-click SAVETIME.DOC.

Save the document with a new name

Give the document a new name so the changes you make in this lesson will not overwrite the original document.

1 From the File menu, choose Save As (ALT, F, A).

2 Under File Name, type *your initials***time**

For example, type **jptime**

3 Choose the OK button.

4 When Word displays the summary information dialog box, select the name in the author box and type your own name if it does not already appear there.

5 Choose the OK button.

Create a footer

1 From the View menu, choose Header/Footer (ALT, V, H).

Word displays the Header/Footer dialog box.

2 To add text to the bottom of every page, click Footer, and then click the OK button.

Word opens the footer pane at the bottom of the screen.

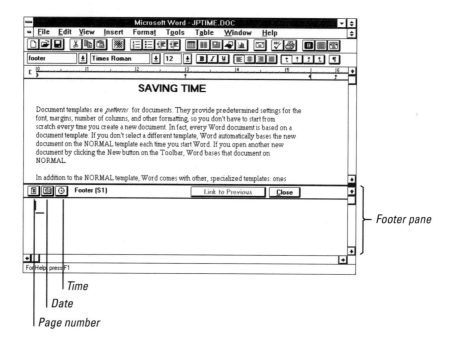

Footer pane

Time
Date
Page number

3 Type **Saving Time**

4 Press the TAB key once. This centers the next text that you type.

5 Type **Introduction**

6 Press the TAB key again. This aligns the next text you type with the right page margin.

7 Type **page** and press the SPACEBAR.

8 Click the page number symbol, as shown in the following illustration.

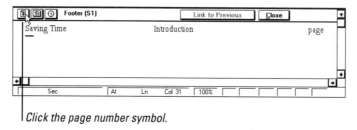

Click the page number symbol.

Tip The text you type in the header or footer pane can be whatever you need. For example, instead of typing text that describes the document, as you did in the last procedure, you could have typed your name and the company name.

Format the footer

You can format the text in a footer, just as you format text in the document.

1 Use the selection bar to select the text and page number.

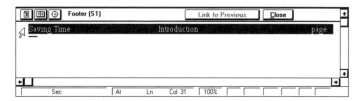

Italic

2 On the ribbon, click the Italic button.

3 To close the footer pane, choose the Close button. You won't see the footer in the document until the next procedure.

View the footer

In the following procedure, you'll view the footer just as it will print. If you find a typing error or if you change your mind about the wording, you can edit the text in the footer just as you edit any other text.

1 From the View menu, choose Page Layout (ALT, V, P).

2 Use the down scroll arrow to scroll to the bottom of the page and view the footer.

3 To see another page, click the Page Forward button at the bottom of the scroll bar, as shown in the following illustration.

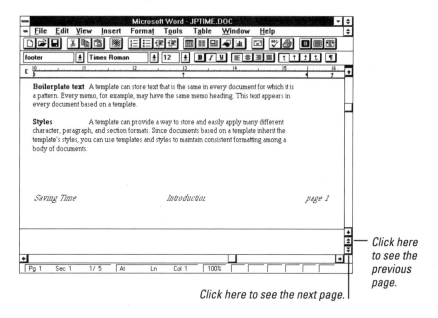

Click here to see the previous page.

Click here to see the next page.

Zoom 100 Percent

Switch to normal view

You'll work in normal view for the next portion of the lesson.

▶ On the Toolbar, click the Zoom 100 Percent button.

Changing Headers or Footers Within a Document

You've learned the skills you need to create headers or footers. Now you'll learn to create different headers and footers for different sections of the document. You'll use the procedures you just learned to create a footer, plus a new technique—inserting a *section break*.

By inserting section breaks, you can divide a document into *sections* and then format each separately, changing the format of the page numbers within sections and changing the text in headers or footers.

The rest of the lesson shows you how to insert a section break and change the footer to look like this example.

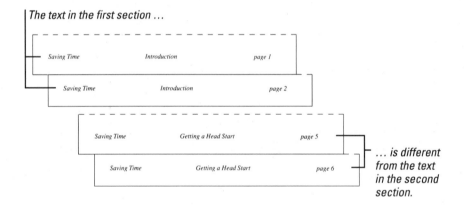

The text in the first section ...

Saving Time   Introduction   page 1

Saving Time   Introduction   page 2

Saving Time   Getting a Head Start   page 5

Saving Time   Getting a Head Start   page 6

... is different from the text in the second section.

Search for text

You need to insert a section break before the heading "Getting a Head Start." You could scroll to see the heading, but this is a long document and that would take time. Let Word find the text for you.

1 From the Edit menu, choose Find (ALT, E, F).

2 Type **Getting**

3 Select the Match Case option so that Word looks for "Getting," not "getting."

4 Choose the Clear button if it is available, to clear any formatting from a previous search.

5 Choose the Find Next button.

Word searches for an exact match and displays the text.

TROUBLESHOOTING: **If "Getting" is not found**   Check your spelling. Make sure the text in the Find What box matches step 2 exactly.

6   To close the Find dialog box, choose the Cancel button.

Insert a section break

You're ready to insert a section break before "Getting a Head Start."

1   Click outside the selection to clear the highlighting.

2   Position the insertion point before the word "Getting."

3   From the Insert menu, choose Break (ALT, I, B).

4   Under Section Break, select Next Page so this section will begin on a new page.

5   Choose the OK button.

In Normal view, Word inserts a double dotted line to mark a section break; these lines do not print.

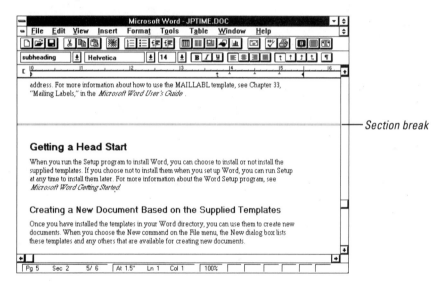
—— *Section break*

TROUBLESHOOTING: **If you do not see double dotted lines**   If you do not see double dotted lines on your screen, you may be working in page layout view. To switch to Normal view, click the Zoom 100 Percent button on the Toolbar or, from the View menu, choose Normal.

Change the footer for the second section

1   Make sure the blinking insertion point is below the section break. If it is not, click anywhere below the section break to position the insertion point in the new section.

2   From the View menu, choose Header/Footer (ALT, V, H).

3 Select Footer and then choose the OK button.

Word displays the footer pane for the second section. Note that "Footer (S2)" appears in the title bar of the pane.

4 Select the word "Introduction."

5 Type **Getting a Head Start**

6 To close the footer pane, choose the Close button.

You will not see the footer until you switch views in the next procedure.

View the new footer

1 From the View menu, choose Page Layout (ALT, V, P).

Word displays the page that contains the insertion point.

2 Use the down scroll arrow to scroll to the bottom of the page to view the footer. Click the Page Forward button or the Page Back button to view other pages. Your document will look similar to the following illustration.

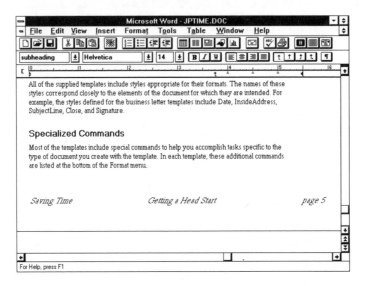

Tip When you are working in page layout view, you can choose the Header/Footer command from the View menu and choose either Header or Footer. Word scrolls to the header or footer for you.

Save the document

Save

▶ On the Toolbar, click the Save button. Word saves this version of the document in place of the previous version.

Remember that you will not see a change in the document or screen display as Word saves the document.

Print the document

You can print the sample document now to see the footers, or, if you are going to work through the One Step Further portion of the lesson, you can wait to print the document then. The five-page document you've been working with describes the head start that Word provides for letters, memos, reports, proposals, and other common documents. Using the procedures described in the document, you can create great-looking documents by simply responding to prompts for information. This is good information to add to your quick reference notebook and to share with co-workers.

Print

1   Make sure the printer is on.

2   On the Toolbar, click the Print button.

One Step Further

▶ You can edit and format headers and footers in page layout view. Try selecting the footer and changing the font or point size. Click the Page Forward or Page Back buttons on the scroll bar to view the different pages. Note that your changes affect only the section in which you made the change.

If you want to continue to the next lesson

1   From the File menu, choose Close (ALT, F, C).

2   If Word displays a message asking if you want to save the changes, choose the Yes button to save your latest work. Otherwise, choose No.

If you want to quit Word for now

1   From the File menu, choose Exit (ALT, F, X).

2   If Word displays a message asking if you want to save the changes, choose the Yes button to save your latest work. Otherwise, choose No.

Lesson Summary

To	Do this
Number all pages except the first	Choose the Page Numbers command from the Insert menu.
Create a header or footer	Choose the Header/Footer command from the View menu. In the pane Word opens, create the header or footer text you want.
View page numbers and headers or footers	Choose Page Layout from the View menu.
Search for text	Choose the Find command from the Edit menu, type the text you want Word to locate, and then choose the Find Next button.
Insert a section break	Position the insertion point where you want a section break. Then choose Break from the Insert menu. In the Break dialog box, select the option you want under Section Break.
Create different headers or footers for different sections of a document	Insert a section break and position the insertion point in the new section. Then open the header or footer pane and change the existing header or footer text to the text you want for the new section.

For more information on	See the *Microsoft Word User's Guide*
Page numbers	Chapter 22, "Numbering Pages"
Headers and footers	Chapter 30, "Headers and Footers"
Page layout view and normal view	Chapter 24, "Viewing Documents"
Sections	Chapter 10, "Sections: Formatting Parts of a Document"
Searching for text	Chapter 12, "Finding and Replacing Text or Formatting"

For an online lesson about	Do this
Adding headers and footers	Click the Help menu. Click Learning Word. Click Formatting. Click Formatting Pages.
	Follow the instructions on the screen.
	To exit a lesson at any time, click the Controls button and then click Exit.

Preview of the Next Lesson

In the next lesson, you'll learn to copy text from one document to another. This lets you take advantage of work you've already done in other documents and makes it easy to share your work with co-workers.

You'll also learn to move and size windows so that you can display step-by-step instructions on the screen as you work in dialog boxes and in your document. Finally, you'll print a document that tells you about some of the "safety features" in Word.

Working with Windows

Microsoft Windows provides a powerful work environment that streamlines many tasks and gives you more control over the way you work. With Windows, you can work with Microsoft Word and other applications at the same time. Within Word, you can display more than one document at a time. You can also arrange windows on the screen, just as you move papers around on a desk.

In this lesson, you'll open two Word documents and copy information from one document into the other. You'll also learn to size the Help window so you can read Help instructions as you work in a document or in a dialog box.

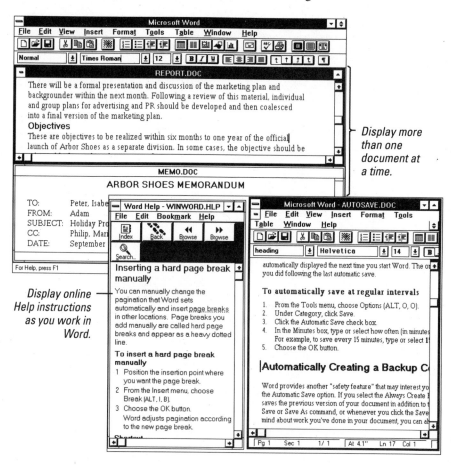

Display more than one document at a time.

Display online Help instructions as you work in Word.

This lesson explains how to do the following:

- Display more than one document on the screen at a time
- Copy text from one document to another
- Move and size windows
- Display step-by-step instructions as you work

Estimated lesson time: 35 minutes

Windows Basics

A window is a rectangular area on your screen in which you work on a document. You can open, move, size, scroll through, switch between, or close windows—just as you might spread out or leaf through books and papers on your desk and put them aside when you're finished with them. You can have many windows open on your screen and can work with several files at once by moving from window to window.

When you start Word and open a document, you are looking at a window within a window—a document window within the Word window.

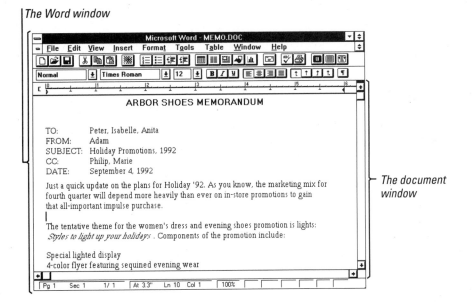

The Word window

The document window

The Word window controls the size of the area in which Word and all Word documents can be displayed. By making this window smaller, you can display and work with other applications at the same time you are working in Word.

Within the Word window, each Word document you open is displayed in its own window. You can make a document window smaller and display several documents at one time within the Word window. This gives you the opportunity to work on more than one document at once, as shown in the following illustration.

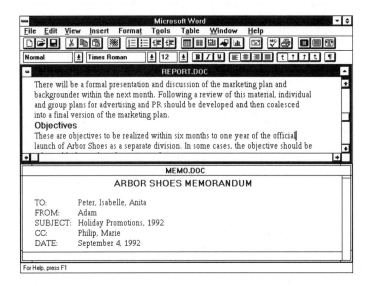

For example, if you think you can use parts of a monthly report in a memo, you can display both the report and the memo in the Word window at the same time. Then you can scroll through the monthly report, copy a paragraph, paste it into the memo, and return to the monthly report to look for other paragraphs that you can use.

In addition to working on more than one document at a time, Windows gives you an advantage with online Help. Word displays online Help in its own window. You can size and move the Help window so you can display step-by-step instructions as you work in a document or a dialog box. The following illustration shows Help arranged next to the Word window, instead of overlapping it.

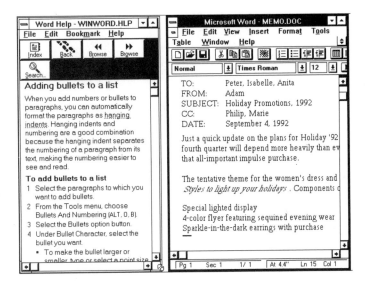

The Word window, Help window, and document windows have many features in common. (You'll work with these features during this lesson; don't try using them yet.) You can close any window and close Word itself by double-clicking the Control-menu box for that window.

Double-clicking this Control-menu bar closes Word.

Double-clicking this Control-menu bar closes the document.

The button on the far right changes depending on the size of the window. If the window is as large as possible, the button is called the Restore button. Clicking it restores the window to a previous, smaller size. If the window is less than its maximum size, the button is called the Maximize button. Clicking it quickly enlarges the window to the largest possible size.

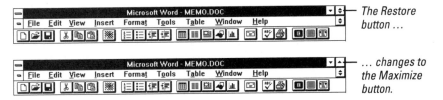

The Restore button ...

... changes to the Maximize button.

There is one feature that the Word window has that document windows do not have—a Minimize button. The Minimize button shrinks Microsoft Word to an icon, so that you can do other work on your computer without Word or any documents displayed, and then quickly return to Word.

Clicking the Minimize button shrinks Word to an icon.

Displaying More Than One Document at a Time

Although you can open many documents at one time, only one is *active*—the one containing the insertion point. Any command you choose affects only the active document.

If any documents are currently open

For this lesson you'll need to close any open documents, including the new document that Word automatically opens when you start Word.

▶ From the File menu, choose Close (ALT, F, C).

Repeat this step for each open document. When all documents are closed, the menu bar will display the only two menus that are still available: File and Help.

Open a sample document

Open

1 On the Toolbar, click the Open button.

2 Under Directories, make sure the PRACTICE directory is open. If it is not, select the drive where the Step by Step practice files are stored and open the appropriate directories.

3 Double-click GOODNEWS.DOC.

If you share your computer with other Word users, they may have changed the screen display. Before you begin this lesson, make sure the Toolbar, ribbon, ruler, and scroll bars are displayed. The ruler should display approximately 6 inches, or the equivalent. The Word window and the sample document should completely fill the screen. If you need assistance in changing the screen display, see "Getting Ready," earlier in this book.

Open another sample document

1 On the Toolbar, click the Open button.

2 Double-click AUTOSAVE.DOC.

The second document hides the first, just as though you'd placed one sheet of paper on top of another.

Switch between the two documents

You now have two open documents. To display one and hide the other, you use the Window menu. A check mark on the menu indicates which document is the active one. Use the following procedure to experiment with switching between documents.

1 From the Window menu, choose GOODNEWS.DOC.

Word displays this document on top of the other.

2 From the Window menu, choose AUTOSAVE.DOC.

Arrange the documents on the screen

Instead of switching between two full-size document windows, you can display both document windows on the screen at once.

▶ From the Window menu, choose Arrange All (ALT, W, A).

Word sizes the document windows evenly. Each window has a ruler so Word can accurately reflect the indents and margins in that document. The Toolbar and ribbon work for whichever window contains the insertion point.

Hide the rulers

When you are working in only one document, it's very useful to display the ribbon, ruler, and Toolbar. When you display more than one document, you may prefer to hide the ruler. You can also hide the ribbon and Toolbar, but these are used more often than the ruler.

Note that your command affects the document that contains the insertion point—the active document.

1 Take a moment and note which document contains the blinking insertion point. Then, from the View menu, choose Ruler (ALT, V, R).

Word hides the ruler for the document that contains the insertion point.

2 Click in the other document to make it active.

The title bars change in color or intensity to indicate which window is active.

3 From the View menu, choose Ruler (ALT, V, R).

Copying Text from One Document to Another

In earlier lessons you used the Cut, Copy, and Paste buttons on the Toolbar to copy and move text within a document. The buttons work the same between documents, and even between Windows applications.

Save AUTOSAVE.DOC with a new name

You will continue working on AUTOSAVE.DOC in this lesson. Give it a new name so the changes you make will not overwrite the original. You don't need to rename GOODNEWS.DOC; after the next procedure, you'll close it without making changes.

1 From the File menu, choose Save As (ALT, F, A).

2 Under File Name, type *your initials***save**

3 Choose the OK button.

4 When Word displays the summary information dialog box, type your name in the author box.

5 Choose the OK button.

Copy text between documents

1 If GOODNEWS.DOC is not currently active, click anywhere in its window to make it the active document.

2 To quickly select all the text in the document, from the Edit menu, choose Select All (ALT, E, A).

Copy

3 On the Toolbar, click the Copy button. You will not see a change in either document.

4 Click anywhere in AUTOSAVE.DOC to make it active.

5 Position the insertion point before the bold heading "To automatically save at regular intervals," as shown in the following illustration.

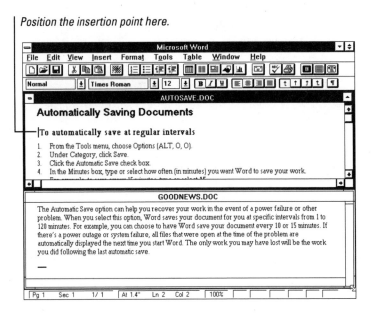

Position the insertion point here.

Paste

Save

6 On the Toolbar, click the Paste button.

Word pastes the text from GOODNEWS.DOC into AUTOSAVE.DOC.

Save the new version of AUTOSAVE.DOC

1 Make sure the insertion point is in your new version of AUTOSAVE.DOC.

2 On the Toolbar, click the Save button. Word saves this version of the document in place of the previous version.

Remember that you will not see a change in the document or screen display as Word saves the document.

Close one of the documents

In earlier lessons you closed documents by choosing the Close command from the File menu. Double-clicking the Control-menu box is a shortcut that works for all windows as it does in the following procedure.

1 Click in the GOODNEWS.DOC window to make it active.

2 Double-click the Control-menu box to the left of "GOODNEWS.DOC," as shown in the following illustration.

If Word displays a message asking if you want to save changes, click No.

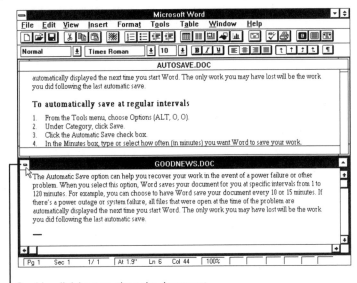

Double-click here to close the document.

TROUBLESHOOTING: **If a menu is displayed below Control-menu box**   If a menu drops open when you click the Control-menu box, it means the mouse clicked the Control-menu box only once. This displays a menu that controls the window. To close the menu, click in the text of GOODNEWS.DOC. Try closing the window again by double-clicking the Control-menu box. The speed at which you click the mouse is important.

3   To make the remaining document window the largest size possible, click the Maximize button to the right of the title bar, as shown below.

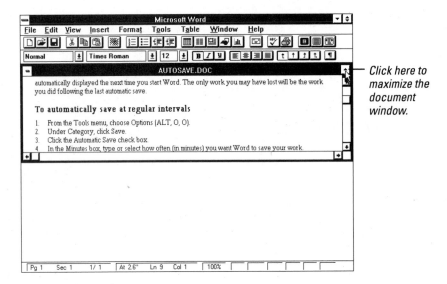

Click here to maximize the document window.

Moving and Sizing Windows

When you have several documents open, the Arrange All command divides the screen space equally among the documents. For example, if you have two open documents, each fills half the screen, as you saw earlier in this lesson. Sometimes it's helpful to make windows uneven sizes, displaying more text in one window than in another. You can move and size windows within Word, or you can move and size Word itself so you can work in Word and in another application at the same time.

The online Help system for Word is actually a separate application. By moving and sizing the Help window and the Word window so that they do not overlap, you can display step-by-step instructions in the Help window as you work in Word.

The next procedures explain how to set up the screen to look similar to the following illustration. You'll be able to scroll through the Help instructions as you work in Word.

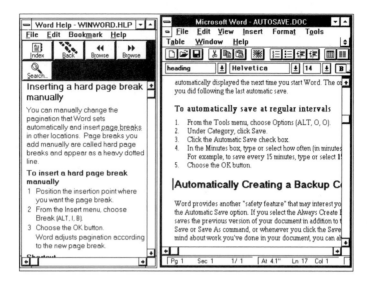

Display a Help topic

To practice moving and sizing windows, suppose that you want to use Help to learn how to insert a page break in the document. Before you size the window, use the following procedure to search for a topic in Help.

1 Press the F1 key.

2 In the Help window, click the Search button.

Word displays the Search dialog box.

3 Type **page**

Word scrolls through the list of categories and displays categories related to "page."

TROUBLESHOOTING: **If Help does not display a list of categories related to "page"** Try again by clicking in the document text and pressing F1 only once. (You may have pressed it twice last time, which carried you to a special Help index.) Then repeat step 3.

4 Select the category "Page breaks: inserting and removing."

5 Choose the Search button to show topics for this category.

6 In the bottom box, choose the topic "Inserting a hard page break manually."

7 Choose the Go To button.

The Help window displays information about inserting hard page breaks.

Move and size the Help window

As you work through the next procedures, note that a shadow border of the window shows you the location and boundary of the window as you drag. Word does not move or size the window until you release the mouse button.

1   Point to the title bar of the Help window, hold down the mouse button, and drag until the window is in the upper-left corner of the screen, as shown below.

If you share your computer with others, they may have already resized the Help window so it does not match the following illustration. You can move it and resize it.

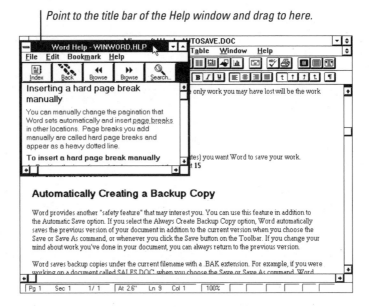

Point to the title bar of the Help window and drag to here.

TROUBLESHOOTING: **If the Help window completely fills the screen**   You must click the Restore button in the upper-right corner of the window before you can move or size the Help window when it fills the screen.

2   Point to the lower-right corner of the Help window. When the mouse pointer changes to a two-headed arrow, hold down the mouse button and drag the corner until the Help window covers about one-third of the screen, as shown in the following illustration.

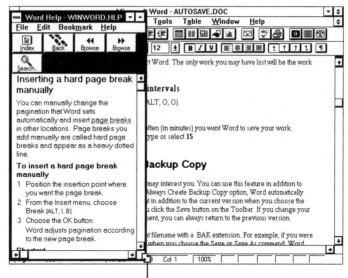

Point to this corner of the Help window and drag to this size.

Size the Word window

You're ready to size the Word window so it's no longer covered by the Help window. You cannot move a window that is *maximized*—that is, that completely fills the screen—there's no room to move it. You'll need to make the Word window smaller and then adjust it to the exact size you want.

1   Click in the document. The Word window will hide the Help window until the end of this procedure.

2   Click the Restore button in the upper-right corner of the Word window, as shown below. This restores the window to a previous, smaller size.

Click here to make the window smaller.

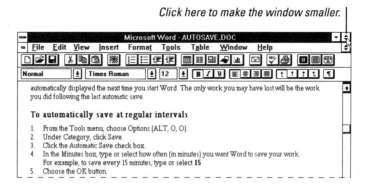

TROUBLESHOOTING: **If the Word window disappears** If the Word window disappears from your screen, you clicked the Minimize button, which shrinks Word to an icon so you can perform other tasks on your computer. Look for the Microsoft Word icon at the bottom of the screen. You may have to drag other windows out of the way to see it. Double-click the icon to display Word again. Repeat step 2, making sure you point to and click the button shown in the preceding illustration.

Note that the size and shape of the Word window on your screen may not match the one shown in the next illustration.

3 Point to the title bar of the Word window and drag the window to the upper right of the screen as shown in the following illustration. Make sure the scroll bar on the right side of the window remains visible.

Point to the title bar of the Word window and drag to here.

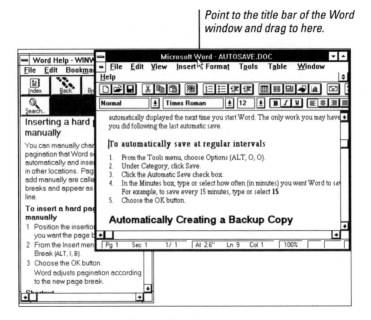

4 Point to the lower-left corner of the Word window. When the pointer becomes a two-headed arrow, drag until the window fills the space not covered by the Help window. You can repeat this step to "fine-tune" the size of the Word window.

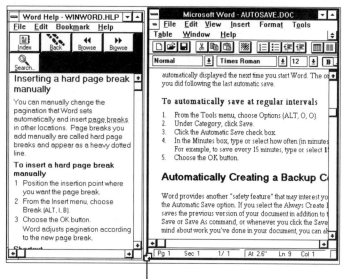

Point to this corner of the Word window, and drag to size the window.

Now you can scroll in either Word or Help to see more text.

Note Next time you choose Help, the Help window will be displayed in the size and position you set in the preceding procedures. It will continue to be displayed that way until you change it. In later work sessions, you'll only need to resize the Word window to work with Help displayed.

Insert a page break

Word automatically breaks pages for you, but occasionally you may want to break a page at a particular location—before a heading, for example. You can do this by manually inserting a *hard page break* at the location that you choose. Word doesn't adjust hard page breaks as you add and delete text. Word does adjust *soft page breaks*—the page breaks that it automatically inserts.

▶ Using the instructions in the Help window, insert a page break before the bold heading "Automatically Creating a Backup Copy," as shown in the following illustration.

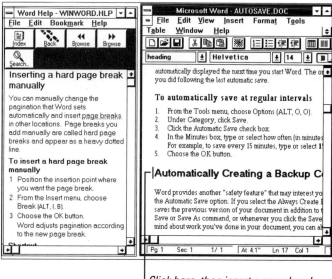

Click here, then insert a page break.

Close the Help window

Earlier in this lesson you closed a document window by double-clicking the Control-menu box at the left of the title bar. You can close the Help window in the same way.

▶ Double-click the Help window Control-menu box, as shown in the following illustration.

Double-click here to close the Help window.

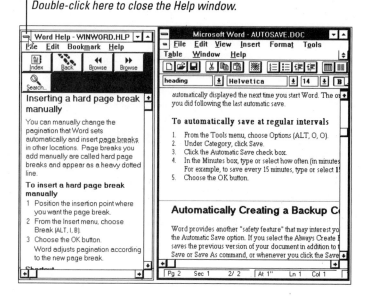

Maximize the Word window

▶ Click the Maximize button on the Word window.

Click here to maximize the window.

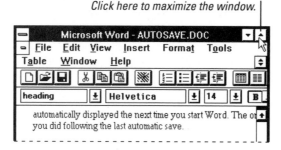

Save the document

Save

▶ On the Toolbar, click the Save button. Word saves this version of the document in place of the previous version.

Remember that you will not see a change in the document or screen display as Word saves the document.

Print the document

The sample document you worked on in this lesson describes something you can do *now* to prevent losing work later if there's a power failure or other problem.

1   Make sure the printer is on.

Print

2   On the Toolbar, click the Print button.

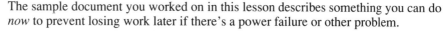

Tip   In addition to printing Word documents, you can also print online Help topics that you find especially useful. To print a Help topic as you view it, choose the Print Topic command from the File menu in the Help window.

One Step Further

Remember that pressing F1 displays the Help window.

▶ Search Help for information about inserting a new section break. When you find and display the topic, scroll down until you see a table that is too wide to fit in the Help window. (All text except tables will wrap within the Help window.) Drag the lower-right corner of the Help window until you can see all of the table. You may want to drag the Help window to a narrower size again after you've finished experimenting.

▶ Dialog boxes are a special kind of window. Do the following to arrange a dialog box and Help on the screen so they do not overlap. You'll be able to scroll through Help and see all of the dialog box. First, from the Format menu, choose Character. Press F1 to display Help about the dialog box. Drag the Character dialog box by its title bar to the far right of the screen. Move and size the Help window so it does not overlap the dialog box. When you are finished experimenting, choose the Cancel button in the dialog box. This closes both the dialog box and the Help that describes the dialog box.

If you want to continue to the next lesson

1 Double-click the Control-menu box for the document window.
–or–
From the File menu, choose Close (ALT, F, C).

Double-click here to close the document.

2 If Word displays a message asking if you want to save changes, choose the No button.

If you want to quit Word for now

1 Double-click the Control-menu box on the left of the Microsoft Word title bar.
–or–
From the File menu, choose Exit (ALT, F, X).

Double-click here to close any open document and exit Word.

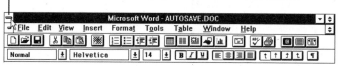

2 If Word displays a message asking if you want to save changes, choose the No button.

Tip No matter how you close a window—by using a command or by double-clicking the Control-menu box—if you've made changes to a document and have not saved them, Word will display a message asking if you want to save the changes.

Lesson Summary

To	Do this
Display several documents at once	Open each document and then, from the Window menu, choose Arrange All.
Copy text from one document to another	Select the text you want to copy. On the Toolbar, click the Copy button. Then, click once in the document in which you want to paste the text to make the document active, and then click again to position the insertion point where you want to paste the text. On the Toolbar, click the Paste button.
Move a window	If a window is its maximum size, click the window's Restore button to make it smaller. Point to the title bar for the window and drag the window to a new location.
Size a window	Point to any border or corner of a window. When the mouse pointer becomes a two-headed arrow, drag the border to make the window the size you want.
Make a window as large as possible	Click the Maximize button for that window.
Display online Help as you work	Size the Help window and the Word window so they do not overlap.
Insert a manual page break	Position the insertion point where you want the page break. Then, from the Insert menu, choose Break and click the OK button.

For more information on	See the *Microsoft Word User's Guide*
Windows	"Your First Word Document"
Using online Help	Chapter 5, "Using Help and Online Lessons"
Page breaks	Chapter 23, "Pagination"

Preview of the Next Lesson

In the next lesson you'll work with tables and learn quick ways to create side-by-side paragraphs or columns of numbers. You'll also learn how to create a chart from the data in a table. At the end of the lesson, you can print two pages of tips about working in tables, to add to your quick reference notebook.

3 Arranging Text and Graphics

Lesson 9 Creating Tables and Charts

Lesson 10 Creating Columns

Lesson 11 Adding Graphics and Emphasizing Text

Creating Tables and Charts

Word tables provide a quick and easy way to arrange columns of numbers in a document as well as a way to place text paragraphs side by side. You can insert a table in your document simply by clicking a button on the Toolbar. After you type the table text, you can adjust column widths; add, rearrange, or delete columns and rows; or format the table with borders and shading. You can also create a chart based on the numbers in a table.

In this lesson, you'll create a simple table and experiment with various formatting options. Then, for practice, you can apply what you've learned to a sample table already created for you. At the end of the lesson, you can print the sample document and add it to your quick reference notebook. It provides helpful information about working with tables.

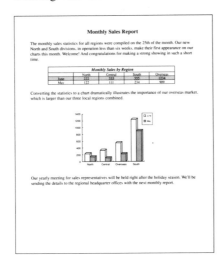

This lesson explains how to do the following:

- Insert a table into a document, type text in the table, and adjust the width of table columns

- Insert additional rows and columns, and format text

- Merge several table cells into one, and add borders and shading to a table

- Create a chart from the numbers in the table

Estimated lesson time: 30 minutes

Creating a Table

You can think of a table as rows and columns of boxes, called *cells*, that you fill with text and graphics. Within each cell, text wraps just as it does between the margins in other parts of a document. You can start new paragraphs within each cell by pressing ENTER, and you can easily add or delete text without affecting the columns of your table.

When you insert a table, Word outlines each cell with dotted gridlines so you can see which row and column of cells you're working in. Just as a paragraph mark ends every paragraph, an *end-of-cell mark* shows the end of every cell. Neither gridlines nor end-of-cell marks print; they are for your convenience as you work. You can hide them using the Show/Hide ¶ button on the ribbon when you want to see what the table will look like when printed.

Open a sample document

Open

1   On the Toolbar, click the Open button.

2   Under Directories, make sure the PRACTICE directory is open. If it is not, select the drive where the Step by Step practice files are stored and open the appropriate directories.

3   Double-click TABLE.DOC.

You may need to scroll down the list of file names to see TABLE.DOC.

If you share your computer with other Word users, they may have changed the screen display. Before you begin this lesson, make sure the Toolbar, ribbon, ruler, and scroll bars are displayed. The ruler should display approximately 6 inches, or the equivalent. The Word window and the sample document should completely fill the screen. If you need assistance in changing the screen display, see "Getting Ready," earlier in this book.

Save the document with a new name

Give the document a new name so the changes you make in this lesson will not overwrite the original document.

1   From the File menu, choose Save As (ALT, F, A).

2   Under File Name, type *your initials***table**

For example, type **jptable**

3   Choose the OK button.

4   When Word displays the Summary Info dialog box, select the name in the author box and type your own name if it does not already appear there.

5   Choose the OK button.

Show/Hide ¶

Display paragraph marks

▶   If paragraph marks are not currently displayed on the screen, click the Show/Hide ¶ button on the ribbon.

Insert a table

1   Position the insertion point as shown below.

> **Monthly·Sales·Report¶**
> ¶
> The·monthly·sales·statistics·for·all·regions·were·compiled·on·the·25th·of·the·month.··Our·new·North·and·
> South·divisions,·in·operation·less·than·six·weeks,·make·their·first·appearance·on·our·charts·this·month.·
> Welcome!·And·congratulations·for·making·a·strong·showing·in·such·a·short·time.¶
> ¶

Click here.

2   Press ENTER to create to a new line.

This will leave a blank line between the paragraph and the table.

3   On the Toolbar, click the Table button to display the grid.

Table

Click here.

4   Drag across the grid to select two rows and three columns, as shown below, and then release the mouse button.

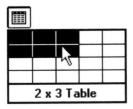

When you release the mouse button, Word inserts an empty table with the number of columns and rows that you selected.

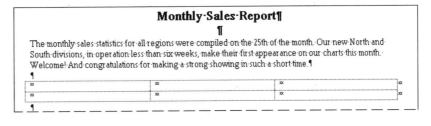

TROUBLESHOOTING: **If you do not see the boxes shown in the previous illustration** Word makes it easy to display the boxes, called *gridlines*, or hide them. For this lesson, you'll need them displayed. To display the gridlines, from the Table menu, choose Gridlines.

Type the text

When you insert a table, Word positions the insertion point in the first cell, ready for you to type.

1 Type **North**

2 Press TAB to move to the next cell.

3 Type **Central** and press TAB.

4 Type **South** and press TAB.

Word moves the insertion point to the first cell in the next row.

5 Fill in the rest of the table as shown in the following illustration, pressing TAB to move from cell to cell. Pressing TAB when the insertion point is in the last cell in the table creates a new row. Make sure you type the number "1" on the keyboard instead of typing a lowercase letter "L."

North°	Central°	South°	°
222°	333°	555°	°
122°	111°	234°	°

Adjust the width of the columns

You can use the ruler to adjust the width of the columns so they are a better fit for the text. When the insertion point is in a table, the ruler displays a column marker, which looks like the letter "T," at each column boundary. When you drag a column marker, the column boundary moves.

The ruler shows the exact width of the columns. It's a good idea to scroll so the table is close to the ruler when you are adjusting the column widths. This makes it easy to compare the table to the ruler.

1 If the ruler is not displayed, from the View menu, choose Ruler (ALT, V, R).

2 Click the down scroll arrow until the table is close to the ruler.

3 Drag the first T on the ruler to approximately 1 inch, so the column boundary is closer to the word "North," as shown below.

TROUBLESHOOTING: **If "T's" do not appear on the ruler**   The "T's" appear only when the insertion point is in the table. If you click outside the table, the ruler changes to reflect the indents and margin settings for the paragraph that contains the insertion point. Clicking in the table will display the "T's" again.

4   Use the same method to make the other columns more narrow.

North	Central	South	
222	333	555	
122	111	234	

Experiment with column widths

This is a good time to experiment with column widths.

▶   Try dragging one of the "T's" that marks a column boundary to make a column wider, just as you dragged to make the columns more narrow.

▶   You can adjust the width of the columns without changing the width of the table. Hold down SHIFT as you drag one of the two middle "T's" on the ruler. Note that the right edge of the table does not change as you adjust the width of the column. Also note that Word wraps text within the cells if the cells get too narrow for the text.

▶   Instead of dragging the "T's" on the ruler, you can drag the gridlines that mark the column boundaries. You might want to experiment with this method to see which you prefer. When you position the mouse pointer over one of the gridlines that marks a column boundary, the mouse pointer changes to a two-headed arrow. Drag the gridline to the left or right to adjust the column boundary.

When you finish experimenting, adjust the column boundaries so each column is approximately one inch wide.

Inserting and Deleting Rows and Columns

You've already learned the basic skills for working with tables. Most of the time, these will be the only skills you need: You'll insert a table that has the number of columns that you want, and you'll fill it in top to bottom, pressing TAB to add rows as you go.

Sometimes, however, you may need to add or delete a column. Or you may need to add or delete a row. This is easy to do. All the commands you need are on the Table menu.

When you add a row, existing rows move down to make room for the new row. Columns move to the right to make room for new columns. Once you insert a new column or row, you can type text and change the column widths as you did earlier in this lesson.

The next portion of this lesson gives you practice in modifying a table. You'll start with the table you created and insert a row and two columns, so your table will look like the following.

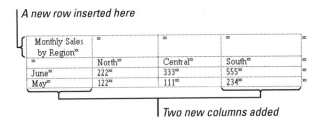

A new row inserted here

Two new columns added

Insert a column

You can insert a column anywhere within a table. Practice by adding a column before the first column.

1   Position the mouse pointer at the top of the first column. When the pointer becomes a down arrow, click. This selects the entire column.

2   From the Table menu, choose Insert Columns (ALT, A, I).

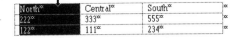

Word inserts an empty column to the left of the selected column.

Type text in the new column

Earlier in this lesson you pressed TAB to move you through the cells one after the other. You can also press arrow keys to move directly to a cell. This may be faster for you as you type. The arrow keys are often clustered together on your keyboard; each is marked with an arrow that points left, right, up, or down.

1   Click in the second cell of the new column and type **June**

2   Press the DOWN ARROW key to move down one cell and then type **May**

xx	North	Central	South	xx
June	222	333	555	xx
May	122	111	234	xx

Insert a column at the end of the table

Word provides *end-of-row marks* so you can add columns to the right side of a table. You select these marks just as though they were an actual column.

1 Position the mouse pointer above the end-of-row marks as shown below. When the pointer becomes a down arrow, click.

¤	North¤	Central¤	South¤	¤
June¤	222¤	333¤	555¤	¤
May¤	122¤	111¤	234¤	¤

When the pointer becomes a down arrow ...

... click to select the column of end-of-row marks.

¤	North¤	Central¤	South¤	¤
June¤	222¤	333¤	555¤	¤
May¤	122¤	111¤	234¤	¤

2 From the Table menu, choose Insert Columns (ALT, A, I).

¤	North¤	Central¤	South¤	¤	¤
June¤	222¤	333¤	555¤	¤	¤
May¤	122¤	111¤	234¤	¤	¤

3 Click in the top cell of the new column and then type text in each cell so the table looks like the following:

¤	North¤	Central¤	South¤	Overseas¤	¤
June¤	222¤	333¤	555¤	1234¤	¤
May¤	122¤	111¤	234¤	909¤	¤

Type this text in the new column.

Insert a row

You can insert a row anywhere within a table using the same procedure you used to insert a column. You simply select a row or several rows and choose a command from the Table menu. Word inserts as many rows as you selected.

In earlier lessons you used an invisible selection bar to the left of paragraphs to quickly select lines and paragraphs. There is a selection bar to the left of tables, which you use to select entire rows.

1 Point to the left of the first row as shown below. When the mouse pointer changes to an arrow pointing at the row, click. This selects the entire row.

¤	North¤	Central¤	South¤	Overseas¤	¤
June¤	222¤	333¤	555¤	1234¤	¤
May¤	122¤	111¤	234¤	909¤	¤

Each cell also has an invisible selection bar. Make sure you click well to the left of the row so you do not select the first cell by itself.

2   From the Table menu, choose Insert Rows (ALT, A, I).

xx	xx	xx	xx	xx	xx
xx	North^{xx}	Central^{xx}	South^{xx}	Overseas^{xx}	xx
June^{xx}	222^{xx}	333^{xx}	555^{xx}	1234^{xx}	xx
May^{xx}	122^{xx}	111^{xx}	234^{xx}	909^{xx}	xx

3   Click in the first cell of the new row and type **Monthly Sales by Region**

Note that the text wraps within the cell as you type. Your text may wrap differently than the text in this example, depending on the width of your column.

Monthly Sales by Region^{xx}	xx	xx	xx	xx	xx
xx	North^{xx}	Central^{xx}	South^{xx}	Overseas^{xx}	xx
June^{xx}	222^{xx}	333^{xx}	555^{xx}	1234^{xx}	xx
May^{xx}	122^{xx}	111^{xx}	234^{xx}	909^{xx}	xx

Delete a column

Deleting a row or column is just like inserting one. If you'd like to try it, you can follow this procedure and then click the Undo button to put the column back in the table.

1   Select the column labeled "Central" by positioning the mouse at the top of the column and clicking when the pointer changes to a down arrow.

2   From the Table menu, choose Delete Columns (ALT, A, D).

Monthly Sales by Region^{xx}	xx	xx	xx	xx
xx	North^{xx}	South^{xx}	Overseas^{xx}	xx
June^{xx}	222^{xx}	555^{xx}	1234^{xx}	xx
May^{xx}	122^{xx}	234^{xx}	909^{xx}	xx

Word removes the column and moves the other columns over to fill the space.

Undo

3   On the Toolbar, click the Undo button to put the column back in the table.

Rows can be deleted in the same way. You select the row and then choose the Delete Rows command from the Table menu.

Tip   You can delete the contents of a table row or column without deleting the row or column itself. To do this, select the row or column whose contents you want to delete, and then press the DEL key.

Polishing the Look of the Table

In this portion of the lesson you'll polish the look of the table by merging cells to create a heading that spans all columns of the table. You'll also center text within the table, center the table between the margins, and add borders and shading.

Merging Cells

You may sometimes want to combine, or merge, two or more selected cells within a row to create a single cell. For example, you can merge cells to create a heading that spans several columns.

It's a good idea to insert all the columns and adjust their widths before merging cells.

Merge the cells in the top row

1   Select the first row by pointing to the left of the row and clicking.

2   From the Table menu, choose Merge Cells (ALT, A, M).

The selected cells merge into one.

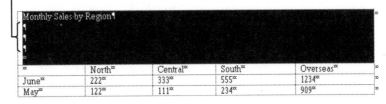

These cells merge into one cell.

The end-of-cell marks become paragraph marks.

3   To delete all the paragraph marks in the first cell, you must first remove the highlighting by clicking in any other cell in the table. Then press the arrow keys to move the insertion point back into the top cell. Press BACKSPACE until all paragraph marks have been removed.

Format the heading

You edit and format text in a table just as you do any other document text.

Bold   *Italic*

1   Select the heading "Monthly Sales by Region" and then click the Bold or Italic button on the ribbon, or click both.

Note that some printers cannot print both bold and italic.

2   Experiment with the point size to make the text in the heading larger than the rest of the text in the table. For example, try enlarging it to 14 points.

Monthly Sales by Region ❑				
	North	Central	South	Overseas
June	222	333	555	1234
May	122	111	234	909

Centering Text and Centering the Table

You can center the text in a cell, and you can center the table itself between the margins of the page. The following procedures show you how to do both.

Center the text in each cell

1   To select all the cells in the table, from the Table menu, choose Select Table (ALT, A, A).

Centered Text

2   On the ribbon, click the Centered Text button.

Your table will look similar to the following:

Monthly Sales by Region ❑				
	North	Central	South	Overseas
June	222	333	555	1234
May	122	111	234	909

Center the table between the margins

You can center one or more rows, or you can center the entire table. The number of rows you center depends on your selection.

1   Select the entire table if it is no longer selected.

2   From the Table menu, choose Row Height (ALT, A, H).

All the options that affect individual rows are available through this command.

3   Under Alignment, select Center.

4   Choose the OK button.

This centers the table between the margins of the page.

Adding Borders and Shading

Although the gridlines you see on your screen make it easy to tell one cell from another, they do not print. If you want table borders to print, you can apply them on top of the gridlines. To apply borders, you first select the cells you want to have borders and then you use the Border command.

Place a border around each cell

1   Select the entire table if it is no longer selected.

2   From the Format menu, choose Border (ALT, T, B).

3   Under Preset, select the Grid option.

4   Choose the OK button.

To see how the borders look, click outside the table to clear the selection. A thick border outlines the entire table, and lighter borders outline individual cells.

Apply shading to the first row of numbers

1   Select the row that begins with "June."

Make sure that you click well to the left of the row so that you select the entire row, not just the first cell.

2   From the Format menu, choose Border (ALT, T, B).

3   Choose the Shading button.

4   The Pattern box indicates the pattern is "Clear." Click the down arrow next to the Pattern box and then click 20%.

5   To close the Shading dialog box, choose the OK button.

6   To close the Border dialog box, choose the OK button.

Word applies shading to the selected cell. Click outside the selection for a better look at the shading.

Bold

7   Shaded text is often easier to read if it is bold. Select the entire shaded row and then click the Bold button on the ribbon.

Tip   Twenty percent is a good starting point for shading. Later, you may want to experiment with different percentages. For example, try 10 percent for lighter shading or 30 percent for fairly dark shading.

Creating Charts

You can select all or part of a table that contains numbers and create column charts, pie charts, and line charts similar to those in the Microsoft Excel spreadsheet program. By default, Word creates a column chart.

The Setup program you use to install Word on your computer gives you the option to install or not install Microsoft Graph. If the feature is not installed, a message will be displayed during the following procedure. You can run the Word Setup program again and specify that you want to install Microsoft Graph only. For more information on the Setup program, see *Microsoft Word Getting Started*.

Create a chart of the sales figures

1   Select the last three rows in the table by positioning the mouse to the left of the second row, holding down the mouse button, and dragging down the selection bar to select the other rows.

Graph

2   On the Toolbar, click the Graph button.

Click here.

Word displays a column chart in its own window. Microsoft Graph is a special Word feature that has its own title bar—Microsoft Graph—and its own menu bar. You'll use these menus until you return to your document.

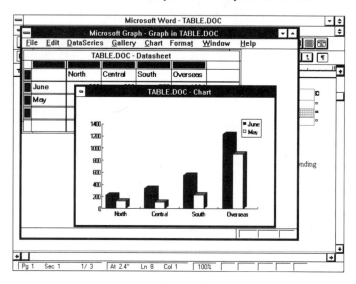

3   From the File menu in the Microsoft Graph window, choose the Exit And Return command (ALT, F, X).

4   When Word asks if you want to update changes, choose the Yes button.

Word inserts a blank line below the table and then inserts the chart.

The large, blinking, vertical line next to the chart is the insertion point, which is always the height of the line it is in. In this case, the line is as tall as the chart.

5   Press ENTER to insert a blank line between the chart and the following text.

Size the chart

You size a chart in the same way that you size a picture: by dragging the sizing handles that surround it. If you drag a corner handle, Word maintains the ratio of height to width as you drag. A dotted line indicates the size of the chart as you drag. You can compare the line to the ruler and drag the chart to a particular width.

1 Click the chart once to display the sizing handles that surround it.

2 Experiment with the size of the chart by positioning the mouse pointer over the lower-right sizing handle until the mouse pointer turns into a two-headed arrow. Drag diagonally upward to make the chart smaller. A dotted line above the two-headed pointer indicates the width of the graph as you drag.

When you release the mouse button, Word resizes the chart. If you want to try again, drag the lower-right corner to a new size.

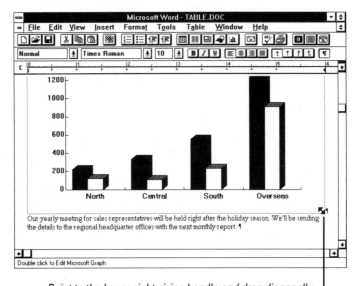

Point to the lower-right sizing handle and drag diagonally.

Tip Charts can be positioned anywhere on the page. Lesson 11, "Adding Graphics and Emphasizing Text," shows you how. For more information, see Chapter 21, "Positioning Text and Graphics on the Page," in the *Microsoft Word User's Guide*.

Save

Save the document

▶ On the Toolbar, click the Save button. Word saves this version of the document in place of the previous version.

Print the document

There are several tables of tips for you at the end of the document that is currently on your screen. You can print one copy of the entire document by clicking the Print button on the Toolbar. If you'd like to print only the pages that contain the tips, use the following procedure.

If you print the document now, you'll note that the first table of tips has no borders, shading, or other formatting. If you want to format that table, go on to "One Step Further," experiment with formatting, and then print the document again.

1   From the File menu, choose Print (ALT, F, P).

2   Under Range, type **2** in the From box.

   If you do not type a number in the To box, Word prints from page 2 to the end of the document.

3   Choose the OK button to print the document.

One Step Further

The first table of tips that follows your chart is an unformatted table. Although gridlines appear on the screen, they do not print. You can use some of the skills covered in this lesson to give the table a more polished look.

Scroll down to see the first table of tips and then try any of the following.

▶   Try editing text in one of the cells. You can drag to select only the amount of text that you want to edit, or you can select all the text in the cell by clicking in the invisible selection bar at the left of the cell. Click the Undo button after you edit the text to reinstate the original text.

▶   Use the ruler to make the columns narrower and wider. If you make the columns too wide, they may extend so far beyond the margin that they will not print. You can choose the Print Preview command on the File menu to see how the table will look when printed.

▶   Practice adding and deleting rows. Add a row at the end of the table by pressing TAB. (The insertion point must be in the last cell of the last row.) Then, select the entire new row and delete it.

▶   Select the entire table and add a border around each cell using the Border command on the Format menu. Under Preset, select the Grid option.

If you want to continue to the next lesson

1   If you've made changes to the first table of tips while you were experimenting that you'd like to print, from the File menu, choose Print. Then, print page 2 only by typing **2** in both the From and To box in the Print dialog box.

2   From the File menu, choose Close (ALT, F, C).

3   If Word asks if you want to save changes, choose the Yes button.

If you want to quit Word for now

1 From the File menu, choose Exit (ALT, F, X).

2 If you've made changes to the the first table of tips while you were experimenting that you'd like to save, choose the Yes button.

Tips About Tables

For more information about any of these tips, see Chapter 17, "Tables," in the *Microsoft Word User's Guide*.

■ You can insert a decimal tab in a table cell so that all numbers containing a decimal point align within the column. For more information about inserting tabs, see Chapter 7, "Paragraph Formatting," in the *Microsoft Word User's Guide*.

■ If a row won't fit on the current page, Word inserts a page break before the row containing that cell. Word cannot, however, insert a page break within a cell.

■ You can drag and drop rows and columns to reorganize a table, just as you drag and drop text to reorganize a document.

■ You can cut, copy, and paste cells within a table, within a document, and between documents.

■ When you insert a new table into your document, all cells in the table initially have the text format of the paragraph that contained the insertion point. You can use the ruler, ribbon, and commands on the Format menu to change the text formatting within the cells, just as you do in the paragraphs in the rest of your document.

■ You can sort the rows in a table to arrange them in alphabetic or numeric order. For example, if you type a membership list in a table so that each member's last name is in a column, you can alphabetize the membership list by sorting the last names. For details about using the Sort command on the Tools menu, see Chapter 15, "Sorting," in the *Microsoft Word User's Guide*.

■ If you have used Microsoft Excel, tables will seem very familiar. In fact, if you insert a Microsoft Excel worksheet in your Word document, you can work with the spreadsheet data just as you would a Word table. For example, you can add borders and change the widths of the columns. The reverse is also true: If you create a table in Word, you can insert the table in a Microsoft Excel worksheet and work with it as you would other spreadsheet data.

■ If you would like more information about creating charts, see the *Microsoft Graph User's Guide*.

Lesson Summary

To	Do this
Insert a table	Click the Table button on the Toolbar and then select the number of columns and rows you want.
Move to a new table cell	Press the TAB key or use the arrow keys.
Select an entire column or row	Click above the column or in the selection bar to the left of the row; select an entire table by choosing the Select Table command on the Table menu.
Adjust the widths of table columns	Drag the column markers on the ruler.
Insert a new row or column	Select a row or column in the existing table and then choose the Insert Rows or Insert Columns command from the Table menu.
Merge several cells into one cell	Select the cells and then choose the Merge Cells command on the Table menu.
Center text within table cells	On the ribbon, click the Centered Text button.
Center a table between the page margins	Choose the Row Height command on the Table menu, and then select the Center option under Alignment.
Add borders to a table	Choose the Border command from the Format menu and then select the Grid option under Preset.
Add shading to a table row	Select Border from the Format menu, choose the Shading button, and then select 20% under Pattern.
Create a column chart	On the Toolbar, click the Graph button and then from the File menu in the Microsoft Graph menu bar, choose Exit And Return.
Size the column chart	Click the chart to display the sizing handles and then drag the sizing handles.

For more information on	See the *Microsoft Word User's Guide*
Tables	Chapter 17, "Tables"
Setting tabs	Chapter 7, "Paragraph Formatting"
Sorting a table	Chapter 15, "Sorting"
Working with spreadsheet data	Chapter 36, "Exchanging Information"

For an online lesson about	Do this
Creating and editing tables	Click the Help menu. Click Learning Word. Click Tables, Frames, and Pictures. Click Creating a Table or Modifying a Table. Follow the instructions on the screen. To exit a lesson at any time, click the Controls button and then click Exit.

Preview of the Next Lesson

In the next lesson, you'll learn to format text into multiple columns and customize the look of the page by adding vertical lines between columns and breaking columns exactly as you want them. You'll learn the best ways to see the multiple-column document take shape on the screen. When you finish the lesson, you can print two documents for your quick reference notebook that give you more information about the *views*—different perspectives on a document—that Word provides.

Creating Columns

With Microsoft Word, you can produce "snaking" columns, in which text flows from the bottom of one column to the top of the next, as in newspaper columns. Word automatically breaks the columns when the text reaches the bottom margin. You can insert manual column breaks if you want the columns broken differently.

In this lesson you'll format two different documents. In the first, you'll change the number of columns for the entire document. In the second, you'll create a different number of columns for each section of the document.

Create two or more
columns in a document

Change the number of
columns on a page

This lesson explains how to do the following:

- Create multiple columns
- Insert manual column breaks
- Add lines between columns
- Vary the number of columns within a document
- Change the view, or display, of a document to concentrate on different aspects of it
- Reduce or enlarge the display of the document on the screen

Estimated lesson time: 40 minutes

Creating Columns

You can use a button on the Toolbar to create columns in a document or to change the number of columns. Word automatically breaks each column at the bottom of the page and moves the next text up to the top of the page. You can also adjust where the columns break by inserting manual breaks.

Word provides several *views,* or ways of displaying a document. Each view helps you concentrate on a different aspect of the document. As you work with columns, you will find that certain views better suit the task at hand. For example, normal view, the view you've used in all preceding lessons, is best for typing and editing text. When you create columns in normal view, Word displays them in their actual width, but not side by side, as they will look when printed. To see the columns side by side, you switch to page layout view.

Open the sample document

Open

1   On the Toolbar, click the Open button.

2   Under Directories, make sure the PRACTICE directory is open. If it is not, select the drive where the Step by Step practice files are stored and open the appropriate directories.

3   Double-click COLUMN.DOC.

If you share your computer with other Word users, they may have changed the screen display. Before you begin this lesson, make sure the Toolbar, ribbon, ruler, and scroll bars are displayed. The ruler should display approximately 6 inches, or the equivalent. The Word window and the sample document should completely fill the screen. If you need assistance in changing the screen display, see "Getting Ready," earlier in this book.

Save the document with a new name

Give the document a new name so the changes you make in this lesson will not overwrite the original document.

1   From the File menu, choose Save As (ALT, F, A).

2   Under File Name, type *your initials***column**

For example, type **jpcolumn**

3   Choose the OK button.

4   When Word displays the Summary Info dialog box, select the name in the author box and type your own name.

5   Choose the OK button.

Switch to page layout view

In page layout view, you can edit the document as well as see how it will look when printed.

Page layout view shows how your document will look when it is printed. When you choose page layout view, you'll see the top "edge" of the page, and you'll see columns positioned side by side. You can edit and format text in page layout view.

▶ From the View menu, choose Page Layout (ALT, V, P).

Experiment with multiple columns

You can change the number of columns as many times as you like. Repeat the following procedure a few times, creating four-column, then three-column, then two-column formats.

1 On the Toolbar, click the Columns button.

Columns

Click here.

A sample box drops open.

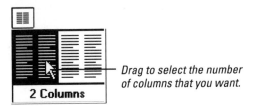

Drag to select the number of columns that you want.

2 Point to the left column in the box, press the mouse button, and drag to the right to select the number of columns you want. When you release the mouse button, Word creates the columns in the document.

3 Experiment by repeating steps 1 and 2, selecting a different number of columns each time. When you finish experimenting, leave the document in two-column format, as shown in the following illustration.

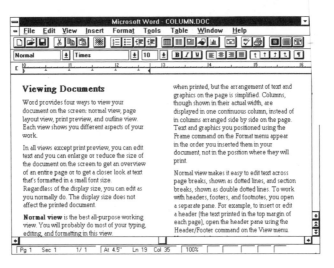

Insert a manual column break

Word automatically breaks each column when the column reaches the bottom of the page, moving the text that follows the break to the top of the next column. If you want to break the columns differently, you can insert manual column breaks.

The next procedure shows you how to insert a manual column break in the sample document, so the bold text "Normal View" appears at the top of the second column.

Dragging the scroll box is a quick way to scroll to the end of a document.

1 Scroll down to see the bottom of the page and position the insertion point where you want the new column to begin. In this case, position the insertion point in front of the bold text "Normal View," as shown in the following illustration.

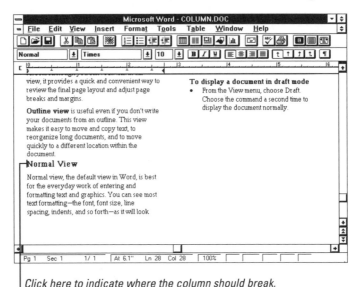

Click here to indicate where the column should break.

2 From the Insert menu, choose Break (ALT, I, B).

3 Select the Column Break option by clicking it.

4 Choose the OK button.

The text that follows the column break moves to the top of the next column. Your document should look similar to the following illustration.

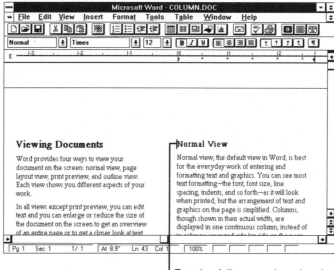

Text that follows a column break moves to the top of the next column.

Add lines between columns

Word provides a Columns command that offers special options. For example, you can use this command to place vertical lines between columns. You see the vertical lines when you print or when you change to another view—print preview. Print preview shows every aspect of your document, just as it will print. While you cannot edit text in this view, you can view two pages at a time.

1 From the Format menu, choose Columns (ALT, T, O).

2 Select the Line Between option by clicking it.

3 Choose the OK button.

Now switch to print preview to see the line.

4 From the File menu, choose Print Preview (ALT, F, V).

Word displays the document as shown in the following illustration.

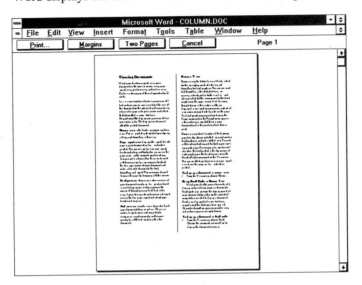

Save the document

Save

▶ From the File menu, choose Save (ALT, F, S).

Choosing this command has the same effect as clicking the Save button on the Toolbar. Word saves this version of the document in place of the previous version.

Remember that you will not see a change in the document or screen display as Word saves the document.

Print the document

It's a good idea to look at a document in print preview right before you print it, to check its final appearance. You can print the document without switching out of print preview. Your document prints the same regardless of which view is on the screen when you print.

The sample document you've been formatting is the first of two short documents that describe the different ways you can view, or display, a document in Word. You can print out the second document at the end of this lesson and then add both to your quick reference notebook.

Stay in print preview and use the following procedure to print the document.

1 Click the Print button at the top of the print preview window.

2 When Word displays the Print dialog box, choose the OK button.

Close the document

Close the document to get ready for the next portion of the lesson.

▶ From the File menu, choose Close (ALT, F, C).
  –Or–
  Double-click the document Control-menu box, which is located to the left of the menu names.

Varying the Number of Columns Within a Document

You've learned all the skills you need to create multiple columns throughout a document. If you need a more complex page layout, you can vary how many columns appear on a page or in various sections of the document. To vary the number of columns, you use the procedures taught in the first portion of this lesson plus one more—inserting a *section break*.

When you insert a section break, you can indicate that you want the break to be *continuous*—one section following immediately after the other on the page.

You can insert a section break that starts sections on new pages, on the next even-numbered page, or on the next odd-numbered page. For multiple-column situations, you usually want a continuous section break. That's what you'll work with in this lesson.

When you insert section breaks, you divide a document into *sections*. You can then format each section separately.The following illustration shows a page that has been divided into four sections. Each section is formatted with a different number of columns. Double dotted lines mark each section break; these lines do not print.

The rest of the lesson shows you how to format a document to look like this example.

Inserting Section Breaks

In normal view, a section break shows on the screen as a double dotted line extending the width of the page. These lines make it easy to see where section breaks occur, which is helpful when you format the sections. After you insert section breaks and create columns in each section, switch to page layout view to see columns side by side, as you did in the first part of this lesson.

Open the second sample document

Open

1 On the Toolbar, click the Open button.

2 Under File Name, double-click SECTIONS.DOC.

Save the document with a new name

Give the document a new name so the changes you make in this lesson will not overwrite the original document.

1 From the File menu, choose Save As (ALT, F, A).

2 Under File Name, type *your initials***sect**

For example, type **jpsect**

3 Choose the OK button.

4 When Word displays the Summary Info dialog box, select the name in the author box and type your own name if it does not already appear there.

5 Choose the OK button.

Switch to normal view

▶ From the View menu, choose Normal (ALT, V, N).

Insert a section break

1 Position the insertion point as shown in the following illustration to indicate where you want to change the number of columns.

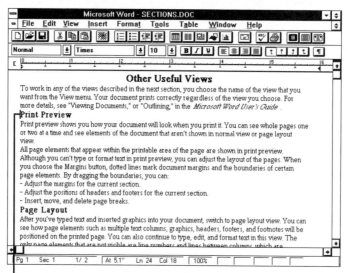

| Position the insertion point here.

2 From the Insert menu, choose Break (ALT, I, B).

3 Under Section Break, select Continuous so the new section will print right after the previous section.

4 Choose the OK button.

Word inserts the section mark—a double dotted line. Now the document has two sections: one above the section mark and one below the section mark.

Insert another section break

1 Scroll down and position the insertion point as shown in the following illustration.

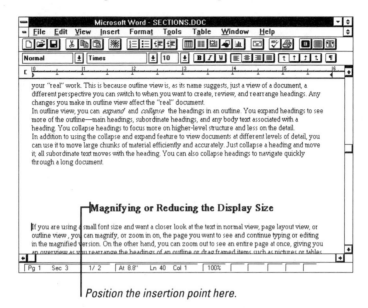

Position the insertion point here.

2 From the Insert menu, choose Break (ALT, I, B).

3 Under Section Break, select Continuous.

4 Choose the OK button.

Insert a section break below the heading

▶ Position the insertion point and insert a continuous section break as shown in the following illustration.

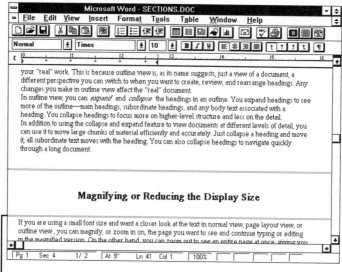

Insert a continuous section break here

Now you can format each section with the number of columns that you want.

Creating Columns in Each Section

To create a different number of columns in each section, use the Columns button on the Toolbar just as you used it during the first part of this lesson. The only difference is that the column formatting will affect only the section that contains the insertion point.

Remember that the document is displayed in normal view. The columns will show in their actual width after you format them, but not side by side. You can see them side by side when you switch to page layout view.

Format each section

The fastest way to scroll is to drag the scroll box.

1 Scroll to the top of the document.

The first section should remain formatted as one column. You do not need to do anything to that section.

2 Click to position the insertion point in the second section.

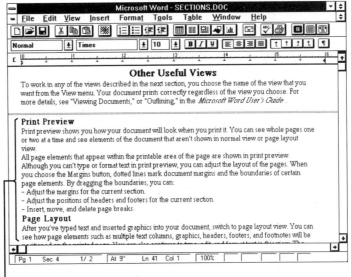

Click anywhere in this section.

Columns

3   Use the Columns button on the Toolbar to create three columns. In normal view, you will see the columns in their actual widths, but not side by side.

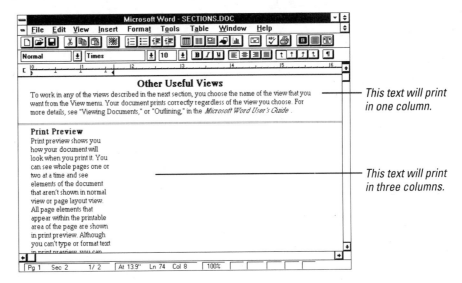

This text will print in one column.

This text will print in three columns.

Click a scroll arrow to scroll line by line.

4   Scroll down to view the next two section breaks.

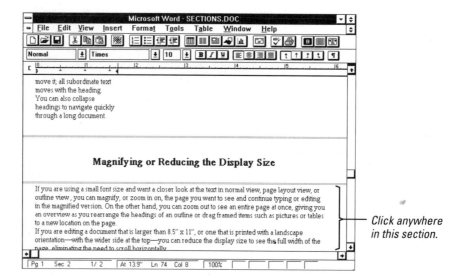

Click anywhere
in this section.

5   Click to position the insertion point in the section below the heading.

6   Create two columns. Your document will look similar to the following illustration. The next procedure will show you how to see the columns side by side.

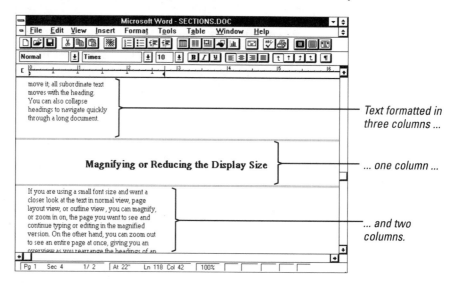

Text formatted in
three columns ...

... one column ...

... and two
columns.

Note As you scroll through the sample document, you may notice a single dotted line. That line indicates an automatic page break.

Getting an Overview of the Layout

Word provides three buttons on the Toolbar that are very useful when you are working with columns. The buttons do not change the document in any way; they only change the view—the way you see the document on the screen.

These buttons change the view of your document.

This button	Has this effect
Zoom Whole Page	Adjusts the level of magnification to show the entire page, and switches to page layout view to show items in the position they will print.
Zoom 100 Percent	Sets the level of magnification to 100 percent and switches to normal view.
Zoom Page Width	Adjusts the level of magnification to show the entire width of the page, regardless of the view.

Change your view of the document

Zoom Whole Page

▶ Click the Zoom Whole Page button for a quick look at the entire page.

Clicking this button does two things. It reduces the size of the display so you can see the whole page, and it switches to page layout view so columns appear side by side.

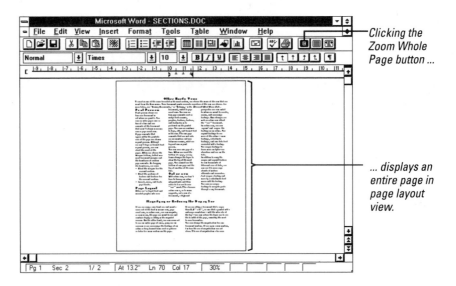

Clicking the Zoom Whole Page button ...

... displays an entire page in page layout view.

Experiment with formatting

▶ With the document display still reduced, click in any of the sections and change the number of columns. Try formatting the three-column section as two-column or four-column. When you are finished experimenting, format the section as three columns again.

Zoom 100 Percent

Return to normal view

▶ Click the Zoom 100 Percent button.

Word enlarges the display to 100 percent magnification and returns to normal view.

View the columns at full size

To view the columns side by side at 100 percent magnification, switch to page layout view as you did in the first part of this lesson. This is the best view for editing multiple-column text, because you can easily see the effect of your changes on the columns. Word adjusts the columns as you add or delete text.

▶ From the View menu, choose Page Layout (ALT, V, P).

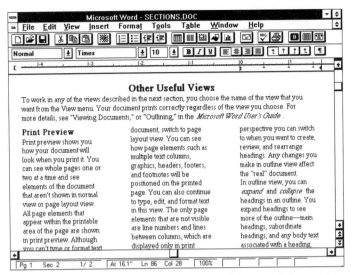

In page layout view, you can edit just as you edit in normal view, and you can see how your changes affect the columns.

Tip Inserting sections gives you a great deal of flexibility in how you format documents. You can vary other kinds of formatting besides columns from section to section. For example, in Lesson 7 you changed the header or footer between sections. For more information about sections, see Chapter 10, "Sections: Formatting Parts of a Document," in the *Microsoft Word User's Guide*.

Print the document

Print

The document you've been formatting describes the different views in Word and suggests uses for each. Use the following procedure if you want to print the document for later reference.

1 Make sure the printer is on.

2 On the Toolbar, click the Print button.

One Step Further

Inserting manual column breaks and adding vertical lines also work in documents you have divided into sections. Using the sample document still open on your screen, experiment with inserting section breaks and applying different formats to different sections.

▶ Switch to normal view and insert another continuous section break before the heading "Page Layout." Then format the new section with a different number of columns and view the entire page in page layout view to see the results.

▶ In page layout view, try adding or deleting text in one of the multiple-column sections. When you edit the document in page layout view, you can see the effect of your changes on the overall layout. The columns adjust as you edit.

▶ Switch to normal view and click in the selection bar to the left of the section mark that follows the first section This selects the section mark. Then click the Cut button on the Toolbar. Note that the first section has taken on the two-column format of the section below it. This is because each section mark stores the formatting for the text above it, including the number of columns. When you delete a section mark, the section takes on the formatting of the section below it.

Click the Undo button to restore the section break and along with it, the formatting instructions for the text above it.

If you want to continue to the next lesson

1 From the File menu, choose Close (ALT, F, C).

2 If Word displays a message asking if you want to save changes, choose the No button.

If you want to quit Word for now

1 From the File menu, choose Exit (ALT, F, X).

2 If Word displays a message asking if you want to save changes, choose the No button.

Lesson Summary

To	Do this
Create columns	On the Toolbar, click the Columns button, and then drag in the sample box to select the number of columns you want.
Insert manual column breaks	From the Insert menu, choose the Break command and then select Column Break.
View and edit a document as it will look when printed	From the View menu, choose Page Layout.
Add lines between columns	From the Format menu, choose Columns and then select the Line Between option. To preview the line, from the File menu, choose Print Preview.
View a miniature version of a document showing how it will look when printed	From the File menu, choose Print Preview.
Divide a document into sections	From the Insert menu, choose Break, and then select the Continuous option under Section Break.

To	Do this
Format each section in a document separately	Click in the section you want to format, and then apply formatting.
View an entire page in page layout view	On the Toolbar, click the Zoom Whole Page.
Return to 100 percent magnification, showing the document in normal view	On the Toolbar, click the Zoom 100 Percent button.

For more information about	See the *Microsoft Word User's Guide*
Columns, column breaks, and lines between columns	Chapter 18, "Columns"
Working with sections	Chapter 10, "Sections: Formatting Parts of a Document"
Changing the view of a document	Chapter 24, "Viewing Documents"

For an online lesson about	Do this
Formatting columns	Click the Help menu. Click Learning Word. Click Formatting. Click Formatting Columns.
	Follow the instructions on the screen.
	To exit a lesson at any time, click the Controls button, then click Exit.
Working in different views	Click the Help menu. Click Learning Word. Click Viewing and Printing.
	Follow the instructions on the screen.
	To exit a lesson at any time, click the Controls button, then click Exit.

Preview of the Next Lesson

In the next lesson, you will learn to emphasize important text by adding borders and shading. You'll try your hand at turning words into art. And you'll learn to insert and size graphics and position them exactly where you want them on the page. At the end of the lesson, you'll have a document for your quick reference notebook that describes WordArt and clip art—two features that can quickly dress up a document.

Adding Graphics and Emphasizing Text

You can add graphics to Word documents to illustrate a point or to add interest to a document. The graphics can be created in any one of several graphics programs and edited as you work in Word, or you can create graphics with Microsoft Draw, a special feature of Word. Another optional feature in Word, WordArt, makes it easy to create special effects with text, such as curving, rotating, flipping, or stretching the text. In this lesson, you'll learn to work with both Microsoft Draw and WordArt. You'll also learn to position text and graphics on the page and wrap text around them.

Insert graphics in a document.

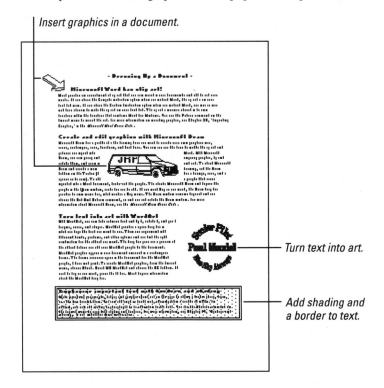

— *Turn text into art.*

— *Add shading and a border to text.*

This lesson explains how to do the following:

- Insert, size, and edit a graphic
- Drag graphics and text to a new location on the page
- Add shading, borders, and special effects to text

Estimated lesson time: 40 minutes

Open a sample document

Open

1   On the Toolbar, click the Open button.

2   Under Directories, make sure the PRACTICE directory is open. If it is not, select the drive where the Step by Step practice files are stored and open the appropriate directories.

3   Double-click ART.DOC.

If you share your computer with other Word users, they may have changed the screen display. Before you begin this lesson, make sure the Toolbar, ribbon, ruler, and scroll bars are displayed. The ruler should display approximately 6 inches, or the equivalent. The Word window and the sample document should completely fill the screen. If you need assistance in changing the screen display, see "Getting Ready," earlier in this book.

Save the document with a new name

Give the document a new name so the changes you make in this lesson will not overwrite the original document.

1   From the File menu, choose Save As (ALT, F, A).

2   Under File Name, type *your initials* **art**

For example, type **jpart**

3   Choose the OK button.

4   When Word displays the Summary Info dialog box, make sure your name is in the author box.

5   Choose the OK button.

Inserting and Sizing Graphics

You can import graphics from many graphics programs into Word. When you insert a graphic into a Word document and then click the graphic, eight sizing handles appear around it. You can use the sizing handles to make the graphic larger or smaller. You can also use the handles to trim, or *crop,* the graphic, hiding the portions you don't want to be displayed or printed. The sizing handles do not print.

Insert a graphic

Word provides a collection of clip art—graphics that you can insert in documents and edit to suit your needs. The following procedure shows you how to insert a clip art graphic of three-dimensional arrows.

1 Position the insertion point at the beginning of the line below "Microsoft Word has clip art!" as shown in the following illustration.

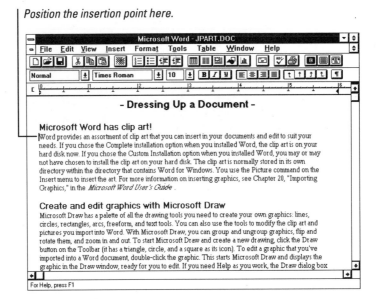

Position the insertion point here.

2 From the Insert menu, choose Picture (ALT, I, P).

3 Double-click the directory where Word for Windows is stored.

4 In the Directories box, double-click CLIPART to open the folder icon next to it. If you do not see the CLIPART directory, see "Troubleshooting," following this procedure.

5 Under File Name, double-click 3DARROW1.WMF.

Word inserts the graphic in the document at the location of the insertion point. The large blinking line is the insertion point. It's the same height as the graphic.

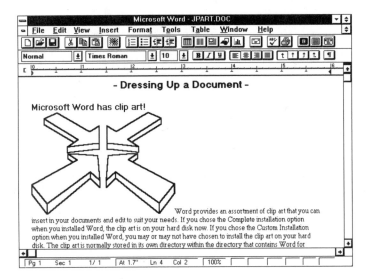

TROUBLESHOOTING: **If you do not see the CLIPART directory**   Make sure the directory that contains Word for Windows is open. If it is and you do not see the CLIPART directory, the art may not have been installed at the time Word was installed—clip art is one of Word's optional features. The Step by Step practice files provide a copy of the graphic for such situations. To insert the graphic, open the drive and directory that contain the Step by Step practice files. Under File Name, double-click ZARROW.WMF.

TROUBLESHOOTING: **If Word displays a message that the filter is unavailable**   Word requires a *filter* to display the graphic. The Setup program you use to install Word on your computer gives you the option to install or not install filters. Run the Word Setup program again, choose Custom Installation, and choose the Conversions button. Select the Windows Metafile Filter to install the correct filter for this graphic.

Crop the graphic

The graphic shows four arrows. You need only one—the one on the upper left. Use the following procedure to hide the others.

1   Click the graphic once to select the graphic and display the sizing handles.

If the Microsoft Draw window appears, see "Troubleshooting," following this procedure.

2   Hide the right half of the graphic by holding down the SHIFT key and pointing to the middle sizing handle on the right, as shown in the following illustration. When the pointer changes to a two-headed arrow, drag to the left. A shadow border indicates the size of the graphic until you release the mouse button.

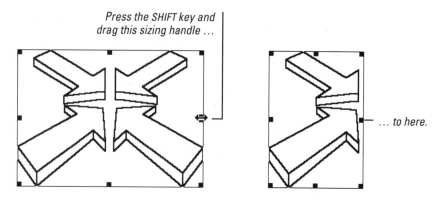

Press the SHIFT key and
drag this sizing handle ...

... to here.

3   Hold down the SHIFT key and drag the middle sizing handle on the bottom until the
graphic looks like the following illustration.

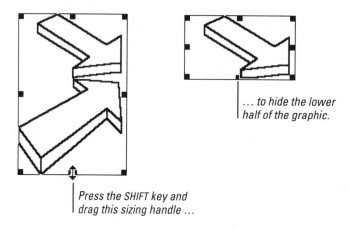

... to hide the lower
half of the graphic.

Press the SHIFT key and
drag this sizing handle ...

TROUBLESHOOTING: **If the Microsoft Draw window appears**   Clicking a graphic once selects the graphic.
Double-clicking a graphic displays the Microsoft Draw window, in which you can edit
the graphic. To return to the document, from the File menu in the Draw window,
choose Exit And Return. If Word displays a message asking if you want to update the
document, choose the No button.

Experiment with the sizing handles

When you drag a sizing handle while holding down the SHIFT key, you *crop* the
graphic, hiding part of it. Dragging a sizing handle without holding down the SHIFT
key changes the size of the graphic. The following procedures show you how to drag
any side to stretch the graphic, and how to drag a corner to make the graphic smaller
or larger proportionally.

1   If the ruler is not displayed, from the View menu, choose Ruler (ALT, V, R).

2 Drag the middle handle on the bottom of the graphic downward three or four lines to see the effect on the graphic.

Undo

3 Click the Undo button on the Toolbar after you've seen the effect.

Remember: You must click the Undo button immediately to undo the last action you took.

4 Drag the middle handle on the right toward the right to stretch the graphic.

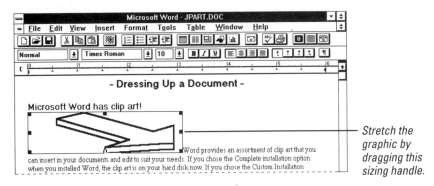

Stretch the graphic by dragging this sizing handle.

5 Click the Undo button after you've seen the effect.

6 Make the graphic larger proportionately by dragging the bottom-right corner until the graphic is 3 inches wide. Use the ruler at the top of the screen to determine the width of the graphic.

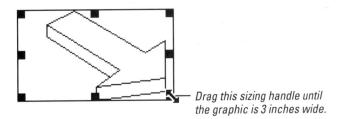

Drag this sizing handle until the graphic is 3 inches wide.

7 Make the graphic smaller proportionately by dragging the bottom-right corner until the graphic is approximately 1 inch wide.

Framing a Graphic

You've learned the basic skills for working with graphics—inserting, cropping, and sizing. The following procedures show you how to wrap text around a graphic and how to drag the graphic to any location on the page.

You'll accomplish both of these tasks by inserting a *frame* around the graphic. Frames do not print; they simply make it easier to create interesting layouts. When you work with framed items, it's best to work in page layout view. Page layout view displays framed items in their correct location on the page. In normal view, framed items appear aligned with the left margin, marked by small, nonprinting bullets.

Insert a frame around the graphic

1 You must select the graphic before you can insert a frame around it. If you can see the sizing handles, the graphic is selected. If you cannot see the sizing handles, click the graphic once to display them.

Frame

2 Click the Frame button on the Toolbar. The symbol on the button shows an item with sizing handles around it.

Click here.

3 If Word displays a message asking if you want to switch to page layout view, choose the Yes button.

You'll see the top "edge" of the page on the screen in page layout view. Word inserts a frame around the graphic. You will not see a change in the outline of the graphic. However, note that framing an item allows text to flow around it. The solid line that marks the frame does not print.

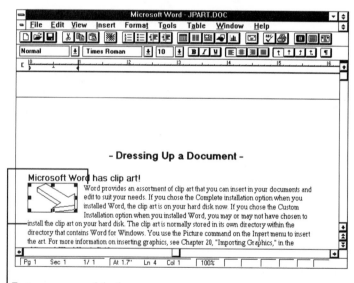

Text wraps around the frame.

TROUBLESHOOTING: **If the mouse pointer turned into a crosshair pointer** If the mouse pointer changed to a crosshair pointer, it means the graphic was not selected when the Frame button was clicked. The crosshair pointer (+) is used to create empty frames as placeholders. To try again, click the Undo button on the Toolbar. Then click the graphic once to select it, and then click the Frame button on the Toolbar.

Tip If later you don't want text to flow around a graphic, you can choose that option using the Frame command on the Format menu.

Position the graphic on the page

In addition to allowing text to flow around an item, frames allow you to drag an item anywhere on the page, using a special, four-headed mouse pointer. Use the following procedure to experiment a bit.

1   If the graphic is not currently selected, click it once to display the sizing handles.

2   Try dragging the graphic to the position shown in the following illustration. You can repeatedly drag with the four-headed arrow and release the mouse button to fine-tune the placement on the page.

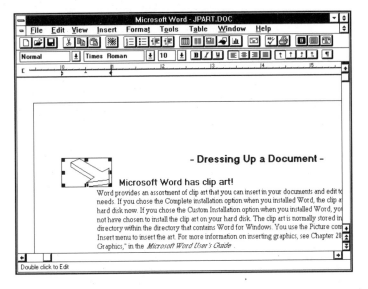

3   Click outside the graphic to hide the sizing handles and view the overall effect.

Save the document

Save

▶   On the Toolbar, click the Save button.

Word saves this version of the document in place of the previous version. You will not see a change in the document.

Making Changes to Graphics

In addition to inserting, sizing, cropping, and positioning graphics, you can edit them using an optional feature called Microsoft Draw. You use Draw to create graphics of your own and to edit graphics that you've imported. This part of the lesson shows you how to edit one of the clip art graphics that come with Word.

Insert a graphic

1 Click the down scroll arrow until "Create and edit graphics with Microsoft Draw" is at the top of the document window.

2 Position the insertion point at the beginning of the paragraph below "Create and edit graphics with Microsoft Draw," as shown in the following illustration.

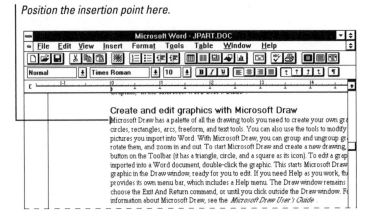

Position the insertion point here.

3 From the Insert menu, choose Picture (ALT, I, P).

4 Under File Name, double-click 2DOORVAN.WMF.

Word inserts the graphic at the location of the insertion point.

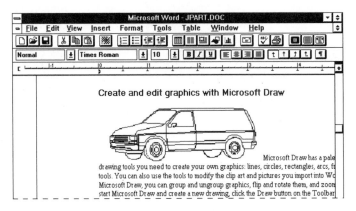

TROUBLESHOOTING: **If you do not have clip art installed**   A copy of the graphic file that you need is available in the directory that contains the Step by Step practice files. Double-click VAN.WMF to insert it.

Start Microsoft Draw

With Microsoft Draw, you can edit graphics, create special effects, and add text to graphics. You can also draw your own art.

1   Double-click the picture of the van to start Microsoft Draw.

2   To make the window as large as possible, click the Maximize button to the right of the Draw window's title bar.

Click here to make the window as large as possible.

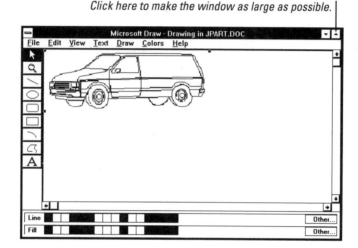

Maximizing the window does two things: It gives you more room in which to work, and it hides Word's menu bar, reminding you that all the commands you need for Draw are available in the Draw window.

TROUBLESHOOTING: **If Word does not display the Draw window**   Try double-clicking the graphic of the van again at a different speed if Word did not display the Draw window. If Word still does not display the Draw window, Draw may not be installed. To check, from the Insert menu, choose Object. If Microsoft Drawing does not appear in the list of features, you can install it by running the Word Setup program. For more information about installing Microsoft Draw, see *Microsoft Word Getting Started.*

Edit the graphic

1   From the Draw menu, choose Rotate/Flip.

2   Select Flip Horizontal.

Draw flips the graphic so the van is facing to the right.

3   Click the Text tool, as shown in the following illustration, then click in the Draw window below the van. A blinking insertion point appears.

Arrow tool   Draw menu

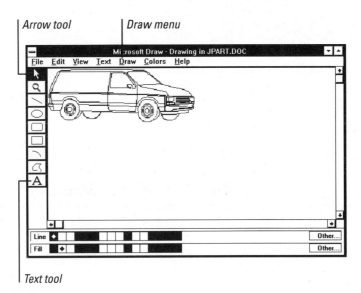

Text tool

4   Type your initials in uppercase letters.

5   Click the Arrow tool so the pointer changes to an arrow.

6   From the Text menu, choose Bold.

7   From the Text menu, choose Size. Then select 10 points.

Move your initials onto the graphic

1   Point to your initials and hold down the mouse button. When a dashed box appears around your initials, drag the dashed box onto the side of the van, as shown in the following illustration. Then release the mouse button.

Drag your initials from here ...

... to here.

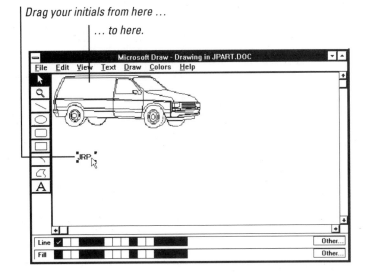

2 Click outside the van to see the effect.

Return to the document

1 From the File menu, choose Exit And Return (ALT, F, X).

2 When Word displays a message asking if you want to update the document, choose Yes to replace the graphic in your document with the graphic you just edited.

Word closes the Draw window and the edited graphic replaces the previous version.

Size the graphic

1 If the sizing handles aren't displayed, click the graphic once.

2 Drag the lower-right sizing handle up and left until the graphic is 2.5 inches wide. Use the ruler to measure the width.

This sizes the graphic proportionately.

Frame the graphic

1 Make sure the sizing handles are displayed around the graphic, indicating that it is selected. If the handles are not displayed, click the graphic once.

Frame

2 On the Toolbar, click the Frame button.

If Word displays a message asking if you want to switch to page layout view, choose the Yes button.

Text wraps around the graphic.

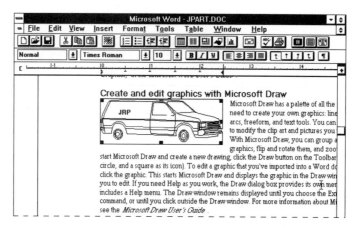

3   Click outside the graphic to hide the sizing handles and see the overall effect.

Save

Save the document

▶   On the Toolbar, click the Save button. Word saves this version of the document in place of the previous version.

Working with WordArt

With WordArt, you can create graphic effects with text, such as flipping, rotating, and curving. Once you insert WordArt in a document, you can work with it as you work with graphics. You can drag sizing handles to stretch or crop the WordArt. You can frame WordArt so that text flows around it and drag it to other locations on the page. You'll have a chance to experiment first. Then you can create WordArt for the sample document.

Display the WordArt dialog box

1   Scroll down so that "Turn text into art with WordArt" is close to the ruler. Position the insertion point as shown in the following illustration.

Position the insertion point here.

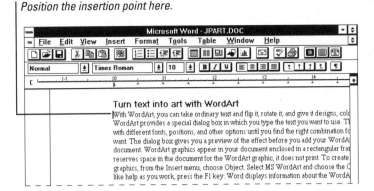

2 From the Insert menu, choose Object (ALT, I, O).

Word displays a dialog box that lists optional features you can use to create "objects," such as equations, graphs, charts, or drawings.

3 Double-click MS WordArt.

Word displays the WordArt dialog box.

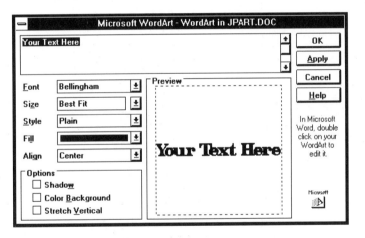

TROUBLESHOOTING: **If you do not see MS WordArt in the list** WordArt is an optional feature. It may not have been installed during setup. For information about installing WordArt, see *Microsoft Word Getting Started*.

Experiment with WordArt

First use the following procedure to experiment with WordArt options. The effect of each option you select is displayed in the Preview box. Do not choose the OK button yet; just experiment with options. When you've finished experimenting, go to the next procedure, where you'll select final options and insert the WordArt in your document.

1   Type your name at the top of the dialog box so you'll have text to experiment with.

    When you begin selecting options, your name will appear in the Preview area.

Remember that you can scroll the list of options.

2   Experiment with WordArt style options by clicking the down arrow next to the Style box to display the list of options. Then click any option. Repeat these steps to see the other effects you can create.

3   Experiment with the special WordArt fonts. Display the list of fonts, then select a font to see the results.

4   In the Size box, experiment with the different size options. Select "12 pts" when you are finished experimenting, so the text is small enough for WordArt to align it in different positions in the next step.

5   Experiment with the options in the Align box.

6   Experiment with the Fill options.

    If you do not have a color printer, the WordArt graphic is printed in shades of gray, depending on the capability of your printer.

7   Experiment with the Shadow, Color Background, and Stretch Vertical options.

Create a button effect

Now that you've experimented with various WordArt options, use the following procedure to edit the WordArt text you typed, select final options, and insert the art in your document.

1   Position the insertion point immediately before your name and type your title. Press ENTER. Perhaps for this exercise, you'd like to be the president of the company.

2   Position the insertion point at the end of your name and press ENTER.

3   Type your company name, or type **Blue Sky Airways**

4   Select the following options.

Option	Setting
Font	Bellingham
Size	Best Fit
Style	Button
Fill	Black, or if you have a color printer, the color of your choice
Align	Center
Shadow	Select the check box
Color Background	Select the check box
Stretch Vertical	Select the check box

The results in the Preview area should look similar to the following illustration.

```
┌────────────────────────────────────────────────────────────────┐
│ ▭        Microsoft WordArt - WordArt in JPART.DOC              │
├────────────────────────────────────────────────────────────────┤
│ Senior Pilot                                        ▲  ┌──────┐ │
│ Paul Mendel                                         │  │  OK  │ │
│ Blue Sky Airways                                    ▼  └──────┘ │
│                                                        ┌──────┐ │
│                              ┌─Preview──────────────┐  │Apply │ │
│  Font   │Bellingham   │ ▼    │                      │  └──────┘ │
│                              │                      │  ┌──────┐ │
│  Size   │Best Fit     │ ▼    │    Senior Pilot      │  │Cancel│ │
│                              │                      │  └──────┘ │
│  Style  │Button       │ ▼    │                      │  ┌──────┐ │
│                              │                      │  │ Help │ │
│  Fill   │        o    │ ▼    │   Paul Mendel        │  └──────┘ │
│                              │                      │ In Microsoft│
│  Align  │Center       │ ▼    │                      │ Word, double│
│ ┌Options──────────────┐      │   Blue Sky Airways   │ click on your│
│ │  ☒ Shadow           │      │                      │ WordArt to  │
│ │  ☒ Color Background │      │                      │ edit it.    │
│ │  ☒ Stretch Vertical │      │                      │ Microsoft   │
│ └─────────────────────┘      └──────────────────────┘           │
└────────────────────────────────────────────────────────────────┘
```

Insert the WordArt graphic in your document

▶ Choose the OK button.

Word inserts the WordArt graphic at the location of the insertion point. Note that a blinking insertion point the size of the WordArt graphic appears next to it.

Insert a frame around the WordArt graphic

Use the following procedure to insert a frame around the WordArt graphic, so that text will flow around it and so you can drag it to a new location.

1 The WordArt graphic must be selected before it can be framed. Click the WordArt graphic once to display the sizing handles.

Frame

2 On the Toolbar, click the Frame button.

If Word displays a message asking if you want to switch to page layout view, choose the Yes button.

Text wraps around the WordArt graphic. The dotted line that marked the edge of the WordArt graphic is replaced by a solid line that marks the frame.

TROUBLESHOOTING: **If the mouse pointer turns into a crosshair pointer** If the mouse pointer changes to a crosshair pointer (✛) when you click the Frame button, the WordArt graphic was not selected when the Frame button was clicked. The crosshair pointer is used to create empty frames as placeholders. To try again, press the ESC key, click the WordArt graphic once to select it, then click the Frame button on the Toolbar.

Size the WordArt

▶ Drag the lower-right corner sizing handle until the WordArt graphic is approximately 1 3/4 inches wide (1.75"), as shown in the following illustration.

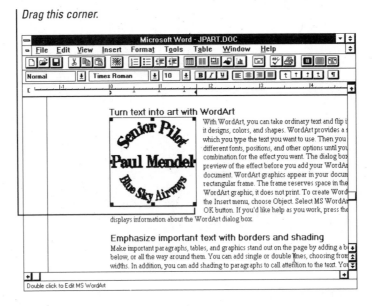

Drag this corner.

Save

Save the document

▶ On the Toolbar, click the Save button. Word saves this version of the document in place of the previous version.

Framing and Sizing Text

You can insert a frame around regular text, just as you do around a graphic. If you size the frame, the text wraps within it. When you frame text, Word automatically provides a box border around the text; the border will print. If you prefer a different style of border—perhaps a double line instead of a single line—or if you do not want a border, you can change the border that Word provides. You can format framed text just as you normally format text.

Zoom Page Width

1 On the Toolbar, click the Zoom Page Width button, to display the full width of the page on the screen.

The font may look different on the screen, but the line breaks remain accurate.

2 Scroll to the bottom of the document if necessary to display the last heading and paragraph in the document. The heading begins "Emphasize important text ..."

3   Drag in the selection bar to select the heading and final paragraph as shown below.

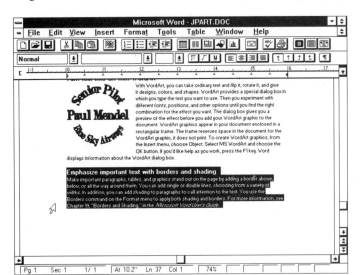

Frame

4   On the Toolbar, click the Frame button.

The text now has a border that will print and sizing handles that do not print.

5   With the two-headed arrow, drag the right side of the frame until it is slightly wider than the heading, as shown below.

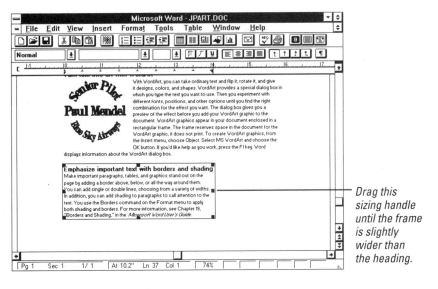

Drag this sizing handle until the frame is slightly wider than the heading.

6   Click outside the frame to hide the sizing handles and view the overall effect.

Add shading to the text

You can add shading to any paragraph, whether it has a frame or not. You can also change the style of border around framed paragraphs. Use the following procedure to add 10 percent shading and place a double-line border around the heading and paragraph.

1 Click the framed text with the four-headed arrow to display the sizing handles.

2 From the Format menu, choose Border (ALT, T, B).

3 Choose the Shading button.

4 The Pattern box currently shows "Clear." Display the list of Pattern choices by clicking the down arrow.

5 Select 10%.

6 Choose the OK button to close the Shading dialog box.

7 To change the line around the text, click the thin, double-line option under Line.

8 Choose the OK button.

Word changes the border to a double line and adds shading to the text.

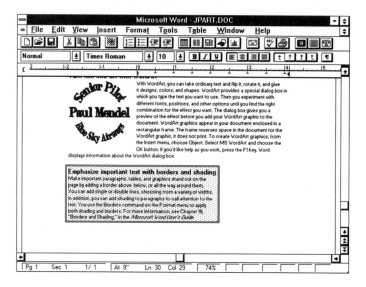

Fine-tune the layout

Zoom Whole Page

1   On the Toolbar, click the Zoom Whole Page button to view the entire page.

Click this button ...

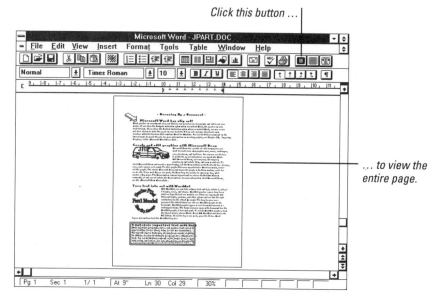

... to view the entire page.

2   Click each framed item in turn to display the sizing handles, and then, with the four-headed arrow, drag to position each item on the page so the document looks similar to the illustration that follows step 3.

3   Try resizing the framed text so it extends margin to margin. With the two-headed arrow, drag the right side of the frame until it extends as far as the other text on the page.

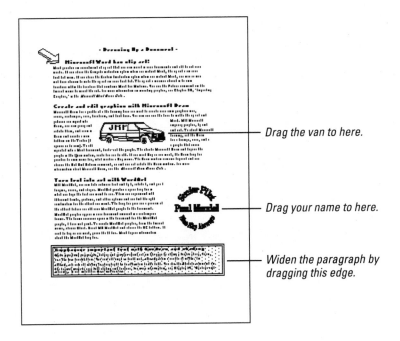

Drag the van to here.

Drag your name to here.

Widen the paragraph by dragging this edge.

Save

Save the document

▶ On the Toolbar, click the Save button.

Word saves this version of the document in place of the previous version. You will not see a change in the document.

Return to 100 percent magnification

Any new window you open displays the document in the last level of magnification that you used. In this case, the new window would display the entire page in page layout view. You probably want to begin other documents in normal view.

Zoom 100 Percent

▶ On the Toolbar, click the Zoom 100 Percent button to display the document in normal view at 100 percent magnification.

Word displays the framed items aligned with the left margin. Nonprinting bullets in the left margin indicate an item is framed.

In normal view, nonprinting bullets indicate an item is framed.

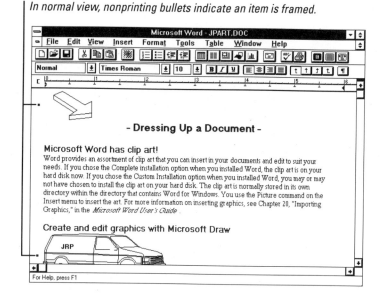

Print the document

Print the document so you can see graphics and the borders and shading. The document describes the features you've been working with—clip art, Microsoft Draw, WordArt, borders and shading—and tells where you can get more information about each.

When you print graphics, you get the best results when you print the most dots per inch (dpi) your printer can print. The more dots per inch, the better the resolution. Graphics printed with low resolution have a "grainy" look to them, which can be useful for special effects. Most often though, you'll want to use the highest resolution available for graphics, using the following procedure. Your printer may not offer a choice of settings. The following procedure shows how you can check.

Print

1   Make sure the printer is on.

2   From the File menu, choose Print Setup (ALT, F, R).

3   Make sure the printer you want to use is selected, then choose the Setup button.

4   In the Resolution box, select the option that offers the most dots per inch.

If the currently selected printer does not offer a choice of settings, omit this step and proceed to Step 5.

5   Choose the OK button to close the Setup dialog box.

6   Choose the OK button to close the Print Setup dialog box.

7   On the Toolbar, click the Print button.

One Step Further

Zoom Page Width

▶ It's easy to add a caption to a framed graphic. On the Toolbar, click the Zoom Page Width button. Select the arrow graphic and then press ENTER. Word creates a blank line below the graphic and positions the insertion point, ready for you to begin typing. Type a caption such as **This arrow is from the clip art collection.** The text wraps within the frame. You can drag to select the text in the caption and change the font or point size. For example, try 8 points. If you drag the frame with the four-headed arrow, the caption moves with the graphic.

▶ If you change the page orientation, take a moment to experiment with margin settings. You learned in Lesson 3 how to adjust the margins using the ruler. Here's a way to set very precise margins. From the Format menu, choose Page Setup. Select the Margins option. In the Left box, select the text and type **2**. Choose the OK button. The margin setting changes, but you need to drag the graphics with the four-headed arrow to adjust their positions on the page.

If you want to continue to the next lesson

1 From the File menu, choose Close.

2 If Word displays a message asking if you want to save changes, click the No button. You do not need to save the changes made while experimenting.

If you want to quit Word for now

1 From the File menu, choose Exit (ALT, F, X).

2 If Word displays a message asking if you want to save changes, click the No button. You do not need to save any of the changes you made while experimenting.

Lesson Summary

To	Do this
Insert a graphic	The online Help for WordArt. From the Insert menu, choose Picture. Select the name of the graphic you want to insert.
Size a graphic	Click the graphic once to display sizing handles. Drag corner handles to size the graphic proportionately, or drag the middle handles to stretch the graphic.
Crop a graphic	Hold down the SHIFT key as you drag a sizing handle to hide the portion of the graphic you do not want to display or print.
Position graphics or text on the page	Select the item you want to position. On the Toolbar, click the Frame button. With the four-headed arrow, drag the item to position it on the page.

To	Do this
Add shading to text	Select the text. From the Format menu, choose Border. Choose the Shading button. In the Pattern box, select the percentage of shading that you want.
Change the border of a framed text paragraph	Click the frame to select it. From the Format menu, choose Border. Under Line, click the type of line you want, then choose the OK button.
Add a caption to a graphic	Select the graphic, press ENTER, and type the caption.

For more information on	See
Inserting and sizing graphics	Chapter 20, "Importing Graphics," in the *Microsoft Word User's Guide*
Positioning graphics and text on the page	Chapter 21, "Positioning Text and Graphics on the Page," in the *Microsoft Word User's Guide*
Editing a graphic	The *Microsoft Draw User's Guide*
Creating and editing WordArt	The online Help for WordArt. From the Insert menu, choose Object. Double-click MS WordArt. Choose the Help button in the WordArt window.
Adding borders and shading	Chapter 19, "Borders and Shading," in the *Microsoft Word User's Guide*

For an online lesson about	Do this
Frames or graphics	Click Help. Click Learning Word. Click Tables, Frames, and Pictures. Click Creating and Modifying Frames or Working with Pictures and Objects.
	Follow the instructions on the screen.
	To exit a lesson at any time, click the Controls button, then click Exit.

Preview of the Next Lesson

In the next lesson, you'll learn to locate files that you have very little information about. For example, you'll find files when you know only two letters of the file name. You'll also find a file when you know only one word that it contains. You'll also learn how you can open, copy, delete, or print more than one file at a time. Finally, after an electronic scavenger hunt, you can print either of the two documents you find, or you can print both—at the same time.

4 Managing and Printing Files

Lesson 12   Finding and Printing Multiple Files

Lesson 13   Creating Merged Documents

Finding and Printing Multiple Files

Over time, you will probably create many documents that contain information you want to reference or reuse. With Word, if you want to locate a quotation, reuse a graphic, review a document's contents, or compare information with a co-worker, you can quickly locate the information you need from any drive or directory to which you have access.

You can locate a document by searching for almost any information you can recall— or guess—about the document. For example, if you remember the name, or even part of the name, of the file that contains the information, you can search by file name. If you want to find all files that contain a phrase, such as "annual income," you can search specifically for that phrase. If you need to recall information from a memo that a colleague wrote last May, you can search for files on that subject created by your colleague during the month of May.

In this lesson, you'll search three times for files. The first time, you'll search for files knowing only two letters of the file names. The second time, you'll search for a file when you know only one word that the file contains. And the third time, you'll search for files knowing only a keyword that was typed in the Summary Info dialog box when the files were first saved. You'll also learn the quickest method to open, copy, print, or delete several files at once.

This lesson explains how to do the following:

- Search for an incomplete file name
- Search for text in a document
- Search for summary information
- Print multiple files at once

Estimated lesson time: 25 minutes

Using the Find File Command

If you already know the file's name and location, the simplest way to open a file is to click the Open button on the Toolbar or choose Open from the File menu, as you've done throughout these lessons.

However, if you choose one of these commands, you can work with only one file at a time. If you want to open, print, copy, or delete more than one file at a time, or if you need to locate a file before you work with it, you can do so using the Find File command on the File menu.

The first time you choose the Find File command, Word searches the current directory for all Word files and then lists the files in the Find File dialog box. Word document files have the extension .DOC after the name; for example, MEMO.DOC would be the name of a Word document.

From the Find File dialog box, you can learn a file's location, display its contents, and view other information about the file without opening it. You can also perform file-management tasks such as opening, printing, copying, and deleting one or more files.

Word also lists the drives and directories that were searched to create the File Name list. By default, Word displays files with the file names in alphabetical order and displays the content of the file you select from the list.

Shows the sort order chosen in the Options dialog box

Shows drives and directories searched to create the list

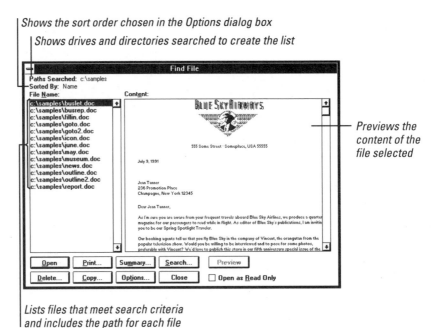

Previews the content of the file selected

Lists files that meet search criteria and includes the path for each file

Searching for Files

The search button within the Find File dialog box carries you to the Search dialog box. When you search for a file, you need to provide two types of information: where to search and what to search for. The Search dialog box provides the options you need to do both. You can type the path that you want to search, or for convenience, you can choose the Edit Path button and choose drives and directories from lists.

The information you use to locate a document—file name, author, subject, and so on—are called the search criteria. Each time you change the search criteria, Word creates a list in the Find File dialog box of the files that meet the new criteria. The criteria remain operative until you change them again.

You can locate files that contain any summary information—title, subject, author, keywords, and comments. You can further modify your search by specifying all drives, or a specific drive, on your computer or a network. You can search for files with a specific extension, such as graphics files with the extension .BMP.

After Word creates a list in the Find File dialog box of the files that meet the search criteria, you can return to the Search dialog box, change the search criteria, and create a new list, add to the current list, or search only the current list.

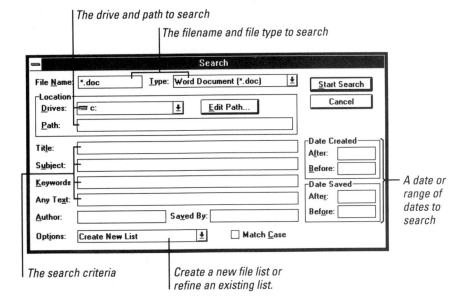

The drive and path to search

The filename and file type to search

The search criteria

Create a new file list or refine an existing list.

A date or range of dates to search

Change the search path

The *path* is a list of drives and directories that you want Word to search through. If you want to search everywhere possible, you can choose the All Drives option in the Path box. For convenience, you can search through several drives and directories to locate files. For speed, you should search the fewest drives and directories that will include the files you want.

The path you set for a search remains in the Search dialog box until you change it. Use the following procedure to add the Step by Step Practice directory to the path that Word searches.

1   From the File menu, choose Find File (ALT, F, F).

Word searches the path that's currently set in the dialog box and displays all files that match the current search criteria.

2   Choose the Search button.

3   In the Search dialog box, choose the Edit Path button.

4   In the Drives box, select the drive where Word for Windows is stored.

5   In the Directories box, double-click the directory where Word for Windows is stored.

6   In the Directories box, double-click the Practice directory.

7   Choose the Add button to add the Practice directory to the search path.

8   Choose the Close button.

Word closes the Edit Path dialog box.

Search using an incomplete file name

Now that you've indicated where to search, you need to indicate what to search for. The following procedure shows how to search for a file when you are not sure of the file name. Throughout these lessons, you've created new names for the practice files by adding your initials to the beginning of each file name. You can find all the files that begin with your initials by using *wildcards*—placeholders—for the other letters in the file names.

1   In the File Name box, type *your initials****.***

For example, if your initials were J.P., you would type **jp*.***

The asterisks indicate that you want to find file names that contain any characters after your initials.

2   In the Options box (at the bottom of the dialog box), make sure the Create New List option is selected.

This option gives you a fresh start by displaying only those file names that begin with your initials, instead of adding any files that are found during the search to the current list of files. ·

3   Make sure all other text boxes are empty so that Word searches only for files that begin with your initials. The dialog box should look similar to the following illustration. The exact path may be different.

Path should end with "practice."

Type here.

```
┌─────────────────────────────────────────────────────────────────┐
│ ▬                          Search                                 │
│                                                                   │
│ File Name: │ip*.doc      │   Type: │Word Document (*.doc)│ ±│  ┌──────────────┐│
│ ┌Location─────────────────────────────────────────┐     │ Start Search ││
│ │ Drives: │📁Path Only    │ ±│   │ Edit Path... │  │     └──────────────┘│
│ │                                                  │     ┌──────────────┐│
│ │ Path:  │c:\winword;c:\winword\practice        │  │     │    Close     ││
│ └──────────────────────────────────────────────────┘     └──────────────┘│
│  Title:   │                              │      ┌Date Created─────┐  │
│                                                  │ After:  │      │ │  │
│  Subject: │                              │      │                 │  │
│                                                  │ Before: │      │ │  │
│  Keywords:│                              │      └─────────────────┘  │
│                                                  ┌Date Saved───────┐  │
│  Any Text:│                              │      │ After:  │      │ │  │
│                                                  │                 │  │
│  Author:  │            │  Saved By: │       │   │ Before: │      │ │  │
│                                                  └─────────────────┘  │
│  Options: │Create New List            │ ±│   □ Match Case           │
└─────────────────────────────────────────────────────────────────┘
```

Make sure Create New List is selected.

Leave these text boxes empty.

4 Choose the Start Search button.

Word closes the Search dialog box, locates the files that match the criteria you specified, lists them in the Find File dialog box, and displays the contents of the first file in the list.

Note If you preview the content of a Word for Windows file, Word displays all of the text as it would appear in Normal view with formatting. If the file includes both text and graphics, you can see both in the file. If the selected file is a graphics file or is in another format, you must choose the Preview button to display the graphics and formatting.

Search using the contents of a file

Now that you know how to find files using file names, you can try another common way to search for a file. Suppose that a co-worker needs a letter someone in your office wrote to someone in Paris. You do not remember the file name or author, or even when the letter was written, but you guess that the letter contains the word "Paris." That's all you need to know to search for the file.

The Search dialog box still contains the information you used in your last search. You'll use the following procedure to clear that information and add the new search criterion—"Paris."

1 In the Find File dialog box, choose the Search button.

2 In the Type box, select "Word Document (*.doc)" as the type of file you want to find.

Word changes the File Name box to show "*.doc" so that any file name with a .DOC extension will be included in the list of files.

3   In the Options box, make sure the Create New List option is selected.

4   In the Any Text box, type **"Paris "**

Make sure you include the quotation marks and the space after the word.

The quotation marks and the space indicate that you want to find only that word. You do not want "comparison" or any other word that contains the same letters in the same order.

5   Choose the Start Search button.

Word displays the names of any files that contain the word "Paris." The list should include LETTER.DOC.

Tip   The more criteria you specify, the more you narrow the list in the Find File dialog box and the faster you can locate the exact file you want. For example, when you search for Any Text, Word searches the entire contents of each file, including headers, footers, footnotes, and hidden text. If you have numerous files and Any Text is the only criterion you specify, the search may take a long time. You can speed the search by adding other search criteria. Perhaps you know that the file was created during a certain month, or you know the name of the author. Adding either of these search criteria—or any other you can recall—will speed the search.

Searching for Files by Using Summary Information

Several of the types of search criteria are automatically part of a file—the file name, text, the date a file was created, the date a file was last saved, and even the author's name as it was entered when you set up Word. But several other categories are optional information that you provide.

You provide the optional information in the Summary Info dialog box that Word displays when you save a file or when you save a file with a new name. If you fill in the dialog box when you save the file, you can search for the file later based on the information you provided—a title of the document, a description of the subject, or keywords that remind you of the file such as client names or account numbers. You can type as many as 255 characters, including spaces and punctuation, for each category of information.

You've worked in the Summary Info dialog box during these lessons. In Lesson 1 you created a new document and filled in the Summary Info dialog box. In later lessons, when you've saved a sample document with a new name, the Summary Info dialog box already contained information, which was typed there when the practice file was created. You simply typed your name in the Author box.

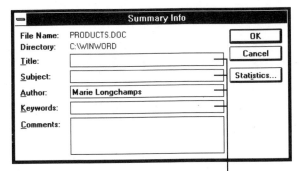

You can search for information
typed in these text boxes.

Word displays the Summary Info dialog box when you first save a file.

Title   The title of the the active document. The title can be longer and more descriptive than the file name to make it easier for you to remember.

Subject   A description of the document's contents.

Author   By default, the name assigned to your copy of the Word program during setup. You can change the author for the active document by typing a new name. You can change the author for all future documents by choosing Options from the Tools menu, selecting the User Info category, and then typing a new name in the Name box.

Keywords   General topics in the document or other important information, such as client names and account numbers.

Comments   Comments are notes you type to yourself or to a co-worker. You cannot use Comments as a search criterion.

Search using a keyword

Included in the Step by Step files are two documents you may find useful. One lists all the keyboard shortcuts for Word and another lists the mouse shortcuts. When the documents were created, the word "shortcuts" was entered as a keyword for each file. Use the following procedure to locate both files.

1   Click the Search button.

2   In the Any Text box, select the text left from the last search and press the BACKSPACE or DEL key.

3   In the Keywords box, type **shortcuts**

You do not need to enclose summary information in quotation marks as you did earlier for the text in a document.

4   Click the Start Search button.

Word locates the files that have the keyword "shortcuts" in their Summary Info dialog box and displays the contents of the first file in the list.

Working with Multiple Files

In this lesson you've used only one of the many capabilities of the the Find File dialog box. In addition to searching for files, you can open, print, copy, or delete more than one file at a time simply by selecting the file names from the list and then choosing the appropriate button.

You can use the following procedure to print two files at once. THOMAS.DOC, two pages long, is a comprehensive list of the mouse shortcuts in Word. VINCENT.DOC, 10 pages long, is a comprehensive list of the keyboard shortcuts in Word. You can either select the file you want to print, or you can print them both, using the following procedure.

Print multiple files

1 Make sure the printer is on.

2 To select two or more file names at once, first select one. Then hold down CTRL while you select the second file name you want. In this case, use this procedure to select both THOMAS.DOC and VINCENT.DOC.

3 Choose the Print button.

Word displays the Print dialog box.

4 If you would like to print the summary information for each file, choose the Options button in the Print dialog box. Select Print Summary Info. The summary information will print on a separate page at the end of each document.

5 Choose the OK button.

Word prints the files in the order they are listed.

One Step Further

▶ Word automatically inserts the name you typed during the setup program into the author box of each Summary Info dialog box. If you share your computer with others, it's best to change the name in the author box when you save a file for the first time. If you are the only one to use the computer, you can make sure that the name Word inserts is exactly what you want. From the Tools menu, choose Options. Select the User Info category (on the left of the dialog box). In the Name box, type the name you want to use.

If you want to continue to the next lesson

1 To close any open documents, from the File menu, choose Close (ALT, F, C).

2 If Word asks if you want to save changes to a document, choose the appropriate button.

If you want to quit Word for now

1 From the File menu, choose Exit (ALT, F, X).

2 If Word displays a message asking if you want to save changes to a document, choose the appropriate button.

Lesson Summary

To	Do this
Find a file	From the File menu, choose Find File. If the path is not what you want, choose Edit Path and select the drives and directories you want to search. Specify any search criteria such as date or author. Choose the Search button.
Select multiple file names in the Find File dialog box	From the File menu, choose Find File. Search if necessary to display the file names you want to work with. Hold down the CTRL key and click to select the files you want. If you accidentally select a file name that you do not want, hold down the CTRL key and click the file name again to remove the highlighting.
Print multiple files	From the File menu, choose Find File. Search if necessary to display the file names of the files you want to print. Select the file names and choose the Print button in the Find File dialog box.

For more information on	See the *Microsoft Word User's Guide*
Finding files or working with multiple files	Chapter 26, "Finding and Managing Files"

For an online lesson about	Do this
Printing more than one document	Click the Help menu. Click Learning Word. Click Viewing and Printing. Click Printing a Document.
	Follow the instructions on the screen.
	To exit a lesson at any time, click the Controls button and then click Exit.

Preview of the Next Lesson

In the next lesson you'll learn to create a basic letter to send to many people. You'll also learn to create a list of names and addresses that Word automatically inserts into the basic letter for you to produce customized form letters.

Creating Merged Documents

With Word, you can create form documents that contain information common to each copy and information unique to each copy. These documents are called *merged documents*. The most common use of merged documents is form letters. The names, addresses, and perhaps certain aspects of the content differ from letter to letter, but the main part of the letter and the closing remain the same. The Print Merge command on the File menu makes it easy to create form letters and print individualized copies for each recipient.

Preparing any type of merged document typically involves two files: a *main document* and a *data file*. The main document contains the standardized text and graphics you want in each version of the merged document. The data file contains the information that varies with each version—for example, names, addresses, account numbers, and product codes. You insert special instructions called *merge fields* to indicate where you want the variable information printed in the main document. When you merge the data file and the main document, Word inserts the appropriate information from the data file.

The data file contains information ...

title	firstname	lastname	company	address	city	state	postcode
Mr.	Adam	Bendel	LitWare Inc.	1234 Central	Denton	WA	00123
Ms.	Marie	Gabor	Arbor Shoes	111 Main	Pecos	TX	12233
Mr.	Paul	Tanner		213 Davis	Aloha	MN	12345

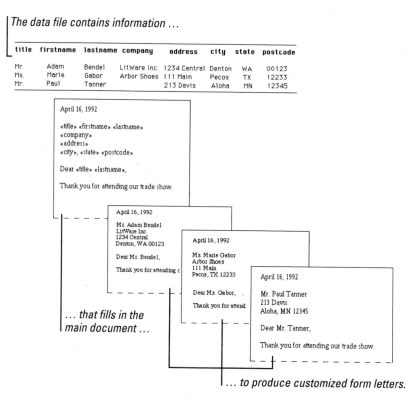

April 16, 1992

«title» «firstname» «lastname»
«company»
«address»
«city», «state» «postcode»

Dear «title» «lastname»,

Thank you for attending our trade show.

April 16, 1992

Mr. Adam Bendel
LitWare Inc.
1234 Central
Denton, WA 00123

Dear Mr. Bendel,

Thank you for attending c

April 16, 1992

Ms. Marie Gabor
Arbor Shoes
111 Main
Pecos, TX 12233

Dear Ms. Gabor, .

Thank you for attend:

April 16, 1992

Mr. Paul Tanner
213 Davis
Aloha, MN 12345

Dear Mr. Tanner,

Thank you for attending our trade show.

... that fills in the main document ...

... to produce customized form letters.

This lesson explains how to do the following:

- Create a data file of names and addresses
- Create a main document with instructions for inserting a name and address
- Merge the data file information into the main document

Estimated lesson time: 35 minutes

Merging Documents: Basic Techniques

Whether you're printing mailing labels or personalizing a form letter, you use the same basic techniques to create the final, merged documents. The Print Merge command on the File menu guides you through the steps:

- Open a new or existing document and attach a data file to it. You can attach an existing data file or you can attach a new one that you fill in. Attaching the data file makes the active document the *main document.*
- Insert merge field names into your main document to indicate where you want the variable information such as names and addresses. The names must exactly match those in the data file.
- Merge the main document with the data file, and either print the merged documents or store them in a new file for viewing on the screen and editing.

When you merge the data file and the main document, the variable information from each data record is combined with the main document to produce a unique merged document—one form letter, for example, or one printed mailing label.

Open and name a new document

You can type the main document from scratch or use an existing document that is similar to what you want. In this lesson you'll name and save a new, empty document that will become the main document. You will not type any text in the new document until you've created the data file. Follow the instructions below to open a new document and save it with the name MYMAIN.DOC.

New

Save

1 If a new, empty document is not already open on the screen, click the New button on the Toolbar.

2 On the Toolbar, click the Save button.

3 Under Directories, make sure the PRACTICE directory is open. If it is not, select the drive where the Step by Step practice files are stored and open the appropriate directories.

4 Under File Name, type **mymain** and press ENTER.

   If Word displays a message that there is another document by this name, type a different file name. For example, use your initials instead of "my." Then press ENTER.

5 Fill in the summary information by clicking in each box and typing a word or phrase that will help you find this document later. Press TAB to move from box to box. Press ENTER when you are finished filling in the dialog box.

For example, you might type something similar to what is shown in the following illustration.

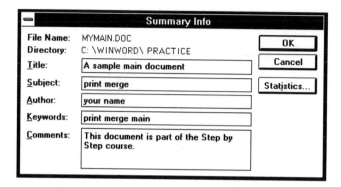

Working with Data Files

Now that you've named and saved a document that can be the main document, you're ready to create a data file. A data file contains the text and graphics that vary with each version of a merged document. In this lesson, the data file will contain names and addresses. Each set of related information makes up one *record* in the data file. The different categories of information in each record—title, first name, last name, company, street address, city, state, and postal code—are called *fields*.

In this lesson, you'll create a data file similar to the following illustration.

The first row contains the field names. The row is called the header record.

title	firstname	lastname	company	address	city	state	postcode
Mr.	Adam	Bendel	LitWare Inc.	1234 Central	Denton	WA	00123
Ms.	Marie	Gabor	Arbor Shoes	111 Main	Pecos	TX	12233
Mr.	Paul	Tanner		213 Davis	Aloha	MN	12345

Each row after the first is simply called a record.

Create and attach a data file

Using the Print Merge command, you can open an existing data file or create a new one; Word then attaches the data file to the document currently open on the screen—in this case, MYMAIN.DOC. In the following procedure, you will create a new data file by first typing field names—names for each category of information in the data file.

When you finish typing the field names, Word will organize them into a table, so you can insert information into each field. This will be your data file.

Note that each field name in a data file must be unique and can have as many as 32 characters. You can use letters, numbers, and underscore characters, but not spaces. The first character must be a letter.

1 From the File menu, choose Print Merge (ALT, F, M).

Word displays the Print Merge Setup dialog box.

2 Choose the Attach Data File button.

Word displays a dialog box. You can select an existing data file to attach to the main document, or you can open another dialog box to create a new data file.

3 Choose the Create Data File button.

Word displays a dialog box for you to type field names.

4 In the Field Name box, type the following names, pressing ENTER after each one.

title

firstname

lastname

company

address

city

state

postcode

5 Choose the OK button.

Word displays the Save As dialog box for you to save the data file.

6 Under File Name, type **testdata**

7 Choose the OK button.

Word opens a new document window and inserts a table. This is your data file. The field names you typed in the Create Data File dialog box are listed in the first row of the table, as the header record. The table extends beyond the right edge of the screen, but Word adjusts the display as you fill in the table. The next procedure shows you how to fill in the name and address for each data record.

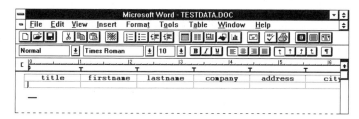

Fill in the records

▶ Type the information shown in the following illustration, pressing TAB to move to the next box, or *cell,* in the table. When you come to the end of a row, press TAB to create the next blank row. If you make a typing mistake, press BACKSPACE and correct the mistake.

title	firstname	lastname	company	address	city	state	postcode
Mr.	Adam	Bendel	LitWare Inc.	1234 Central	Denton	WA	00123
Ms.	Marie	Gabor	Arbor Shoes	111 Main	Pecos	TX	12233
Mr.	Paul	Tanner		213 Davis	Aloha	MN	12345

Press TAB to skip this field.   *Press TAB at the end of the row to create the next blank row.*

TROUBLESHOOTING: **If you see "x's" in the table** If you're working with paragraph marks displayed, you'll see "x's" at the end of each cell. These simply mark the end of the cell the same way a paragraph mark indicates the end of a paragraph. You can ignore them.

Check your typing

Take a moment to make sure the information in the table is correct.

1 If you are not working with paragraph marks displayed, click the Show/Hide ¶ button on the ribbon. This shows you the blank spaces between words. It also displays the end-of-cell markers.

2 If you typed extra spaces after the last character in a cell or in an empty cell, the extra spaces will appear in your merged documents. Should you find an extra space, click to the right of the space and press BACKSPACE to delete the mark. You can click the arrows on the horizontal scroll bar at the bottom of screen to display text that is to the left or the right of the screen area.

Cut

3 There should be one empty cell in your table—this particular person did not have a company name as part of his address. (See the preceding illustration.) If you accidentally typed in that cell, drag to select the text and click the Cut button on the Toolbar. Select the text in the cells that follow the blank cell and type the correct text.

4 If you see any typing errors that you'd like to correct, you can select and edit the text as you normally do in a document.

Working with Main Documents

Now that the data file is complete, you are ready to return to the main document and fill it in. The main document will contain the standard text, spaces, and punctuation you want printed in all versions of the merged document. To tell Word where you want variable information such as the name and address printed, you insert the merge field names—the categories of information— exactly as they are spelled in the data file. When you merge the main document with the data file, Word replaces the merge field names with the corresponding information from each record in the data file.

The following procedures show you how to create a main document that looks like the following illustration:

```
April 16, 1992¶
¶
«title» «firstname» «lastname»¶
«company»¶
«address»¶
«city», «state» «postcode»¶
¶
Dear «title» «lastname»,¶
¶
Thank you for attending our trade show. We will be in «city» next month. We would like to show you
our newest product line.¶
```

Display the main document

▶ From the Window menu, choose MYMAIN.DOC.

Word displays the main document and hides the data file. Note the print merge bar above the ruler; it provides the information and options you'll use to merge documents. Word displays the print merge bar every time you open a document that has a data file attached to it.

Display paragraph marks

The merge field names reserve a place for the text in the data file; they act as *placeholders.* You must insert the same spacing and punctuation between the placeholders as you would between the words. For example, you need to insert a space between the «title» and «firstname» fields and a comma and space between the «city» and «state» fields. Displaying paragraph marks makes it easier to see the spaces between words and the "empty paragraphs," or blank lines, in the document.

Show/Hide ¶

▶ If paragraph marks are not currently displayed on the screen, click the Show/Hide ¶ button on the ribbon.

Insert the date

Use the Date And Time command to insert the current date into the main document. Word will automatically update the information each time you print the document.

1   From the Insert menu, choose Date And Time.

2   Under Available Formats, select the date format you want.

3   Choose the OK button.

Word closes the dialog box and inserts the date into the document. Each time you print MYMAIN.DOC, Word will insert the current date.

4   Press ENTER twice to leave a blank line below the date.

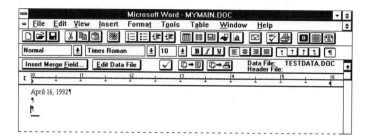

TROUBLESHOOTING: **If you see "{TIME\ ...}" on the screen instead of today's date** If {TIME\ ...} is displayed in place of today's date, it means you are viewing the main document with the field codes displayed. These codes instruct Word to insert information into the document. It's a little easier to read the main document if these codes are hidden. To hide them, from the View menu, choose Field Codes. How you view the main document doesn't affect how the main document is merged or printed.

Inserting Field Names in the Main Document

When you insert the merge field names into the main document, you are telling Word where you want the variable information from the data file to print. Word encloses each field name in chevrons (« »).

Insert the title, first name, and last name

1 On the print merge bar, click the Insert Merge Field button.

Click here.

2 The merge field name "title" is already selected. Choose the OK button to insert it into the document.

3 Press the SPACEBAR to insert a blank space between the title and the first name.

4 Click the Insert Merge Field button to insert the next field name.

5 Double-click "firstname."

6 Press the SPACEBAR to insert a blank space between the first name and the last name.

7 Click the Insert Merge Field button.

8 Double-click "lastname."

9 Press ENTER to move to the next line.

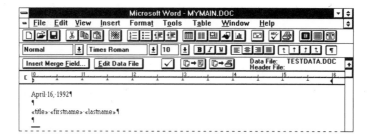

Insert the company name

1 Click the Insert Merge Field button.

2 Double-click "company."

3 Press ENTER to move to the next line.

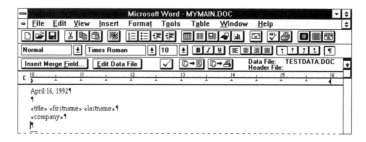

Insert the address

▶ Insert the address by using the same steps you used to insert the company name.

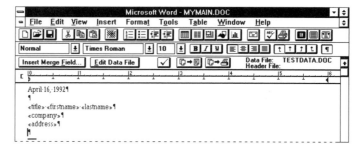

Insert the city, state, and postal code

1 Click the Insert Merge Field button.

2 Double-click "city."

3 Type a comma and press the SPACEBAR so that the punctuation will be correct between the city and state.

4 Click the Insert Merge Field button.

5 Double-click "state."

6 Press the SPACEBAR to insert a blank space between the state and the postal code.

7 Click the Insert Merge Field button.

8 In the Print Merge Field box, scroll down if necessary to see and double-click "postcode."

9 Press ENTER twice to leave a blank line.

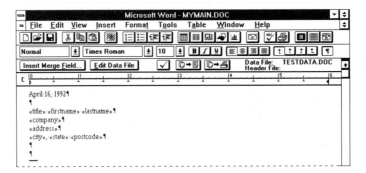

Type the salutation

You can use a merge field name more than once in a document. The following procedure inserts "Dear «title» «lastname»," which will print as "Dear Mr. Tanner," or as "Dear Ms. Gabor," when the main document is merged with the data file.

1 Type **Dear** and press the SPACEBAR. Do *not* press ENTER yet.

2 Click the Insert Merge Field button.

3 Double-click "title."

4 Press the SPACEBAR to leave a space between the title and the last name.

5 Click the Insert Merge Field button.

6 Double-click "lastname."

7 Type a comma, and then press ENTER twice to leave a blank line.

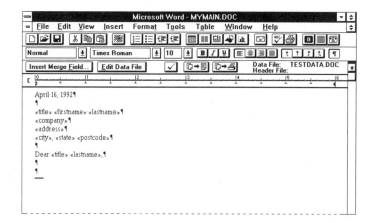

Finish typing the letter

You can use a merge field name within the body of the letter to customize the text. The following procedure inserts the name of the city in each letter.

1 Type **Thank you for attending our trade show. We will be in**

Do *not* press ENTER yet.

TROUBLESHOOTING: **If you pressed ENTER at the end of your typing**   If you accidentally pressed ENTER just now and your insertion point moved to a new line, press BACKSPACE to delete the paragraph mark.

2 If you have not already typed a space following "We will be in" press the SPACEBAR now.

3 Click the Insert Merge Field button.

4 Double-click "city."

5 Press the SPACEBAR.

6 Type **next month. We would like to show you our newest product line.**

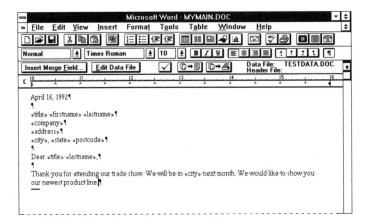

Format a field

When Word inserts a name, address, or other information in a merge field, the text automatically takes on the formatting of the merge field. In this procedure you'll format the «city» merge field so the city name prints bold in the body of each letter.

1   Within the body of the letter, select the merge field «city» as shown in the following illustration.

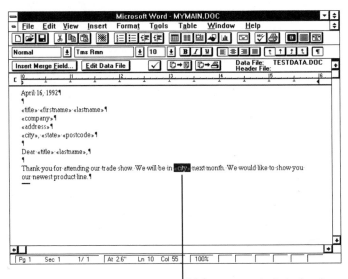

*Make sure you include the chevrons (« »)
that surround the word "city" in your selection.*

B

Bold

2   On the ribbon, click the Bold button.

When the main document is merged, the city name will appear in bold.

Save

Save the main document

▶ On the Toolbar, click the Save button.

Merging Documents

Once you've attached a data file to a main document and inserted merge field codes into the main document, you are ready to merge. You have three choices, each made available by clicking on of the buttons on the print merge bar. You can:

- Use the Check For Errors button to have Word check the main document and the data file and alert you to errors.

- Use the Merge To File button to merge the main document and data file, and store the resulting documents in a new document called Form Letters1. You can then view each version of the merged document on your screen and check formatting, spacing, and other details. You can save the Form Letters1 document and print it later. That is what you will do in this lesson.

- Use the Merge To Printer button to merge the main document and data file, and immediately print each resulting document.

Merge To File

Merge the information into one file

▶ To merge the main document and the data file and store the results in a new file, click the Merge To File button.

| Click here.

Word merges the documents and stores the results in a document named Form Letters1. Each letter is separated with a double dotted line that indicates a section break. Each section is automatically formatted to begin on a new page.

View and edit the letters

As you scroll through the letters, note that the name of the city appears in bold in the body of each letter. Also note that the first two letters have a company name in the address, but that the third letter does not. Word skips this field in the third letter because you left the company field blank in the data file. You can edit any of the text as you would edit any other document.

1 Click the down scroll arrow on the scroll bar to read through each letter.

2 In the last letter, select the word "month" and type **week** instead. Then position the insertion point at the end of the last sentence, press the SPACEBAR, and type **Please contact Maria Mendel to set up an appointment.**

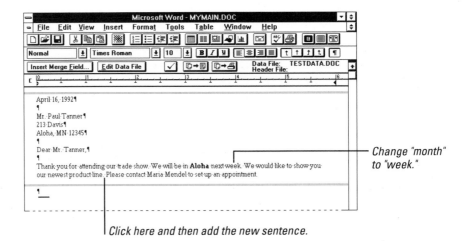

Change "month" to "week."

Click here and then add the new sentence.

Print the merged letters

Print

▶ On the Toolbar, click the Print button.

Close the merged document file

1   From the File menu, choose Close.

2   Choose the No button. You do not need to save this file.

Attaching an Existing Data File

Once you create a data file, you can use it with any main document, as long as the field names in the data file match those that are inserted in the main document. You can attach data files that were created in Microsoft Excel, in a database application, or in a word processor other than Word for Windows. The Step by Step practice files provide another data file so you can practice attaching an existing data file to a main document.

1   If MYMAIN.DOC is not currently displayed on the screen, from the Windows menu, choose MYMAIN.DOC.

2   From the File menu, choose Print Merge (ALT, F, M).

3   Click the Attach Data File button.

4   In the Directories box, select the directory containing the Step by Step practice files.

5   In the File Name box, double-click MOREDATA.DOC.

Word attaches the data file MOREDATA.DOC to the main document in place of the previous data file. Note that the right end of the print merge bar shows the name of the data file that is currently attached.

Merge To File

6 To merge the main document with the new data file and store the results in a file, click the Merge To File button.

Close the merge document file

Take a moment to scroll through the document to see the new names and addresses. If you'd like to print these letters, click the Print button on the Toolbar. Otherwise, you can use the following procedure to close the file.

1 From the File menu, choose Close (ALT, F, C).

2 Choose the No button. You do not need to save this document.

Save the main document for later use

If you'd like to use the main document as the starting point for other documents, do the following.

1 Delete the sample text below the salutation.

2 On the Toolbar, click the Save button. You will not see a change on the screen.

Save

Tips for Merging Documents

- Unless you choose otherwise, Word merges all records in the data file with the main document. Records are merged in the order in which they occur in the data file. By using the Print Merge command on the File menu to merge the documents, you can select which records are merged. For example, you can select only those records having a certain postal code. For more information, see "Merging and Printing the Documents" in Chapter 32, "Print Merge Basics," in the *Microsoft Word User's Guide.*

- Before merging, close all files you are not using. This provides Word more memory for merging your documents.

Check For Errors

- Once you've attached the data file to the main document and inserted the merge field names, you can click the Check For Errors button (the one with the check mark symbol) to check the main document and data file and alert you to errors. For example, Word notifies you if the main document contains a merge field name that is not defined in the attached data file.

- The data file does not need to be open when you merge. As long as the data file is attached to the main document, Word can find the necessary information.

- In addition to merge field names, you can use other Word fields such as IF, ASK, and SET to control how the variable text is merged with the main document. For example, you can instruct Word to omit a paragraph or include a different phone number if the letter is addressed to a particular city or state. For information about these fields, see "Using Fields in Merged Documents," in Chapter 32, "Print Merge Basics," in the *Microsoft Word User's Guide.*

- You can use data files that you created in an earlier version of Word for Windows, in Microsoft Excel, in a database application, or in a word processor other than

Word for Windows. For step-by-step instructions and some tips on what information to include in a data file, see "Creating and Attaching a Data File," in Chapter 32, "Print Merge Basics," in the *Microsoft Word User's Guide*.

One Step Further

▶ You can easily edit the text in the data file. With MYMAIN.DOC on the screen, experiment by clicking the Edit Data File button. Double-click a first name to select it, and then type your own first name. Double-click to select a last name, and then type your own last name. From the Window menu, choose MYMAIN.DOC. Merge the main document with the edited data file if you'd like to see the results.

To quit Word

1 From the File menu, choose Exit (ALT, F, X).

2 Choose the No button. You do not need to save any of the changes you made while experimenting.

3 Repeat steps 1 and 2 for any other open documents.

Lesson Summary

To	Do this
Create a main document	Open a new or existing document. Choose Print Merge from the File menu and choose the Attach Data File button to attach an existing data file to the active document, or create and attach a new one.
Create and attach a data file	Make sure the document you want to use as the main document is open on the screen. From the File menu, choose the Print Merge command. Then choose the Attach Data File button. Choose the Create Data File button to open the dialog box where you type the field names. Once you name and save the data file, Word opens a document window where you can type the information you want for each field.
Insert merge fields in a main document	With the main document displayed, choose the Insert Merge Field button. Double-click the name of the field you want to insert.
Merge a main document and a data file, and either save the merged documents to a new file or print them	With the main document open on the screen, click the appropriate button on the print merge bar. Click the Merge To File button to merge the information into one file that you can view and print later. Click the Merge To Printer button to merge the information and print the merged documents immediately.

For more information on	See the *Microsoft Word User's Guide*
Merging documents	Chapter 32, "Print Merge Basics"
Form letters	Chapter 34, "Form Letters and Other Merged Documents"
Mailing Labels	Chapter 33, "Mailing Labels"

For an online lesson about	Do this
Merging documents	Click the Help menu. Click Learning Word. Click Viewing and Printing. Click Using Print Merge. Follow the instructions on the screen. To exit a lesson at any time, click the Controls button and then click Exit.

Appendixes

Appendix A   *Installing Word*

Appendix B   *Installing and Selecting a Printer*

Appendix C   *Converting Documents To or From Other Formats*

Appendix D   *New Features in Word*

Appendix E   *Other Ways to Save Time in Word*

Installing Word

The Word Setup program decompresses and copies the Word program and other Word files to your hard disk. Before you can start using Word, you must use Word Setup.

Hardware and Software Requirements

To use Word, your computer must meet the following requirements:

- MS-DOS system computer with an Intel 286 microprocessor or greater, with a hard drive and a 1.2 MB or greater floppy disk drive.

- 1 MB of RAM for the basic Word program. To use all features, including Graph, Draw, Equation Editor, WordArt, and grammar checking, 2 MB of RAM is required.

- Enhanced graphics adapter (EGA) monitor or better resolution.

- Microsoft Windows version 3.0 or later.

In addition, a mouse is required for the Step by Step lessons.

Before You Set Up Word

Use the Windows Setup program to set up Windows on your computer before you set up Word.

With Windows Setup, you install screen fonts to display text on the screen and the printer driver for your printer. The printer driver provides access to printer fonts and instructions for your printer. When you set up Windows, you also choose a port to establish a software connection between your computer and the printer. Finally, you choose the printer and printer settings that you will use with the installed printer driver.

If you set up Windows and did not install a printer, you must do so before printing with Word. For information on installing a printer, see your Windows documentation.

Using the Word Setup Program

The options you choose in Setup determine the amount of disk space you need to install Word. For the Step by Step lessons, you can choose either of two installations.

Complete Installation Installs all of the Word files, including the Word program, Help, online lessons, and the tools for proofing documents, drawing, charting, and creating equations. You need approximately 15 MB of hard disk space for this option, with 5 MB available on the drive where Windows is installed.

Custom Installation   Lets you install only the options you want to use. Disk space requirements vary based on the options you select. As you select options, Setup tells you how much disk space you need. The Step by Step lessons teach you to use the following optional features: WordArt, Draw, Graph, Thesaurus, Grammar Checker, Speller, Help. For the graphics lesson, you will also need the Windows metafile filter, one of the conversion options that Word offers. If space on your hard disk permits, make sure you install these options.

To set up Word on a hard disk

This procedure covers the basics for setting up Word. For technical information about Setup, see "Additional Setup Information," in Microsoft Word Getting Started.

1   If Windows is not already running, type **win** at the MS-DOS prompt.
    −or−
    If Windows is running, close any open applications.

2   Insert the Word Setup disk (Disk 1) in drive A, and close the drive door.

3   From the File menu, choose Run (ALT, F, R).

4   Type **a:\ setup** and then press ENTER.

5   To personalize your copy of Word, type your name in the Name box and your affiliation or business name in the Organization box (maximum 50 characters).

    To move between the boxes, point and click with the left mouse button, or press TAB. To correct errors, use the BACKSPACE key.

    Your name is used as the author name for your documents. Your initials are used for any comments you insert in a document.

6   Click the Continue button, or press ENTER.

    A dialog box asks you to verify the information you typed.

7   To accept the information, click the Continue button, or press ENTER.
    −or−
    To change the information, click the Change button, and then type the correct information.

    After you click the Continue button, Setup asks you where you want to install Word.

8   To accept the path that Setup proposes, click the Continue button.
    −or−
    To choose your own directory, type a new path in the Install To box, and then click the Continue button.

9   If the path in the Install To box indicates a directory that doesn't exist, do one of the following:

    ■   To create the directory, click the Yes button.

    ■   To edit the path, click the No button, edit the path in the Install To box, and then click the Continue button.

10 If Setup detects a previous version of Word in the directory you specified, do one of the following:

- To overwrite the files in the directory, click the Continue button.

- To keep the old version, click the Change Directory button, and then type a different path in the Install To box.

Setup displays a dialog box with three installation options.

11 Click either the Complete Installation or the Custom Installation button.

12 When Setup asks if you want to update the startup file AUTOEXEC.BAT, do one of the following:

- To update the file, click the Update button, or press ENTER.

- To update the file manually, click the Do Not Update button.

13 When Setup is complete, click the OK button, or press ENTER.

Setup automatically creates the Word for Windows 2.0 program group and Word icons.

Once you have set up Word, you can run Setup at any time to add additional features. For more information, see *Microsoft Word Getting Started* booklet that came with Word for Windows.

Installing and Selecting a Printer

There are three steps to printing. The first step, *installing* a printer, you may do only once; the second step, *selecting* a printer, you may do occasionally; and the third step, *printing,* you may do on a daily basis.

Step 1   Installing printers in Windows   When you install Microsoft Windows, you also install one or more printers for all Windows applications to use. When you install the printer, you indicate which *port*—a mechanical connection within the computer—the printer should use. This is called *configuring* the printer.

Step 2   Selecting a printer in Word   If you've installed more than than one printer for all Windows applications to use, you can select, while you are in Word, which of the printers you want Word to use. For example, to print a memo, you might select a less expensive, lower quality printer. If the next document you print is a letter or formal report, you might change to a more expensive, higher quality printer. Your printer selection affects not only printing, but also the screen display and the fonts available in Word. The printer you select remains selected until you select another.

Step 3   Printing a document   To actually print a document, you click the Print button on the Toolbar, or you choose the Print command from the File menu.

If you could not print in Word, or if you printed to a different printer than you wanted to, there are two things to check. First, are printers available to Windows applications in general? Second, does Word know which connection, or *port,* to use to send information to the printer? This appendix shows you how to answer both questions. You begin with the following procedure.

To see a list of available printers

1   From the File menu, choose the Print Setup command.
    –or–
    Hold down the ALT key and press P and S.

2   **If you do not see the name of the printer you want to use**, click the Cancel button and install the printer using the procedure in "If You Want to Install a New Printer," later in this appendix.
    –or–
    If you see the printer you want to use, but "on None" appears after it's name, Word cannot connect to the printer because the printer has not been assigned to a port. Click the Cancel button and use the procedure "To open the Printers-Configure dialog box," later in this appendix.
    –or–
    If you see the printer you want to use and "on LPT*number*" or a similar message appears after its name, simply select the printer and choose the OK button. For more information about selecting a printer and choosing options for that printer, see "Selecting a Printer," later in this appendix.

If You Want to Install a New Printer

If you purchase a new printer, or if for some reason a printer was not installed when you installed Microsoft Windows, you can install a new printer at any time using one of two methods:

Setup Program   The Setup program you use to install Microsoft Windows includes printer setup. You can run the Setup program at any time to install new printers.

Control Panel   The Control Panel is a Windows utility application that you can run while using Microsoft Word. Using the Control Panel is the most convenient way to install a new printer, because you can make changes without leaving Word.

Following are basic procedures for starting the Control Panel application and displaying the printer dialog boxes you would use to install and configure printers. For information about actually installing and configuring printers, see your Windows documentation.

To start Control Panel from Word

1   Hold down the ALT key and press the SPACEBAR and U (ALT, SPACEBAR,U).
   −or−
   Open the Word Control menu by clicking the bar at the left side of the Word title bar, and then choose Run.

   The Word Control menu is displayed.

2   In the dialog box that Word displays, select the Control Panel option button.

3   Choose the OK button.

   The Control Panel window is displayed.

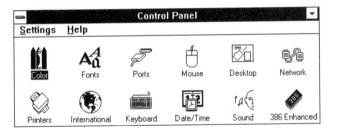

You can do more than install a printer with Control Panel. For example, you can select the Mouse option and change the double-click speed. You can also change other operating environment settings, such as date and time, background colors, and network configuration, with Control Panel. For complete information about Control Panel, see your Windows documentation.

To open the Printers dialog box

You use the Printers dialog box to install and configure new printers. Open the dialog box now, to see which options are available.

1 In the Control Panel window, double-click the Printers icon.

The Printers dialog box is displayed. It lists the printers that are installed on your computer, the default printer, and indicates whether or not the selected printer is active for the port it is assigned to.

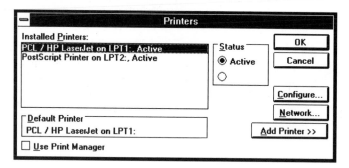

2 Choose the Add Printer button to expand the dialog box and display a list of other printers.

If you want to install another printer, you select the printer you want from the List Of Printers and then choose the Install button. Word displays a message asking you to insert the Microsoft Windows disk that contains the appropriate printer-driver file. At this point either insert the floppy disk that contains the drivers, or indicate where the printer-driver file is located.

3 To close the Printers dialog box and cancel any changes you made, choose the Cancel button.
–or–
To close the Printers dialog box and put any changes you made into effect, choose the OK button.

To open the Printers-Configure dialog box

When you install a new printer, you insert a Microsoft Windows disk with the appropriate printer-driver file and then you *configure* the printer by assigning it to a printer port. You may have more than one printer assigned to a port. If this is the case, you indicate which of the printers assigned to the port should be active. You use the Printers-Configure dialog box to do this.

1 Double-click the Printers symbol in the Control Panel window to display the Printers dialog box.

Make sure the printer you want to use is selected under Installed Printers.

2 Choose the Configure button.

Word displays the Printers-Configure dialog box. The Ports box lists printer ports—the connections through which your computer exchanges data with an installed printer.

- When you install a new printer, you need to assign it to a port. You do that by selecting the appropriate port in the Ports box.

- If the port has more than one printer assigned to it, you need to indicate which printer will be the active one for the port. To indicate which printer should be active, you close the Printers-Configure dialog box and, in the Printers box, select the Active option button under Status.

- Choosing the Setup button in the Printers-Configure dialog box displays print setup options for documents in other Windows applications. To specify print setup options for Word documents, you return to the Word application window and use the Page Setup command on the Word Format menu, as described in "Changing Print Setup Options," later in this appendix.

Close the dialog boxes and quit Control Panel

Use the following procedure to close the printer dialog boxes and return to the Word application window. If you made any changes you're unsure about, be sure to choose the Cancel buttons to close the dialog boxes. For complete information about installing printers, selecting ports, and making printers active, see your Windows documentation.

1 To close the Printers-Configure dialog box and cancel any changes you made, choose the Cancel button.
–Or–
To close the Printers dialog box and put the changes you've made into effect, choose the OK button.

2 To close the Printers dialog box and cancel any changes you made, choose the Cancel button.
–or–
To close the Printers dialog box and put the changes you've made into effect, choose the OK button.

3 Quit Control Panel by holding down ALT and pressing F4 (ALT+F4).

Selecting a Printer

If you have more than one printer installed on your computer, you can use the Print Setup command on the File menu in Word to select the printer you want as you work in Word.

The printer you select controls more than just the final printout; it controls the way the document appears on the screen. Word displays the document using fonts as similar as possible to those that the selected printer can print. One of the most powerful advantages of Word for Windows is that you can see your document on the screen as it will be printed. Word can do this only if you've selected the printer you will use for this document. For this reason, it's important that you select the printer you will use to print a document *when you begin to work on the document*. The printer selection also controls the fonts that are available to you as you work on a document. If you've selected the printer that you will use to print the document, Word lists the fonts that the selected printer can print in the Font box on the ribbon and in the Font box in the Character dialog box.

Word automatically uses the printer you select for the current and future documents until you change it.

To select a printer in Word

1 From the File menu, choose Print Setup (ALT, F, R).

2 Select the printer you want to use.

   If you select a laser printer, you may also need to select a font cartridge by choosing the Setup button and selecting the cartridge.

3 Choose the OK button.

Changing Print Setup Options

On certain printers, you can change the settings for paper orientation (portrait or landscape), paper size, or paper source (such as a specific tray or manual feed). If these options are available on your printer, you can set the default settings for every document template that you use. You can also change these settings for an individual document or for a page of a document. You use the Page Setup command to change these options.

To change the orientation, paper size, or paper source

The page orientation, paper size, or paper source can be set for all documents based on a particular template using the following procedure. In addition, you can change the settings for any document or for part of a document. For more information, see Chapter 9, "Margins, Paper Size, and Page Orientation."

1 From the Format menu, choose Page Setup (ALT, T, U).

2 Select either the Size And Orientation option or the Paper Source option.

   The dialog box changes to display optional settings either for page size and orientation or for paper source.

3 Select the print setup settings you want.

4 If you want to change the settings in another category, repeat steps 2 and 3.

5 To change the settings for the active document only, click the OK button.
−or−
To change the default for the active document and for future documents based on the same template, first, check the settings in all three categories—Margins, Size And Orientation, and Paper Source. All settings will be saved as the default. Then click the Use As Default button. When Word displays a message asking if you want to use all the settings as the default for the template on which the current document is based, choose the Yes button.

Printing Tips

When you make printer and print setup options the default settings, Word automatically uses them; you don't have to specify them every time you print. Then you can print documents simply by clicking the Print button on the Toolbar or choosing the Print command from the File menu. When you print Word documents, keep the following tips in mind:

- Before you print, it's a good idea to check your document by switching to print preview or page layout view, or by clicking the Zoom Whole Page button on the Toolbar. Using one or more of these views will give you a better idea of how your document will look when printed.

- It's also a good idea to save your document before you print. That way, if a printer error or other problem occurs, you won't lose any of the work you've done since you last saved the document.

- If you do not want to print an entire document—only certain pages—and you've edited the document recently, from the Tools menu, choose Repaginate Now. Then, verify the starting and ending page numbers that you want to print.

- You can select a paragraph, a table, a graphic, or any amount of text and graphics and print only the selection. Before choosing the Print command, select the portion of your document you want to print. When you choose the Print command, the dialog box displays the Selection option under Range. Select it and then choose the OK button. If you don't make a selection, Current Page is available under Range; select this option to print only the current page.

For more information on	See
Printing	Chapter 4, "Printing a Document," in the *Microsoft Word User's Guide*
Installing and setting up a printer	Microsoft Windows documentation.

For an online lesson about	Do this
Printing	Click the Help menu. Click Learning Word. Click Viewing and Printing. Click any of the lessons on Printing. Follow the instructions on the screen. To exit a lesson at any time, click the Controls button, then click Exit.

Converting Documents To or From Other Formats

You can open documents created by many other applications directly in Word. Word recognizes the file formats of popular word processors, spreadsheets, and other applications, and converts their files into Word format, preserving the content and, in most cases, formatting of the original documents. You can also save documents you create in Word for use with popular word processing applications. For complete information about converting documents to and from Microsoft Word, see Chapter 35, "Converting File Formats," in the *Microsoft Word User's Guide*.

Word also converts to and from plain text formats, which allows you to move files between applications when a specific conversion isn't available or necessary.

Word provides conversions for the following file formats:

- Word for Windows 1.*x*; Word for DOS 4.0, 5.0, and 5.5; and Word for the Macintosh, 4.0 and 5.0
- WordPerfect 4.1, 4.2, 5.0, and 5.1
- RFT-DCA (for DisplayWrite and IBM 5520)
- Works for Windows and Works for DOS 2.0 (word-processing documents only)
- WordStar 3.3, 3.45, 4.0, 5.0, and 5.5
- Lotus 1-2-3 2.*x* and 3.0 (convert to Word format only, not from Word format)
- Microsoft Excel BIFF 2.*x* and 3.0 (convert to Word format only)
- Multiplan 3.0 and 4.2
- dBASE (II, III, III PLUS, and IV)

Word can open or save text files in three file formats: Text, DOS Text, or Rich Text Format. When you save a document using the Text or DOS Text format, you can choose variations that control how much of the formatting in the document is converted. RTF adds the option to convert all formatting. The differences and potential uses for the options are as follows:

Text only and DOS Text only   Saves the text without the formatting. Newline marks, section breaks, and page breaks are all converted to paragraph marks. Use this basic text file format only if the application to which you're converting the document is unable to read any of the other available file formats.

Text only with line breaks and DOS Text only with line breaks   Saves all of the text in a document without the formatting, but places a paragraph mark at the end of every line, and replaces section breaks and page breaks with paragraph marks. This format is useful when you want to keep your lines at a certain length, for example, when transferring files to an electronic mail system.

Text with layout and DOS Text with layout   Preserves line breaks and also preserves indents, tables, line spacing, paragraph spacing, and tab stop positions by inserting spaces in the file. Section breaks and page breaks are replaced by single paragraph marks. This is useful for converting a document in text file format and maintaining the page layout. You can reformat the document in the new application, using the converted layout as a guideline.

Rich Text Format (RTF)   Saves all of the formatting in the file. Formatting is converted to instructions that other applications can read and interpret. Where there isn't a specific conversion, RTF is useful for converting files from one Microsoft application to another and for transferring files between a Macintosh and a DOS system. You can also use RTF to transfer fully formatted documents using communications software that accepts only text files.

Opening Files Created in Other Applications

With the appropriate converter, you can open files from other applications that have been saved in a non-Word file format. For a list of file formats Word converts, see the introduction to this appendix.

You open files from other applications as you would a Word document, by choosing the Open command from the File menu. You can then use the List Files Of Type box to have Word list the group of files that may contain the one that interests you. Word lists documents according to the three-character file name extension. Word documents, for example, usually end with .DOC, and text files with .TXT.

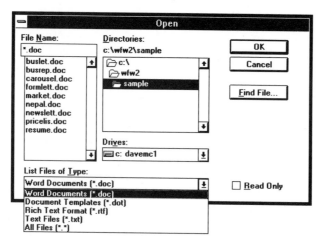

Word uses separate programs, called converters, to convert the text and formatting within a document to a different file format. When converting *to* Word format, Word uses additional programs, called graphics filters, to convert the graphics that are within a file or linked to a file to the graphics format Word recognizes. You install converters and graphic filters with the Setup program, using either the Complete Installation or Custom Installation option. If you have not installed the converter you need, see *Microsoft Word Getting Started* for information on running Setup.

For comprehensive information about each converter, see the file CONVINFO.DOC, included in the Word package.

To open a file created by another application

You must have the appropriate converter installed to convert files from a particular application. For more information on installing converters, see *Microsoft Word Getting Started*.

1   From the File menu, choose Open (ALT, F, O).

2   In the List Files Of Type box, select the type of files you want to display.

If you want to see files of a type not listed in the List Files Of Type box, in the File Name box, type the extension of the types of files you want to display, and then press ENTER. For example, type ***.xls** or ***.wps**

Word will continue to use the file type you select until you select a new one or quit Word.

3   In the File Name box, type or select the name of the document you want to open.

If you do not see the name of the file you want, you can change the file type, the current directory, or the current drive, or you can choose the Find File button to help you locate the file.

4   Choose the OK button.

Word looks at the file to determine as best it can the file format of the document you want to open, and displays the Convert File dialog box if it cannot determine the format.

Saving Word Documents in Another File Format

You can create documents using Word and then save them in file formats that can be used by many other applications. You can then work on the documents using other applications or share them with people who don't have Microsoft Word.

To save a Word document in another file format

When you save a Word document in another file format, you give it a new name and then save it. The Word document that is the base for your save remains open after the save. You may want to save the Word document in Word format in case you need it later.

1   From the File menu, choose Save As (ALT, F, A).

2   In the Save File As Type box, select the file format you want.

The file format is displayed only if the corresponding converter is installed.

3   In the File Name box, type a new name for the document. Word does not allow you to save a file in a different file format with the same name.

If you don't type an extension, Word adds the extension that's characteristic for the file format you selected in the Save File As Type box. Word adds the .TXT extension to all Text and DOS Text formats. For example, Word adds the .DOC extension to documents saved in WordPerfect format.

4   Choose the OK button.

Tip   To make it easier to identify files you've converted to a different file format, you can change the default extension for a particular converter. For example, for WordPerfect documents, you might change the extension from .DOC to .WPF to distinguish these documents from Word documents, which also have a .DOC extension.

To change a converter's default extension, choose Options from the Tools menu, and then select the Win.ini category. In the Application box, select MSWord Text Converters, and in the Startup Options box, select the converter whose extension you want to change. Finally, in the Setting box, scroll to the end of the string of characters and change the three-letter extension that appears there. Then choose the OK button.

New Features in Word

The following table lists the features that are new in Microsoft Word for Windows version 2.0. The table shows the lesson in which you can learn about each feature. For features not described in this book, the appropriate chapter in the *Microsoft Word User's Guide* is listed.

New Features

To learn how to	See *Step by Step*
Move text with a mouse	Lessons 1 and 2
Magnify or reduce your view of a document	Lessons 3 and 11
Use bullets and special characters	Lessons 3 and 4
Preview your formatting changes in the dialog box	Lesson 4
Use online Help for WordPerfect users	Lesson 4
Use WordPerfect keys in your daily work	Lesson 4
Check your documents for correct grammar and language use	Lesson 6
Create envelopes quickly	Lesson 6
Create charts from numeric data	Lesson 9
Create and edit graphics for your documents	Lesson 11
Use the sample clip art that comes with Word	Lesson 11
Rotate, flip, and arrange text in circles and other shapes	Lesson 11
Add borders and shading to text	Lesson 11
Preview the contents of a file before opening it	Lesson 12
Create merge documents with the Print Merge Helper	Lesson 13

To learn how to	See *Microsoft Word User's Guide*
Protect documents with a password	Chapter 2, "Opening, Saving, and Deleting Documents"
Assign different margin settings to paragraphs on the same page	Chapter 9, "Margins, Paper Size, and Page Orientation"
Print different page sizes in the same document	Chapter 9, "Margins, Paper Size, and Page Orientation"
Print both portrait and landscape in the same document	Chapter 9, "Margins, Paper Size, and Page Orientation"
Format text in any of 16 languages	Chapter 14, "Proofing a Document"
Share features with other applications	Chapter 36, "Exchanging Information"
View online Help about macros while you create them in the WordBasic macro language	Chapter 42, "Using Macros"
Create custom dialog boxes quickly	Chapter 42, "Using Macros"
Insert equations in your documents	See the *Microsoft Equation Editor User's Guide*

Other Ways to Save Time in Word

The following list describes Microsoft Word for Windows features not covered in this book. These features offer additional ways you can save time in your daily work. For information about any of these features, see the *Microsoft Word User's Guide*.

Store frequently used text for quick insertion   Store text by name in a glossary, and then insert the text by typing the name. For more information, see Chapter 13, "Glossaries: Storing Items for Reuse."

Organize your documents   Create an outline and restructure your document by rearranging the outline's major headings. Generate a table of contents and an index. Sort paragraphs and items in tables alphabetically or numerically. For more information, see Chapter 27, "Outline View: Creating Outlines and Reorganizing Documents."

Use templates for consistency   Use a template to provide a pattern for the text and layout in your document. For more information, see Chapter 37, "Document Templates."

Automate your work   Use macros to record complex or repetitive actions and carry them out with only a few keystrokes. Use fields to insert information into a document. For more information, see Chapter 41, "Fields," and Chapter 42, "Using Macros."

Insert bookmarks, cross-references, and footnotes   Find text in a document by naming it and searching for it by name. Update cross-references to page numbers, illustrations, tables, and chapter headings automatically. Create footnotes that renumber automatically when you move the associated text. For more information, see Chapter 40, "Bookmarks and Cross-references."

Track changes to documents   Insert annotations (comments) in a document and lock a document so that only annotations can be added without affecting the existing text. Use revision marks (redlining) to highlight revised text. Compare different versions of a document and automatically mark any changes. For more information, see Chapter 31, "Footnotes, Annotations, and Revision Marks."

Perform mathematical calculations   Use the Calculate command to add, subtract, multiply, divide, and calculate percentages in your documents. For more information, see Chapter 16 "Math Calculations."

Customize Word for the way you work   Add and remove commands from menus and the Toolbar. Change keyboard combinations. Create macros to automate repetitive tasks. Create templates to contain the Word commands, macros, and Toolbar buttons you use most often. Set preferences for printing, saving, and viewing documents on the screen. Specify the rules you want Word to apply when proofing your documents. Change the defaults for font, page margins, and tab locations. Specify the language you want to use with Word and the directory in which Word automatically saves your documents. For more information, see Chapter 38, "Customizing Menus, the Keyboard, and the Toolbar," and Chapter 39, "Setting Preferences."

Glossary

alignment   The horizontal position of text within the width of a line or between tab stops. There are three kinds of alignment in Word.

Alignment	Determines
Paragraph	Whether the lines in a paragraph are aligned with the left indent (flush left), aligned with the right indent (flush right), aligned with both indents (justified), or centered between indents (centered).
Tab	Which direction text extends from a tab position.
Section	How paragraphs are placed vertically on a page.

application   A piece of software, such as Microsoft Word or Microsoft Excel.

application Control menu   A menu that includes commands with which you can control the size and position of the Word window and switch to another application. To display the menu with keys, press ALT+SPACEBAR.

application window   A window that contains a running application. The window displays the menus and provides the workspace for any document used within the application. The application window shares its borders and title bar with document windows that are fully enlarged.

arrow keys   The UP ARROW, DOWN ARROW, LEFT ARROW, and RIGHT ARROW keys. Used to move the insertion point or to select from a menu or a list of options.

automatic save   An option that automatically saves your document at specified intervals. You can select or clear the Automatic Save option with the Options command on the Tools menu.

bullet   A mark, usually a round or square dot, often used to add emphasis or distinguish items in a list.

cell   The basic unit of a table. In a table, the intersection of a row and a column forms one cell.

click   To press and release a mouse button in one nonstop motion.

Clipboard   A temporary storage area for cut or copied text or graphics. You can paste the contents of the Clipboard into any Word document or into a file of another application, such as Microsoft Excel. The Clipboard holds the information until you cut or copy another piece of text or a graphic.

column break   A place in text where you designate the end of one column and the beginning of another. In page view and print preview, and when you print your document, text after a column break appears in a new column. A column break appears as a dotted line. A break you insert is called a hard break; a break determined by the page layout is called a soft break.

Control Panel   The Microsoft Windows Control Panel adjusts operations and formats such as the insertion point blink rate, date and time formats, and communications setup. The settings affect both Word and Windows.

crop   To trim away the parts of a graphic you don't want to display.

cut   To remove selected text or a graphic from a document so you can paste it to another place in the document or to another document. The cut information is placed in a temporary storage area called the Clipboard. The Clipboard holds the information until you cut or copy another piece of text or a graphic.

data file   A document that contains text to be merged into a main document to create form letters or other merged documents. For example, a data document for a form letter may contain names and addresses that vary for each letter. If you want to use data from another word-processing program, database, or spreadsheet, first convert the file to Word format.

defaults   Predefined settings such as page margins, tab spaces, and shortcut key assignments. The default template when you create documents is NORMAL.DOT, whose default settings include margins of 1.25 inches and no indents.

dialog box   A box that displays the available command options for you to review or change.

directories   Subdivisions of a disk that work like a filing system to help you organize your files. For example, you can create a directory called LETTERS for all of your form letters.

document Control menu   A menu with commands that control a document window—for example, you can size, position, and split a document window. To display the menu with keys, press ALT+HYPHEN.

document window   A rectangular portion of the screen in which you view and edit a document. You can have up to nine document windows open in the Word window. Each document window can be divided horizontally into two parts, called panes. When you enlarge a document window to maximum size, it shares its borders and title bar with the Word window.

drag   To hold down the mouse button while moving the mouse.

drive   The mechanism in your computer that turns a disk to retrieve and store information. Personal computers often have one hard disk drive labeled C and two drives labeled A and B that read removable floppy disks.

edit   To add, delete, or change text and graphics.

extend selection   To lengthen a selection. When you extend a selection, it grows progressively larger each time you press F8. For example, if you select a word, you can extend the selection to a sentence by pressing F8 once. To shrink the selection, press SHIFT+F8. When you extend a selection, you can also use the arrow keys, or any of the other keys that move the insertion point within text, to enlarge or shrink the selection.

field   The coded instructions that insert many types of information into your document, including the variable data inserted into form letters during printing. You can update fields to automatically insert new information into your document.

field codes   A field that appears as instructions enclosed by field characters ({ }).

field result   Text or graphics inserted into a document because of the action of a field.

file   A document that has been created, then saved, under a unique file name. In Word, all documents are stored as files.

file format   The format in which data is stored in a file. Word usually stores a document in Word's "Normal" file format, which includes the text and all the formatting applied to the document. Word can read and save in several file formats, such as Microsoft Excel BIF, Windows Write, RTF, and WordPerfect.

font   The general shapes for a set of characters. Each font has a name with which you can select the font and apply it to text. Geneva and Modern are examples of fonts.

form letter or document   One of a number of documents created by merging the main document and the data document. The main document contains basic text that is the same in every copy of the letter. The data document contains the information that varies for each letter, such as names and addresses.

format   The way text appears on a page. In Word, a format comes from direct formatting and the application of styles. The four types of formats are character, paragraph, section, and document.

formula   A mathematical statement or expression, such as $3x = 1/2y$. Word provides special codes to create formulas. For information on creating formulas, see the *Microsoft Equation Editor User's Guide*.

frame   A box you add to mark an area of your document —for example, a block of text, a graphic, or a chart —so that you can easily change its position on a page. Once you insert an object into a frame, you can drag it to the position you want in page layout view. Word automatically makes room for the frame at the new location.

global template   In Word, a template with the file name NORMAL.DOT that contains default menus, dialog box settings, and styles. Documents use the global template unless you specify a custom template.

glossary   A place you store text or graphics you want to use again. Each piece of text or graphics is recorded as a glossary entry and assigned a unique name. Global glossary entries are available to all documents.

hanging indent   A paragraph format in which the first line of a paragraph starts farther left than subsequent lines.

header and footer   A header is text or graphics that appear at the top of every page in a section. A footer appears at the bottom of every page. Headers and footers often contain page numbers, chapter titles, dates, and author names. Headers and footers appear in the header or footer pane for editing.

header file   In a print merge process, a document containing a header record that Word substitutes for the header record in a data document.

heading   A title for a part of a document (for example, a chapter title).

hidden text   A character format that allows you to show or hide designated text. Word indicates hidden text by underlining it with a dotted line. You can select or clear the Hidden Text option with the Options command on the Tools menu. You can omit hidden text during printing.

icon   A graphical representation of a file-level object—that is, a disk drive, a directory, an application, a document, or other object that you can select and open.

indent   The distance between text boundaries and page margins. Positive indents make the text area narrower than the space between margins. Negative indents allow text to extend into the margins. A paragraph can have left, right, and first-line indents.

Indents can also be measured relative to columns in a section, table cells, and the boundaries of positioned objects.

insertion point   Vertical blinking line on the Word screen that shows your current location and where text and graphics are inserted. The insertion point also determines where Word will begin an action, such as checking spelling.

landscape   A term used to refer to horizontal page orientation; opposite of "portrait," or vertical, orientation.

leader characters   Characters, usually dots or hyphens, that fill the space between words separated by tab characters to draw the reader's eye across a line. Leader characters are often used in tables of contents. Example: Chapter 1.................Page 5

line break   Mark inserted where you want to end one line and start another without starting a new paragraph. When you select the All option with the Options command from the Tools menu, a line break you insert is represented by the newline character.

line spacing   The height of a line of text, including extra spacing. Line spacing is often measured in lines or points. The following table shows the approximate point equivalents for standard line spacing set with the ruler.

Spacing	Line height in points
Single	12
One-and-one-half	18
Double	24

Note: Two lines = double-spaced; 72 points = 1 inch.

list box   Part of a dialog box that contains a list of valid selections for an option. Some list boxes stay the same size; others drop down to display the list of items.

main document   In a form letter or document, the main document contains text and graphics that are the same for all the merged documents. Within the text, you insert fields that are replaced by information specific to each of the merged documents when you print.

measurement   A measured distance. In Word, you type measurements in a dialog box with one of the following units.

Unit	Equivalent measurements
Centimeters (cm)	2.54 cm = 1 in
Inches (in or ")	1 in = 72 pt = 6 pi
Lines (li)	1 li = 1/6 in = 12 pt
Picas (pi)	1 pi = 12 pt = 1/6 in
Points (pt)	1 li = 1/6 in = 12 pt

menu   A list of commands that drops down from the menu bar. The menu bar is displayed across the top of an application window and lists the menu names, such as File and Edit.

merge   To combine one or more sources of text into a single document, such as a form letter.

message   A notice on the screen that informs you of a problem or asks for more information. Messages appear in the status bar at the bottom of your screen, in a message box, or as bold text in your document. When Word displays a message, you can press F1 for immediate help, with the following exceptions:

>   Field error messages that appear as bold text in your document
>   Some low-memory messages

Note that you can get help on all messages by pressing F1 and choosing the Index button. Choose Messages under Reference Information.

normal view   The view you see when you start Word. Normal view is used for most editing and formatting tasks.

object   A table, chart, graphic, equation, or other form of information you create and edit with an application other than Word, but whose data you insert and store in a Word document.

options   The choices you have in a dialog box.

outline view   An outline shows the headings of a document indented to represent their level in the document structure. In Word, you can display the structure of your documents in outline view. Outline view makes it easy to move quickly through a document, change the importance of headings, and rearrange large amounts of text by moving headings.

overtype   An option for replacing existing characters one by one as you type. You can select overtype by pressing the INS key or by selecting the Overtype option with the Options command on the Tools menu. When you select the Overtype option, the letters "OVR" appear in the status bar at the bottom of the Word window.

page break   The point at which one page ends and another begins. In page view and print preview, and when you print your document, text after a page break appears on a new page. A break you insert is called a hard break; a break determined by the page layout is called a soft break.

page layout view   A view of your document as it will appear when you print it. Items such as headers, footnotes, and framed objects appear in their actual positions, and you can drag them to new positions. You can edit and format text in page layout view.

pane   Each document window can be divided horizontally into two parts, called panes. You can scroll within each pane to view different parts of a document at the same time. In normal view and outline view, you can view and edit headers and footers, footnotes, and annotations in separate panes.

paste   To insert cut or copied text into a document from the temporary storage area called the Clipboard.

path   Drive, directory, and file name. For example, the complete path for Word for Windows might be C:\WINWORD\WINWORD.EXE.

point size   A measurement used for the size of text characters. There are 72 points per inch.

portrait   A term used to refer to vertical page orientation; opposite of "landscape," or horizontal, orientation.

position   The specific placement of graphics, tables, and paragraphs on a page. In Word, you can assign items to fixed positions on a page.

repaginate   To calculate and insert page breaks at the correct point in your document. By default, Word repaginates whenever you make a change in your document.

ribbon   A graphical bar displayed across the top of the Word window for viewing and applying character formatting.

To display the ribbon, choose Ribbon from the View menu. You may need to enlarge the Word window to the full width of the screen to see the entire ribbon.

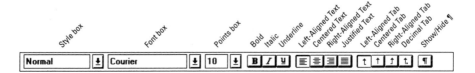

rule   A straight vertical or horizontal line between columns in a section, next to paragraphs, or in a table. You can assign a variety of widths to a rule.

ruler   A graphical bar displayed across the top of the document window. You can use the ruler to indent paragraphs, set tab stops, adjust page margins, and change column widths in a table. You can also use the ruler to view these formatting characteristics. You can change the units of measurement on the ruler with the Options command on the Tools menu. To display the ruler, choose Ruler from the View menu. You may need to enlarge the Word window to the full width of the screen to see the entire ruler.

scale   To change the height and/or width of a graphic by a certain percentage. You can choose to preserve or change the relative proportions of elements within the graphic.

scroll bar   A graphical device for moving vertically and horizontally through a document with a mouse. Scroll bars are located at the right and bottom edges of the document window. You can display or hide scroll bars with the Horizontal Scroll Bar and Vertical Scroll Bar check boxes, View options in the Options dialog box (Tools menu).

section   A portion of a document in which you set certain page formatting options. You create a new section when you want to change options such as line numbering, number of columns, or headers and footers. Until you insert section breaks, Word treats your document as a single section.

section break   The point at which you end one section and begin another because you want some aspect of page formatting to change. A section break appears as two dotted lines.

selection bar   An unmarked column at the left edge of a document window used to select text with the mouse. In a table, each cell has its own selection bar at the left edge of the cell.

special characters   Marks displayed on the screen to indicate characters that do not print, such as tab characters or paragraph marks. You can control the display of special characters with the Options command on the Tools menu, and the Show/Hide ¶ button on the ribbon.

status bar   A line at the bottom of the Word window that displays information about the current status of the document and application.

style   A group of formatting instructions that you name and store. When you apply a style to selected paragraphs, all the formatting instructions of that style are applied at once.

summary information   Descriptions and statistics about a document such as title, author, comments, and revision number. You can view or change summary information with the Summary Info command on the File menu.

tab stop   A measured position for placing and aligning text at a specific place on a line. Word has four kinds of tab stops, each with a different alignment.

Button	Alignment
⊥	Left—Text extends to the right from the tab.
↑	Center—Text is centered at the tab.
↑	Right—Text extends to the left from the tab until the tab's space is filled, and then text extends to the right.
↑.	Decimal—Text before the decimal point extends to the left, and text after the decimal point extends to the right.

table   One or more rows of cells commonly used to display numbers and other items for quick reference and analysis. Items in a table are organized into rows and columns. You can convert text into a table with the Insert Table command on the Table menu.

template A special kind of document that provides basic tools and text for shaping a final document. Templates can contain the following elements: text that is the same in every memo or report, styles, glossary items, macros, menu and key assignments.

text box A box within a dialog box where you type information needed to carry out a command.

title bar The horizontal bar at the top of a window that shows the name of the document or application that appears in that window.

Toolbar A graphical bar with buttons that perform some of the most common commands in Word, such as opening, copying, and printing files.

To display the Toolbar, choose Toolbar from the View menu. You may need to enlarge the Word window to the full width of the screen to see the entire Toolbar.

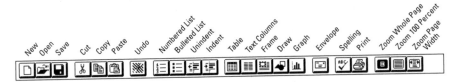

vertical alignment The placement of text on a page in relation to the top, bottom, or center of the page.

view A display that shows certain aspects of the document. Word has five views: normal, draft, outline, page layout, and print preview.

widow and orphan A widow is the last line of a paragraph printed by itself at the top of a page. An orphan is the first line of a paragraph printed by itself at the bottom of a page. The initial settings in Word prevent widows and orphans.

window A rectangular area on your screen in which you view and work on documents. You can have up to nine different document windows open at once.

wordwrap Automatic placement of a word on the next line. When you type text and reach the right margin or indent, Word checks to see if the entire word you type fits on the current line. If not, Word automatically places the entire word on the next line.

Index

A

Active document 122
Addressing envelopes 100, 103
Alignment
    defined 247
    paragraph 13
    vertical alignment, defined 255
Alignment buttons 13
Antonyms, in thesaurus 92
Application(s)
    conversion file formats 239
    defined 247
Application Control menu, defined 247
Application window, defined 247
Arrow keys, defined 247
Arrow tool, Microsoft Draw 184
Art *See* Graphics
ASCII file *See* Text only files
Attribute *See* Character formatting
Author of document
    finding document with 206–207
    typing in summary information 208
AUTOEXEC.BAT file 231
Automatic page break 169
Automatic save, defined 247

B

BIFF conversion file format 239
Blank line, creating 6–7
Bold button 13
Border
    frame 192, 197
    in tables 148–149
Break *See* Column break; Line break; Page break;
  Section break
Bullet defined 247
Bulleted list button 45
Bulleted list, creating 45, 56
Button effect, creating with WordArt 188–189

C

Canceling
    See also Closing; Undoing an action
    dialog box 66–67
Caption, positioning with graphic 196–197
Cell(s)
    See also Table
    borders 148–149
    defined 140, 247
    deleting contents 146
    deleting from table 146
    editing text in 152
    end-of-cell marks 140
    in data file 214
    merging 147, 154
    moving between cells 154
    selecting 144–145
    shading 148–149
Centered Text button 13, 148
Centering paragraphs 13
Character(s)
    formatting *See* Character formatting
    leader characters, defined 250
    spacing between characters 75
    special characters, defined 254
Character formatting
    applying 13, 63–66
    bold 13
    color 75
    finding and replacing 91–92, 102–103
    fonts 14–15
    italic 13
    point size 14–15
    repeating 36
    spacing between characters 75
    special characters, defined 254
    storing as style 79
    underline 13
Chart
    creating 149–150, 154
    sizing 151, 154
Check boxes, selecting/clearing 64
Check For Errors button 221, 223

Checking spelling *See* Spelling check
Click
   See also Mouse
   defined 247
Clip art *See* Graphics
Clipboard
   cutting, copying, and pasting text 29–33
   defined 247
Closing
   documents 125, 134
   online Help 132
   Word 19, 134
Color character formatting 75
Column(s)
   breaks 159, 172, 248
   changing number of 166–168
   creating newspaper-style 157–158, 172
   lines between 160, 172
   newspaper-style *See* Newspaper-style columns
   snaking *See* Newspaper-style columns
   table columns *See* Table
   viewing newspaper-style 158, 160–161, 169–173
Column break
   defined 248
   manual 159, 172
Column chart *See* Chart
Columns button 158, 167
Command
   canceling 66–67
   choosing 58, 60, 63, 76
   choosing with keys 70–71
   getting Help on 62, 76
Computer system required for Word 229
Configuring printer 232–235
Control menu
   application, defined 247
   document, defined 248
Control-menu box
   application 132
   document 125
Control Panel
   defined 248
   installing printer with 233–235
Converting files
   application file formats 239
   converters and filters 240–241
   default file extensions 242
   opening files created in other applications 240–241
   text file formats 239
   Word documents to other formats 241–242
Copy button 30, 124

Copying
   character formatting 36
   multiple documents or files 202, 208
   text
      between documents 123–125, 135
      drag-and-drop method 25–26, 37
      with Clipboard 30–31, 37
Creating new document 211–212
Cropping
   defined 248
   graphics 175, 177–178, 196
Cursor *See* Insertion point
Custom dictionary
   adding word to 98–99, 103
   for multiple languages 102
   overview 98
Cut button 9, 32
Cut, defined 248
Cutting text 32, 37

D

Data file
   See also Print merge
   defined 248
Date, inserting in document 215–216
dBASE files, converting file formats 239
Defaults, defined 248
Deleting
   multiple documents or files 202, 208
   text 8–10
Dialog boxes
   canceling 66–67
   check boxes 64
   choosing options with keys 70–71
   defined 248
   drop-down lists 64–65
   getting Help on 65–66, 76
   moving 133
   overview 62
   selecting options in 58, 62–71, 76
   text boxes 65
Dictionary, custom (user) 98–99, 103
Directories, defined 248
Disk space, required for Word 229–230
DisplayWrite files, converting file formats 239
Document
   See also File
   active document 122
   closing 125, 134
   converting file formats 239–242

Document *(continued)*
    copying multiple 202, 208
    creating new 211–212
    deleting multiple 202, 208
    finding 201–207, 209
    formatting *See* Character formatting; Paragraph
      formatting; Section formatting
    main document, defined 251
    margins *See* Margin(s)
    opening
        existing 22–23, 37
        multiple 122–123, 202, 208
    printing 35–36, 232
    proofing 33–35, 88–104
    proofing tips 102
    renaming 24
    saving 17–19, 24,
    scrolling through 26–29, 37
    statistics 99
    steps in creating xviii–xx
    summary information 206–207, 254
    switching between multiple 123
    typing text in 5–8
    views 52–54
    window *See* Document window
    working with multiple 202–208
Document Control menu, defined 248
Document window
    copying/pasting text between 123–125, 135
    defined 248
    illustration 4
    maximizing 126, 135
    moving 126
    sizing 126
    switching between 123
    viewing all open 123, 135
DOS text files 239–240
Dots per inch (dpi) 195
Drag, defined 248
Drag-and-drop text editing 10–11, 25
Drawing *See* Graphics
Drive, defined 249
Drop-down list, using 64–65

E

Edit, defined 249
Edit menu 61
EGA monitor required for Word 229
Ellipsis (…) following command name 60
End-of-cell mark 140
End-of-row mark 145

Envelope
    creating 100, 103
    printing 101, 103
Envelope button 100
Excel *See* Microsoft Excel
Exiting *See* Closing
Extend selection, defined 249
Extensions for filenames 242

F

Field(s)
    codes, defined 249
    defined 249
    print merge
      defined 212, 249
      merge fields 214–215
      merge fields, formatting 220
      merge fields, inserting 216–220, 224
    result, defined 249
File
    See also Document
    converting formats 239–242
    copying multiple 202, 208
    defined 249
    deleting multiple 202, 208
    extensions 242
    finding 201–207, 209
    header file 250
    managing *See* File management
    opening multiple 202, 208
    printing multiple 202, 208–209
    working with multiple 202–208
File format
    converting 239
    defined 249
File management
    finding files 201–207, 209
    locating directory where file is 203–204
    search criteria 203, 205–207
    searching for specific text 205–206
    summary information 206–207, 254
    using Find File dialog box 202–208
File menu 60
Find File command 202
Finding
    files
      overview 201
      procedure 203–207, 209
      search criteria, specifying 203, 205–207
      summary information 206–207

Finding *(continued)*
    formatting 91–92, 103
    text 89–91, 102–103
First-line indent marker 47, 49
Flesch readability indexes 99
Flipping a graphic 183–184
Font
    changing 14–15
    defined 249
    screen and printer fonts 229
Font size *See* Point size
Footer
    See also Header/footer
    changing for different sections 113–114, 116
    creating 109–111
    formatting 111
    page number, inserting in 110
    viewing 111–112, 114, 116
Form letters
    See also Print merge
    creating 211–221
    defined 249
    overview 210–211
    viewing and editing 221–222
Format, defined 249
Format menu 61
Formatting
    characters *See* Character formatting
    footers 111
    paragraphs *See* Paragraph formatting
    repeating 36
    sections *See* Section formatting
    storing as style 79–80
Formula, defined 249
Frame
    border 192, 197
    caption 196–197
    defined 249
    graphics 179–180, 185, 189
    moving 193
    moving graphic 179, 181
    normal view 194
    positioning
        framed text 193
        graphic 179, 181
    scaling/sizing 190–191, 193
    selecting 180
    text 190–191
    wrapping text around 180, 186
Frame button 180

G

Global template, defined 250
Glossary, defined 250
Grammar checking
    installing 230
    overview 95
    procedure 95–97, 103
    rules 97, 102
    tips for 102
Graph *See* Chart; Microsoft Graph
Graph button 150
Graphics
    caption 196–197
    cropping 175, 177–178, 196
    editing with Microsoft Draw 182–186
    flipping 182
    framing 179–180, 185, 189
    inserting 175–177, 182, 196
    moving 179, 181, 196
    overview 174
    page layout view 179
    positioning 179, 181, 196
    printing 195
    scaling/sizing 178–179, 185, 190, 196
    views, working in 179–180
    wrapping text around framed 179–180, 186
Gridlines, table 140, 142

H

Hanging indent
    creating 49
    defined 250
Hard disk space required for Word 229
Hard (manual) page break, inserting 131–132
Hard return *See* Paragraph mark
Hardware requirements, Word 229
Header file, defined 250
Header/footer
    See also Footer
    changing for different sections 112, 116
    creating 116
    defined 250
    overview 105, 108–109
    pane 108
    viewing 111–112, 114, 116
Heading, defined 250

Help
  closing 66, 132
  finding topics 72–73, 76, 84–85, 127
  for commands 62, 76
  for dialog boxes 65–66, 76
  hiding 66
  installing 229–230
  jumping to related topics 73–74
  moving and resizing window 128–129, 133, 135
  printing topics 133
  returning to previous topic 74
  WordPerfect 74
Help menu 61
Hidden text, defined 250

I

IBM 5520, converting file formats 239
Icon, defined 250
Images *See* Graphics
Importing graphics 175
Indent button 43
Indenting
  defined 250
  displaying markers on ruler 54
  first-line indent 49–50
  hanging indent 49, 250
  left indent 47–48, 51
  paragraphs 43–45, 47–51, 56
  right indent 49
  ruler indent markers 47–51
  setting with Paragraph command 67–69
  to next tab stop 43–45
  unindenting paragraphs 43–44
Insert menu 61
Inserting graphics 175–177, 182, 196
Insertion point, defined 250
Installing
  online Help 229–230
  online lessons 229
  optional tools 229–230
  printers 232–235
  Word 229–231
Italic button 13

J

Justified Text button 13, 84
Justifying paragraphs 13, 84

K

Keyboard
  choosing commands with 70–71
  selecting dialog box options with 70–71
Keywords, finding document with 206–207

L

Landscape page orientation, defined 250
Leader characters, defined 250
Left-Aligned Text button 13
Left indent marker 47–48, 51
Lessons, installing online 229
Letter *See* Form letters
Line
  blank, creating 6–7
  break 251
  spacing 69, 251
Line break, defined 251
Line spacing
  adjusting 69–70
  defined 251
List(s)
  bulleted 45, 56
  numbered 46, 56
List box, defined 251
Lotus 1-2-3, converting file formats 239

M

Mail merge *See* Form letters; Print merge
Mailing labels 211
Main document for print merge
  creating 211–221, 224
  defined 211, 251
Manual page break 131–132
Margin(s)
  adjusting/changing with ruler 53–54, 56
  default 52
  displaying on ruler 52
  overview 51–53
Margin markers 52
Marking text *See* Selecting
Maximize button 126, 133
Maximizing
  windows 133, 135
  Word window xxii, 133
Measurement, defined 251

Menu
    defined 251
    choosing commands from 58
    Word 60
Merge To File button 221
Merging
    cells 147, 154
    defined 251
    documents *See* Print merge
Message, defined 252
Microsoft Draw
    editing graphics with 182–186
    importing graphics into Word files 174
    installing 230
Microsoft Excel
    converting file formats 239
    merging data files from 222
    spreadsheets, using in Word 153
Microsoft Graph
    See also Chart
    creating charts with 150
Microsoft Windows
    overview 118–122
    starting xiv
    version required for Word 229
Microsoft Word *See* Word (program)
Microsoft Word for DOS, converting file formats 239
Microsoft Word for the Macintosh, converting file
    formats 239
Microsoft WordArt
    creating a button effect 188–189
    installing 230
    special text effects 174, 186–190
Microsoft Works, converting file formats 239
Minimize button 130
Misspelled words *See* Spelling check
Monitor required for Word 229
Mouse
    how to use xvi–xviii
    pointer shapes xvi–xvii
    required for lessons 229
Moving
    text
        drag-and-drop method 10–11, 25, 37
        with Clipboard 31–33, 37
    windows 126, 128–131, 135
Multiplan, converting file formats 239
Multiple files *See* File

N

New button 211
New document, creating 211–212
Newspaper-style columns
    changing number of 166–168
    creating 157–158, 172
    inserting column breaks 159, 172
    lines between 160, 172
    overview 156
    viewing 158, 160–161, 169–171, 172–173
Normal style 86
Normal view
    defined 252
    headers/footers in 112
    newspaper-style columns in 170, 173
    page numbers in 107–108
    section breaks in 163
    using 54
Numbered list button 46
Numbered list, creating 46, 56

O

Object
    defined 252
    inserting 187
Online Help *See* Help
Open button 22
Opening
    document 22–23, 37
    files from other applications 240–241
    multiple documents 202, 208
    new document 211–212
Options, defined 252
Orientation, page
    See also Landscape; Portrait
    changing 236–237
Orphan, defined 255
Outline view, defined 252
Overtype, defined 252

P

Page
    break *See* Page break
    in different views 52–54, 169
    margins *See* Margin(s)
    orientation 236–237
Page Back button 107

Page break
  defined 252
  hard (manual) 131–132
  inserting in document 131–132, 135
  soft (automatic) 169
Page Forward button 107
Page layout view
  defined 252
  framed objects in 179–180
  headers/footers in 111, 114, 116
  newspaper-style columns in 158, 170–173
  page numbering in 107
Page numbering
  all pages except first 106–107, 116
  overview 105
  viewing 107, 116
Page orientation
  changing 236–237
  landscape, defined 250
  portrait, defined 253
Pane
  defined 252
  header/footer 108
Paper size, changing 236–237
Paper source, changing 236–237
Paragraph
  alignment 13
  creating new 15–16
  formatting *See* Paragraph formatting
  indenting 43–45, 47–51, 56, 67–69
  shading 192, 197
  spacing, adjusting 69
  typing 6–8
  unindenting 43–44
Paragraph formatting
  applying 67–68
  justified text 84
  storing as style 80
Paragraph mark (¶), displaying on screen 6–7
Paste button 31–32, 125
Pasting
  defined 252
  text 31–32
  text between documents 123–125, 135
Path
  See also Search path
  defined 253
Personal dictionary *See* Custom dictionary
Picture *See* Graphics
Point size
  changing 14–15
  defined 253

Pointer shapes xvi–xvii
Port, printer 229, 232, 234–235
Portrait page orientation, defined 253
Position, defined 253
Positioning *See* Moving
Practice files
  displaying xx–xxi
  installing xiii
Print button 36
Print merge
  checking for errors 223
  data file
    attaching 212–214, 222, 224
    creating in Word 212–214, 224
    field names in 212
    overview 210–212
  form letters *See* Form letters
  main document
    merge fields, formatting 220
    merge fields, inserting 214–220, 224
    overview 210–211
  merge fields
    formatting 220
    inserting 214–220
    overview 210–211
  merging main document and data file
    overview 210–211
    procedure 221, 224
  printing form letters 222
  tips for 223–224
Print preview, newspaper-style columns in 160–161, 172
Print setup options 236–237
Printer
  See also Printing
  configuring 232–235
  driver 229
  fonts 229
  installing 232–235
  port 229, 232, 234–235
  selecting 232, 235–236
  setup options 236–237
  viewing available 232
Printing
  document 35–36, 232
  envelope 101, 103
  graphics 195
  merged documents 222
  multiple documents 202, 208–209
  online Help topics 133

Printing *(continued)*
    selected text 237
    tips for 237
Proofing document 33–35, 88–104

Q

Quitting Word 19, 134

R

Readability of document 99
Record, defined 212
Removing text 8–10
Renaming documents 24
Repaginating
    defined 253
    document 237
Repeating an action 36
Replacing
    formatting 91–92, 103
    text 9–10, 89–91, 102–103
Resizing windows 126, 128–131, 135
Resolution when printing graphics 195
Restore button 129
RFT-DCA files, converting file formats 239
Ribbon
    defined 253
    displaying xxi
Rich Text Format (RTF) files 239–240
Right-Aligned Text button 13
Right indent marker 47, 49
Rotating a graphic 183–184
Row (in tables)
    See also Table
    centering 148
    deleting 146
    end-of-row mark 145
    inserting 142–143, 145–146, 154
    selecting 145, 154
RTF (Rich Text Format) files 239–240
Rule, defined 253
Ruler
    defined 253
    displaying xxi
    hiding 123
    indenting paragraphs with 47–51
    margins, viewing 52
    table columns, adjusting width 142–143

S

Save button 17
Saving
    automatic save, defined 247
    document 17–19, 24
Scale, defined 253
Screen
    changing the display xxi
    fonts 229
Scroll arrow 26–27
Scroll bar, defined 253
Scroll box 26–28
Scrolling through a document 26–29, 37
Search criteria 203, 205–207
Search path 203–204
Searching
    for files 203–207
    for Help topics 72–73, 84–85
Section break
    defined 254
    for headers/footers 112, 116
    inserting 113, 163–166, 172
    overview 162
    viewing 169
Section, defined 254
Section formatting
    headers/footers 112–114, 116
    newspaper-style columns 162, 166–168, 173
    viewing 169
Section mark
    format settings stored in 171
    inserting 164
Selecting
    printer 232, 235–236
    text 8–10, 12–13, 20
Selection bar, defined 254
Setting up Word 229–231
Setup program, Word 229–231
Shading paragraphs 192
Show/Hide ¶ button 6–7, 24
Sizing handles 175
Snaking columns *See* Newspaper-style columns
Soft (automatic) page break 131, 169
Software requirements 229
Space marks, displaying on screen 6–7
Spacing
    between characters 75
    line 69–70, 251
    paragraph 69

Special characters, defined 254
Spelling button 34
Spelling check
    adding words to custom dictionary 98–99, 103
    for multiple languages 102
    installing 230
    overview 33
    procedure for checking the document 34–35, 37
Split box 29
Spreadsheet *See* Microsoft Excel
Standard styles 86
Starting
    Windows xiv
    Word xiv–xv
Statistics about document 99
Status bar, defined 254
Style
    applying 80–83, 87
    changing 83–85, 87
    creating 79, 87
    defined 254
    naming 79
    Normal style 86
    overview 77
    redefining 83–85, 87
    standard styles 86
    storing formatting as 79
Subject of document, finding document using 206–207
Summary information 206–207, 254
Synonyms, in thesaurus 92–94

T

Tab stop, defined 254
Table
    borders 148–149, 154
    cell
        defined 140
        deleting 146
        editing text in 152
        end-of-cell mark 140
        merging 147, 154
        moving between cells 154
        selecting 144–145
        shading 148–149
    centering 148, 154
    centering text in cell 148, 154
    column
        changing width 142–143, 154
        deleting 146

Table *(continued)*
    column *(continued)*
        displaying on ruler 142–143
        inserting 143–145, 154
        selecting 144, 154
    creating 141–142, 154
    defined 254
    deleting contents of cells 146
    formatting 147–148
    gridlines 140, 142
    moving the insertion point 144
    overview 139–140
    row
        centering 148
        deleting 146
        end-of-row mark 145
        inserting 142–143, 145–146, 154
        selecting 145, 154
    selecting 148
    shading 148–149, 154
    tips for 153
Table button 141
Table menu 61
Template
    changing page setup options 236–237
    defined 255
    global template, defined 250
Text
    aligning 13
    border around framed 192, 197
    changing the look of 12–16
    copying
        between documents 123–125, 135
        drag-and-drop method 25–26, 37
        with Clipboard 30–31, 37
    creating special effects with WordArt 174, 186–190
    cutting and pasting 32, 37
    deleting 8–10
    finding and replacing 89–91, 102–103
    formatting *See* Character formatting; Paragraph
        formatting
    framing 190–191
    hidden text 250
    moving
        drag-and-drop method 10–11, 25, 37
        with Clipboard 31–33, 37
    pasting 31–32
    positioning framed 193
    replacing 9–10
    scaling/sizing framed 190–191, 193

Text *(continued)*
    shading paragraphs 192, 197
    typing a document 5 – 8
    wrapping around graphics 180, 186
Text box
    defined 255
    using 65
Text only files 239 – 240
Text tool, Microsoft Draw 184
Thesaurus
    using 92 – 94, 103
    installing 230
Title bar, defined 255
Title of document, finding document using 206 – 207
Toolbar
    defined 255
    displaying xxi
Tools menu 61
Typeface *See* Character formatting; Font
Typing text 5 – 8
Typos *See* Spelling check

U

Underline button 13
Undo button 9
Undoing an action 9
Unindent button 44
Unindenting paragraphs 43 – 44

V

Vertical alignment, defined 255
Vertical scroll bar xxii, 26 – 29
View
    defined 255
    header/footer 111 – 112, 114, 116
    normal view 54, 107, 252
    of document 52 – 54, 56
    outline view, defined 252
    page layout view, 107, 252
    page numbers 107, 116
    zooming page 52 – 53, 169, 193
View menu 61

W

Widow, defined 255
Wildcard, in file search criteria 204
Window
    application window, defined 247
    copying/pasting text between 123 – 125, 135
    defined 255
    document window, defined 248
    maximizing xxii, 126, 133, 135, 183
    moving 126, 128 – 131, 135
    resizing 126, 128 – 131, 135
    restoring to previous size 129
Window menu 61
Windows *See* Microsoft Windows
Word (program)
    converting documents to other formats 241 – 242
    converting file formats 239 – 242
    hardware and software requirements 229
    maximizing the Word window xxii, 133
    menus 60 – 61
    new features in this version 243 – 244
    quitting 19, 134
    saving time with 245
    screen *See* Screen
    setting up 229 – 231
    starting xiv – xv
    steps in creating documents xviii – xx
    tips for using 245
    window, illustrations xv – xvi
Word for DOS, converting file formats 239
Word for the Macintosh, converting file formats 239
Word for Windows, converting file formats 239
WordArt *See* Microsoft WordArt
WordPerfect
    converting file formats 239
    help in switching to Word 74
WordStar, converting file formats 239
Wordwrap, defined 255
Wrapping text around graphics 179 – 180, 186

Z

Zoom 100 Percent button xxii, 54, 108, 169 – 170
Zoom Page Width button 169
Zoom Whole Page button 52, 169
Zooming 52 – 54, 169, 173, 193

Other Titles from Microsoft Press

Outstanding References on Microsoft® Word

WORD FOR WINDOWS™ COMPANION, 2nd ed.

The Cobb Group: Mark W. Crane with M. David Stone & Alfred Poor

This new edition of The Cobb Group classic covers all the exciting features of Word for Windows 2.0—an exceptional tutorial for new users as well as a master reference guide for experienced users. With the hallmark clarity of books from The Cobb Group, this Companion will take you from the basics of document processing to more advanced procedures such as building style sheets, developing outlines and multi-column formats, producing mailing labels and form letters, and using the glossary. Packed with illustrations, examples, and tips to enhance your productivity!

896 pages, softcover   7³/₈ x 9¹/₈ $29.95 ($39.95 Canada)

RUNNING MICROSOFT® WORD FOR WINDOWS™

Russell Borland

This example-rich book is an outstanding reference for intermediate and advanced users. Now completely updated (formerly Working with Word for Windows), it highlights all the new document-processing, desktop publishing, and WYSIWYG features of Word for Windows 2.0. Russell Borland, a former member of the Microsoft Word for Windows development team, has included scores of insights and powertips not found in the documentation or in other Word for Windows books.

592 pages, softcover   7³/₈ x 9¹/₄ $27.95 ($34.95 Canada)

Become a spreadsheet expert the easy way!

MICROSOFT® EXCEL FOR WINDOWS™ STEP BY STEP
Version 4

Microsoft Corporation

If you prefer the timesaving step-by-step approach to learning, *Microsoft Excel Step by Step* is the book-and-software package you need to get up and running with Microsoft Excel 4. Learn to create useful, error-free spreadsheets the most effective way—by combining self-paced lessons, disk-based practice files, and real-world business examples.

325 pages, softcover, with one 3¹/₂-inch disk   7³/₈ x 9¹/₄
$29.95 ($39.95 Canada)

Great Resources for Windows™ 3.1 Users

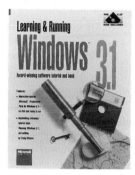

LEARNING & RUNNING WINDOWS™ 3.1

Includes *Microsoft® Productivity Pack for Windows* and *Running Windows 3.1, 3rd ed.*

Microsoft Corporation, Craig Stinson

This is the ideal blending of software and book instruction for users of all levels of experience. If you want to be up and running with Windows 3.1 quickly and easily, this is the place to start. *The Microsoft Productivity Pack for Windows 3.1* (regularly $59.95) combines disk-based lessons with hands-on exercises. RUNNING WINDOWS 3.1 (regularly $27.95) will continue to answer day-to-day questions about Windows long after you've learned the basics from the software tutorial. An unbeatable package at an unbeatable price. Sold separately for $87.90.

560 pages, softcover with one 5¹/₂-inch (HD) disk $39.95 ($54.95 Canada)

RUNNING WINDOWS™ 3.1, 3rd ed.

Craig Stinson

Build your confidence and enhance your productivity with Microsoft Windows, quickly and easily, using this hands-on introduction. This Microsoft-authorized edition—for new as well as experienced Windows users—is completely updated and expanded to cover all the new exciting features of version 3.1. You'll find a successful combination of step-by-step tutorials, helpful screen illustrations, expert tips, and real-world examples. Learn how to install and start using Windows 3.1, use applications with Windows, and maximize Windows performance.

560 pages, softcover $27.95 ($37.95 Canada)

WINDOWS™ 3.1 COMPANION

The Cobb Group: Lori L. Lorenz and R. Michael O'Mara with Russell Borland

This bestseller is now completely updated to cover the important new features of version 3.1. Both a step-by-step tutorial and a comprehensive reference, this book is specifically designed to help you quickly find the information you need—moving from the basics to more advanced information. Learn to take advantage of all the extraordinary improvements and added features of version 3.1, including the new, *faster* File Manager; TrueType font; support for multimedia; the improved Program Manager; the faster Printer Manager; automatic network reconnections; the new "drag and drop" feature. The authors include a wealth of expert tips and tricks and great examples to show you how to use Windows more efficiently.

550 pages, softcover $27.95 ($37.95 Canada)

CONCISE GUIDE TO MICROSOFT® WINDOWS™ 3.1

Kris Jamsa

Instant answers to your Windows 3.1 questions! Clear, concise information on all the key Microsoft Windows 3.1 features. For beginning to intermediate users. A great complement to *Windows 3.1 Companion*.

192 pages, softcover $12.95 ($17.95 Canada)

Microsoft Press books are available wherever quality computer books are sold. Or call 1-800-MSPRESS for ordering information or placing credit card orders. Please refer to BBK when placing your order. Prices subject to change.*

*In Canada, contact Macmillan Canada, Attn: Microsoft Press Dept., 164 Commander Blvd., Agincourt, Ontario, Canada M1S 3C7, or call (416) 293-8141.

In the U.K., contact Microsoft Press, 27 Wrights Lane, London W8 5TZ.

THE WORD FOR WINDOWS™
COURSEWARE DEVELOPMENT KIT

This is the ideal courseware development tool for Microsoft Word for Windows courses. This kit includes all instructor and student materials: the *Microsoft Word for Windows Step by Step* book along with reproduction masters, disk-based practice files, instructor demo files and overheads, and more. A great value at only $295 per kit.

INSTRUCTORS KIT

An Instructors Kit for *Microsoft Word for Windows Step by Step* will be available Spring 1992.

For more information on either The Word for Windows Courseware Development Kit or Instructors Kit, send your request along with your name, address, and the name of your corporation, institution, or school to:

Microsoft Press, Attn: Sales Dept.
One Microsoft Way, Redmond, WA 98052-6399

------- ORDERING INFORMATION -------
3¹/₂-inch Practice File Disk for
MICROSOFT® WORD FOR WINDOWS™ STEP BY STEP

YES ... please send me_____ copies of the MICROSOFT WORD FOR WINDOWSSTEP BY STEP 3¹/₂-inch Practice File Disk at $3.95 each (Check/Money Order, U.S. funds only) .... $ _____

SALES TAX: Please add applicable sales tax for the following states: AZ, CA, CO, CT, DC, FL, GA, HI, ID, IL, IN, IA, KS, KY, ME, MD, MA, MI, MN, MO, NE, NV, NJ, NM, NY, NC, OH, OK, PA, RI, SC, TN, TX, VA, WA, WV, WI. .... $ _____

SHIPPING: $5.00 per disk (domestic orders) .... $ _____

TOTAL: .... $ _____

_____
NAME

_____
ADDDRESS   (   )
_____
                                    DAYTIME PHONE NUMBER

_____
CITY   **STATE**   **ZIP**

Send your prepaid order to:
Microsoft Press, Attn: Word Step by Step Disk
One Microsoft Way, Redmond, WA 98052-6399

Please be sure to include payment (Check/Money Order, U.S. funds only), your name, and complete address. Allow 2–3 weeks for delivery. Offer valid in U.S. only.

3¹/₂-inch disk— 097-000-616